Praise for Dr. Tom Ferguson's HEALTH ONLINE

"Dr. Tom Ferguson's *Health Online* is a definitive resource guide, and more. I chose Dr. Ferguson as the Health domain editor of *The Millennium Whole Earth Catalog* because he knows more about self-health than anyone else I know. If you own a computer and modem and have a health or wellness concern, a disability, or are a caregiver, this book can be a lifeline. Dr. Ferguson goes beyond gathering the best resources and telling you how to access them; his book instills a necessary and potentially powerful mental discipline of self-care."

> Howard Rheingold
> Author, *The Virtual Community*

"The online resources this book describes offer consumers easy access to practical health information, experienced self-helpers, and online medical experts. This electronic empowerment is changing health care dramatically. In *Health Online*, Dr. Ferguson has written the bible of self-care information on the Internet."

> Dean Ornish, M.D.
> Author, *Dr. Dean Ornish's Program for Reversing Heart Disease*;
> President & Director, Preventive Medicine Research Institute

"The real revolution in health care is consumer information. *Health Online* puts every consumer in touch with a world of health information previously reserved to a limited few. This book is an absolute must for any consumer who cares about their own health and the health of their family. *Health Online* is your personal window to the health world. It will revolutionize the way you take care of yourself and those around you. This is a book I'm buying for all my friends!"

> Charles B. Inlander
> President, People's Medical Society

"Self-care pioneer Tom Ferguson is ahead of the wave once again. This book opens the door to the Internet, welcoming online newbies and teaching net vets new tricks. *Health Online* shows us how to find the people, the experts, the self-help groups, the support forums, and the health information we need. Tom then blows our minds by modestly suggesting that online health might be the missing link in reforming health care. This could be the most important book you'll read this year!"

> Joe Graedon
> Author, *The People's Pharmacy*

D1225646

Praise for Dr. Tom Ferguson's HEALTH ONLINE

"Once again self-care pioneer Tom Ferguson has identified a key health care trend and presented it in an accessible, empowering way. *Health Online* presents cyberspace not as a cold universe of bits and bytes, but as a rich, warm world full of people who connect, share, and care for each other. A moving and meaningful profile of the Internet at its best."

> David S. Sobel, M.D., M.P.H.
> Regional Director of Patient Education,
> Kaiser Permanente Medical Care Program

"Health information, decision-making, and social support on the information superhighway will change health care forever. The new online networks discussed in Ferguson's book will be as essential to 21st century medicine as hospitals are today. If you want to understand the power of health resources in cyberspace in the early days of Information Age health care, read *Health Online*."

> Michael D. McDonald, Dr.P.H.
> Senior Adviser, The C. Everett Koop Institute

"A wonderfully innovative, user-friendly introduction to the exciting new world of online support communities. The best available guide to becoming a part of the online self-help movement. A heartfelt labor of love by our leading self-care visionary."

> Edward J. Madara
> Director, American Self-Help Clearinghouse

"One of the biggest dilemmas facing medicine is getting health information and advice to the people who need it. The Internet is certainly one answer. With this book, Tom Ferguson has given us a very useful map to the many medical resources currently available online. It's a swiftly moving target, but Ferguson hits it dead center."

> John Perry Barlow
> Cofounder, The Electronic Frontier Foundation

"The Internet can be a bewildering maze to people in trouble. Tom's book is the most comprehensive, compassionate, and consumer-oriented guide to getting usable online help. I highly recommend it."

> Robert G. Blank, Jr.
> Director of Health Content,
> AT&T Personal Online Services

Health
Online

Other Books by Tom Ferguson

Self-Care Books

Medical Self-Care: Access to Health Tools

The People's Book of Medical Tests, with David Sobel

The No-Nag, No-Guilt, Do-It-Your-Own-Way Guide to Quitting Smoking

Hidden Guilt: How to Stop Punishing Yourself and Enjoy the Happiness You Deserve, with Louis Engel

Helping Smokers Get Ready to Quit

What You Need to Know About Psychiatric Drugs, with Stuart Yudofsky and Robert E. Hales

The Aspirin Handbook, with Joe and Teresa Graedon

Medical Mysteries

No Deadly Drug, with Joe Graedon

Books for Children

The Stethoscope Book & Kit, with Linda Allison

The Get-Well-Quick Kit, with Linda Allison

Health Online

Tom Ferguson, M.D.

Medical Editor, *The Millennium Whole Earth Catalog*
Senior Associate, Center for Clinical Computing, Harvard Medical School

Foreword by **Edward J. Madara**
Director, American Self-Help Clearinghouse

 ADDISON-WESLEY PUBLISHING COMPANY

Reading, Massachusetts   Menlo Park, California   New York
Don Mills, Ontario   Wokingham, England   Amsterdam
Bonn   Sydney   Singapore   Tokyo   Madrid   San Juan
Paris   Seoul   Milan   Mexico City   Taipei

Library of Congress Cataloging-in-Publication Data

Ferguson, Tom, 1943-
     Health online: how to find health information, support groups, and self-help communities in cyberspace / Tom Ferguson.
        p. cm.
     Includes index.
     ISBN 0-201-40989-5
     1. Information storage and retrieval systems—Medicine.
2. Online searching. 3. Medical informatics. 4. Medicine—Information services. 5. Self-care, Health—Information services. 6. Medicine, Popular—Information services. 7. Computer networks—Social aspects. I. Title.
R859.7.D36F47 1996
025.06'3621—dc20

                                       95-45000
                                          CIP

Cover design by Suzanne Heiser
Text design by Gex
Set in 11-point Stone by Gex

1 2 3 4 5 6 7 8 9-MA-0099989796
First printing, February 1996

Addison-Wesley books are available at special discounts for bulk purchases. For more information about how to make such purchases in the U.S., please contact the Corporate, Government, and Special Sales Department at Addison-Wesley Publishing Company, 1 Jacob Way, Reading, MA 01867, or call (800) 238-9682.

Who then can so softly bind up the wound of another
as he who has felt the same wound himself?
—*Thomas Jefferson*

The time has come for a major conceptual shift . . .
from viewing lay people as consumers of health care
to seeing them as they really are:
its primary providers.
—*Lowell Levin and Ellen Idler*

When the wise healer's work is done,
The people say, 'Amazing.
We did it all ourselves.'
—*Lao Tze*

Dedication

To Glenna Tallman (1952–1994), one of my first cyberspace friends. For taking the time and energy to greet and orient a clueless newbie and for sharing her excitement at the wondrous new world of online self-help—when she was facing such monumental problems of her own. It was my early interactions with "GlennaT" that first made me aware of the depth and power of online self-help, and it was with her that I first shared my early thoughts about writing this book. She is online in heaven now, where computers never crash, there is no flaming, and monthly access charges never come due. We'll remember you, Glenna, for your courage, generosity, and grace in playing one of life's more difficult hands.

To all the past, present, and future online self-help group founders, forum coordinators, group leaders, mailing list owners, BBS sysops, Web page producers, and assorted Internet junkies who have devoted thousands of hours of time to helping their fellow humans connect with each other and find the information they seek in the rapidly growing self-help neighborhoods of cyberspace. You are the real heroes of this story.

To you, the reader, hoping you will find what you are looking for and urging you to remember that in virtual support communities it is those who help the most who receive the most benefit. May you find the help you need. And in helping others, may you find yourself tapping into a deep altruistic impulse you never knew you possessed.

Contents

About the Author

Award-winning author Tom Ferguson is president of Self-Care Productions, a health care consulting firm in Austin, Texas. He founded the influential journal *Medical Self-Care* and has served for many years as medical editor of the *Whole Earth Catalog*. He wrote the chapter "Working With Your Doctor" for the book that accompanied Bill Moyers's PBS series *Mind/Body Medicine*.

Tom is a Yale-trained physician who has saved hundreds of lives by refraining from the clinical practice of medicine. As a senior associate at Harvard Medical School's Center for Clinical Computing, he is organizing the first series of conferences on computer networks that support the informed, responsible health consumer. The author of a dozen books for the empowered medical consumer, he speaks and consults widely on the issues discussed in this book.

His hobbies include observing squirrels, collecting old poker chips, and writing medical mystery novels. He lives in Austin with his wife, Meredith, and their two unpredictable cats. You can reach him online at: Dr.TomHO@aol.com.

Foreword

This book is a first-of-its-kind guide to online self-help communities and other helpful online health resources. Though it covers a high-tech topic, *Health Online* is truly written from the heart. The online messages and stories Tom shares in the following chapters provide an accurate and compelling picture of the rich and rapidly growing new world of online self-help.

As a leading advocate of self-care and mutual support for nearly twenty years, Tom Ferguson has helped many of us recognize and understand that self-care is the foundation of all health care. As a futurist, he long ago envisioned the development of the world this book describes. In *Health Online*, he opens the door, invites us in, and provides a guided tour of these new virtual, but very real, communities.

Tom understands that we're not just talking about computers here: We're talking about computers as a way to find vital health information, to receive the comforting "you are not alone" support of those who've walked the same path, to collaborate with medical professionals, and, when needed, to work with others to advocate for new research, new services, or new directions in health policy.

As Tom guides us through the booming self-help neighborhoods of the Net, he is always acutely aware of the person-to-person focus that is at the heart of this remarkable new world. For online self-help is not just a matter of computer users employing modems to download health information. The real story here is the creation of thousands of new online communities of common concern—the rise of a whole new type of grassroots, consumer-based health resource. While information is important, it is, as Tom explains, *information shared in the context of community* that is the very foundation of these new online support networks.

The online communities Tom describes are becoming a major channel for grassroots altruism. Thousands of volunteer self-helpers already use their computers to assist each other with a wide range of problems: from recovering alcoholics to those facing the mental illness of a loved one, from parents of premature infants to families coming to terms with a life-threatening illness. An increasing portion of our population now faces such challenges—chronic illness, disability, addiction, loss, depression, caregiver fatigue, etc.—at a time when the extended family and the neighborhood provide less support than they did in decades past. Online self-help can take up much of the slack.

Health Online is an award-winning medical journalist's groundbreaking report on a major new development that will affect our entire health care system—the rise of electronic support networks run by and for informed, committed layfolk. For nearly twenty years, Tom has been telling us that the recent shift toward the empowered health consumer and the growing interest in self-help represent the early signs of a major transformation of our health care system.

In the chapters that follow, Tom explains how our emerging mega-network of interconnected computers may be the most powerful tool our planet has ever seen for supporting individual empowerment, relieving loneliness, building community—and solving our current health care crisis. At a time when the demand for supportive health services exceeds the supply, electronic self-help groups should be recognized and promoted for their unique ability to transform people with problems into providers and supporters of self-provided health care. As Tom recently told an audience of health and computer professionals:

> By encouraging layfolk to be overly dependent on doctors, we have all too often inadvertently disempowered the populace in health matters, turning potentially powerful, knowledgeable, health-responsible citizens into ignorant, fearful, isolated clients of professionalized health care. The rise of consumer health informatics and online self-help provides the perfect opportunity to remedy this situation.

But the pioneering groups and networks this book describes are only the beginning: It will be people like you, the readers of this book, who will help to build and create our common health care future. You will use the Net to obtain a wide variety of health information. Even more importantly, you will find and tap into—and create—online support communities made up of informed, empowered, supportive layfolk who share your experiences and concerns.

I join with Tom in wishing you the best of luck in this exciting new world. May the chapters that follow bring you as many insights, understandings, and practical tips and guidelines as they have given me.

See you online.

—Edward J. Madara, Director
The American Self-Help Clearinghouse
edmadara@aol.com
70275.1003@compuserve.com

Introduction

How to Use This Book

Online self-help has already reached critical mass. The transformation of health care as we know it has already begun.

"MarshHawk"
RecoveryLink host
on America Online

WHEN SARA STYLES'S DOCTOR prescribed Cotrimoxazole for her recurring bladder infections, Sara went right home, logged on to Prodigy, and read a detailed profile of the drug in the Consumer Reports Drug Database. To her surprise, she discovered that Cotrimoxazole (a combination of the antibiotic drugs sulfamethoxazole and trimethoprim) could interact with the blood thinner, Coumadin, which she was taking to prevent blood clots in her legs. This combination could have produced a potentially fatal hemorrhage. She also learned that the drug could produce skin rashes, itching, or severe sunburn after only a few minutes' exposure to sunlight—and Sara was an avid gardener. She immediately e-mailed her doctor, enclosing copies of her findings, and suggested that a single dose of amoxicillin (which, according to her online research, posed fewer problems) might be a better choice. Sara's doctor agreed, phoned in the new prescription to Sara's local pharmacy, and sent Sara an e-mail note thanking her for helping to avoid the potential problems.

Both Tracy Washington and her brother James travel to their childhood home once or twice a week to help their mother care for their father, who has amyotrophic lateral sclerosis (ALS, or Lou Gehrig's disease). In the beginning, they found it impossible to find up-to-date information on their dad's condition.

Then they discovered *ALS Digest*, an interactive support group newsletter that arrives in their online mailboxes every week. They can now exchange experiences with dozens of families with an ALS-affected loved one. Their online friends have helped them find a computer-assisted communication device that allows their father to "talk" even though his vocal cords are paralyzed. And by following online tips, they've been able to enroll him in a clinical trial of a promising new anti-ALS drug.

Six months ago, Stan Briscoe's life was coming apart. He was behaving erratically at work, he'd lost most of his family's savings on an ill-advised investment scheme, and he was driving his wife crazy. It was only after he'd lost three jobs in a row, his wife had moved out, and he was faced with bankruptcy that he was forced to accept the fact that he had a problem—manic-depressive mood swings made worse by heavy drinking. Luckily, a neighbor referred him to two online support groups: one for alcoholism and one for mood disorders. The friends he met online had been down the same path and refused to fall for his regular excuses. They challenged him to take responsibility for his behavior and urged him to seek psychiatric help. By participating in two support groups and by using online links to track down a top local specialist, Stan was able to successfully put his life back together. Thanks to his present regimen of drugs, therapy, and continuing online support, Stan's problems are now under control. He's doing well at his new job, he and his wife have reconciled, and he's been asked to become a coleader of his mood-swing support group.

Welcome to the Wonderful World of Electronic Self-Help

The problems of cyberspace—rampant commercialism and virtual bad behavior—have gotten all the press. But there is a compassionate, altruistic side as well. It lives in the self-help forums, the support newsgroups, the self-help mailing lists, the online self-help newsletters, and, above all, in the millions of one-to-one e-mail support messages that flow back and forth across the Net each day. It can be found on commercial services, local electronic bulletin boards, and the global Internet—all of which make up what I call the Net. Online self-help has attracted much less attention than the dark sides of the Net. But it may turn out to be considerably more important.

Within the rapidly growing self-help neighborhoods of cyberspace, people routinely go out of their way to help each other. Online Mother Theresas are as common as dandelions on a suburban lawn. Generosity, altruism, and fellow feeling are the rule. Sophisticated computer techies and the technically unsophisticated reach out to each other, joining together in a common pursuit of mutual concerns. And health professionals are beginning to step out of their old authoritarian roles as they use e-mail, shared medical decision making, and other online links to collaborate with their clients in mutually respectful new ways.

Online self-help is already a tremendous resource, helping millions to manage their own health concerns. A single health forum on one of the commercial services currently receives more than a quarter of a million online "hits," or visits, per month. If current predictions hold true, online self-help will become even larger and more important in years to come. And the next decade will see a growing number of links between the online self-help community and the professional health care system.

This book is a report on the first generation of online self-help networks. I've spent the past two years exploring the self-help neighborhoods of cyberspace. What I've found there has astounded, inspired, and heartened me.

I've found people reaching out for help—and others (very often the same people) reaching out *to* help. I've discovered a remarkable and impressive variety of new online support communities that have grown up spontaneously, with no publicity, no government planning, and no professional authorization. I've found people talking and sharing, exchanging information and support, listening and understanding each other: people in ones and twos and small groups and massive far-flung networks, people relating to each other—and to online health professionals—in startling and innovative new ways.

I learned that the information superhighway is not some vague vision just over the horizon. It's out there waiting for us right now. It's not much like a highway at all—more like a giant Brillo pad, with millions of self-helpers connected by modems and phone lines. Forget the 500-channel future. We're up to twenty million "channels" already and we're just getting warmed up.

In the pages that follow, I'll do my best to describe the world of online self-help and to tell you how you can connect to it: how to pick a service, how to log on for the first time. And if I'm lucky, I may be able to give you a glimpse of the magic that can occur when you pass through the looking glass of your computer screen and begin exploring the world of cyberspace support communities.

Who Am I?

Before we go further, let me introduce myself: I'm a physician by training but a self-helper by inclination. I completed my doctoral dissertation on self-help and self-care at Yale Medical School in 1978. I founded and edited a journal called *Medical Self Care* and have served as medical editor for the *Whole Earth Catalog* for nearly twenty years. Because of my interest in online self-help, I was recently invited to become a senior associate at the Center for Clinical Computing at Harvard Medical School and Beth Israel Hospital in Boston.

I think of myself as a self-care person, not a heavy-duty computer-techie type. I bump up against my limits of technical knowledge every time I brew up my morning latte on our home espresso machine. That maddening blue "12:00" still flashes on and off on my VCR twenty-four hours a day—I've never learned to set it. And yet, I *have* learned to connect to the world of online self-help. So I'm confident that if a relative technodolt like *me* can do it, *you* can do it too.

Yes, it was a little scary at first. I had to do battle with my own innate technophobia. But on the whole, it was much easier than I'd imagined. I moved from fear to fascination to near addiction in a matter of weeks.

There were times I needed a helping hand. Luckily, I had friends and colleagues, both online and in real life, to help me through. In the same way, you'll find your real-life friends and neighbors with online experience—and your new online friends—only too willing to help you make the leap.

Why I Wrote This Book

I decided to write this book for both personal and professional reasons. In addition to my professional interest in the field, I'm an active self-helper myself. I've participated in face-to-face support groups for many years and have made extensive use of online resources to help me manage health concerns of my own. As such, I've participated in a number of forums, groups, and networks as both a helper and a helpee, seeking and receiving information and advice on and support for my own special topics of interest.

In my professional role as a physician and writer specializing in self-care and self-help, I wanted to write this book because I believe that the development of online self-help networks will let health-active consumers play a larger and more responsible role in managing their own health care. I would hope that this book might speed the process by which self-help and self-care are accepted as powerful and reliable resources for creating a more humane, more accessible, and more cost-effective health care system.

How to Use This Book

Health Online is divided into three principal parts: Part I covers the basics of the online world—e-mail, online friends, and a bit about the cultures and customs of self-help cyberspace. Part II takes you on a step-by-step tour through the self-help neighborhoods of each of the "Big Three" computer networks—America Online, CompuServe, and Prodigy—with a brief discussion of some of the others. Part III describes some of the most important groups, networks, and information sources on the Internet: mailing lists, newsgroups, World Wide Web sites, and more. The Epilogue provides a perspective on what it all means and speculates on how online self-help may change our health care system.

There's no need to read this book from front to back. Here are some tips for finding the right starting place:

- If you're still somewhat unsure about whether the online world is for you, or if you'd like to consider such basic questions as Why does going online feel so scary? What kind of a computer will I need to go online? Do I have everything I need to go online? or Why would I want to send anybody e-mail anyway? Why not just call them up on the phone? go to Chapter 1, "Going Online the Easy Way."

- If you've made the tentative decision to go online, but still consider yourself a novice in the online world, check out Chapter 2, "What You'll Find When You Get There," Chapter 3, "The Human Side of E-Mail," and Chapter 4, "Online Friends and Cyberspace Angels."

- If you'd like some help deciding which of the commercial computer networks to join, read Chapter 5, "America Online," Chapter 6, "CompuServe," Chapter 7, "Prodigy," and Chapter 8, "The Best of the Other Commercial Services." If you've already chosen a commercial network, zero in on the chapter or section that covers that service.

- If you're already pretty comfortable in the online world and would like to go directly to the listings of self-help resources on the Internet, go to Chapter 9, "Internet Mailing Lists," Chapter 10, "Internet Newsgroups," Chapter 11, "The World Wide Web," and Chapter 12, "Other Online Resources."

- If you'd like to read about the ways that online self-helpers could change our health care system, go to the epilogue, "The Healing Computer."

Several short sections at the end of the book, provide additional information: "How You Can Help Update This Book" explains how you can provide feedback for an updated edition. "A Note to Health and Computer Professionals" gives guidelines for professionals interested in publications and conferences in the new field of consumer health informatics. The Author's Notes provides comments and references for the topics covered in each chapter, and the Acknowledgments give credit where credit is due.

A Mouse Turning into an Elephant

Online self-help is too huge and rapidly growing a phenomenon to be completely covered within the limits of any printed volume. The changes in the online world are now occurring so rapidly that it taxes our ability to assimilate them. In the course of writing this book, I often felt like an artist who'd set out to do a painting of a mouse—only to discover that as I dabbed away at my canvas, my subject was transforming itself into an elephant. It is difficult to believe that when I started the research for this book, hardly anyone I knew had even heard of the World Wide Web.

Many new developments will doubtless take place between the time I write these words and the time you read them. People drop in, drop out, or move to different networks. Newsgroups and mailing lists and online forums change and close, and new ones come into being. Hundreds of new Web sites open every day.

That's why I've done my best to provide you with so many different ways to access the people and the networks and the other resources we've listed. Use the tips provided here as starting places. If you have trouble connecting with any of the online people or places described in the chapters that follow, don't give up; simply try another route.

Once you get online, the best way to find the resources and people you seek is simply to ask. Your online connection makes it easy to post your questions in all the right places. Most online self-helpers will go out of their way to help you find what you're looking for.

Before you begin your trip through the chapters that follow, let me make one final suggestion: When I find a book that means a lot to me, I read it with a selection of writing implements at hand: a yellow highlighter, a red pen, a black pen, and a pencil. As I proceed, I underline, highlight, take notes, turn down corners of pages, and mark any section that has a special meaning to me. I make notes to myself in the margins and use the front and back endpapers of the book to record a variety of impressions, thoughts, ideas, addresses, titles, and other things I want to remember.

As you make your way through *Health Online*, I strongly suggest that you annotate your book—assuming of course it's not a library or borrowed copy. Use the blank pages provided to record essential data: passwords and screen names and e-mail addresses. Record your thoughts and plans and ideas for other online resources you'd like to explore—or create. The more you do, the more this volume will become a customized guidebook to your own personal online information and support network.

Welcome Aboard

Finally, I'd like to speak for the thousands already involved in the world of online self-help: Please log on and join us. We'll be delighted to have you. And because we've been through the same process ourselves, we'll understand your fears and uncertainties about entering this strange new world. We're all part of the same amazing new community, and we'll do all we can to help.

See you online.

—Tom Ferguson, M.D.
DrTomHO@aol.com

The Best of Online Health: The Health Online Awards

In researching the world of online self-help, my colleagues and I have encountered some truly unique and wonderful resources and people that deserve special acknowledgment. We decided to present the Health Online Distinguished Achievement Awards to a few particularly outstanding services, resources, and people in the world of online self-help. As you read through the chapters that follow, you will from time to time come across a heading that looks like this:

Health Online Distinguished Achievement Award

To: Winnie Winner

For: Name of Accomplishment or Resource

While there are doubtless dozens of other online self-helpers and self-help resources that are equally deserving, these awards reflect my personal choices (and those of my advisers) of some of the most impressive people and resources in the world of online self-help.

A Glossary of Common Online Terms

Archive A library of online information available on many online forums and networks. Materials available may include past forum postings, logs of real-time meetings, files and programs contributed by members, databases, news clips, lists of frequently asked questions (FAQs) with answers, and other information.

Bandwidth The range of frequencies that can be transmitted over a given channel. The larger the bandwidth, the more information that can be transmitted. A telephone line has a relatively narrow bandwidth, the coaxial cable that supplies a TV signal has a wider bandwidth, and the bandwidth for fiber-optic cable is even wider.

BBS Bulletin board system, a small computer network, frequently running on a desktop computer, that can provide such online services as e-mail, forums, database access, chat groups, and Internet access. It is often called, simply, a bulletin board.

Bookmark A "memory" function of a Web browser that gives the user an easy way to return to Web pages previously visited. Once you find a site you like, be sure to save its address as a bookmark. You can then check back regularly with a single click of your mouse.

bps Bits per second, the speed at which a modem transmits information. A 14,400-bps modem transmits at 14,400 bits of information per second. Modem speed is also frequently called the baud rate, although technically the terms are not identical.

Chat group Online meetings where a number of self-helpers all log in to the same online "room" at the same time to exchange typed messages. Most self-help chat groups are found on the commercial services and meet at regularly scheduled times. On some commercial services, any member can start a chat group on any topic at any time. Chat groups are also sometimes called live chat or real-time meetings.

E-mail address An Internet address at which a person can receive e-mail. A typical e-mail address (this one happens to be mine) looks like this: DrTomHO@aol.com.

FAQ A list of frequently asked questions, with answers provided by veteran members of that particular forum or other online group. The FAQ contains much of the group wisdom on the topic of interest. It is a good idea for newcomers to any self-help group to ask if there's a FAQ for the group, and if so, to obtain a copy and read it before participating actively in group discussions.

Flame A critical, angry, or verbally abusive online tirade, rarely encountered in self-help cyberspace. Sending such a message is called flaming.

ftp (or FTP) File transfer protocol, a method of sending files to and from a remote computer on the Internet. It is also the name of the type of program used to make the transfer. In Internet addresses, it is always all lowercase.

gopher (or Gopher) An Internet search and retrieval system. A gopher client is software that runs on your computer and lets you get information from a gopher server (more software). A gopher site is a computer that has a gopher server running on it. Gopher sites are text-only sites; files have no graphics or hypertext links. The sites are mostly at university computer centers. Gopher client software can search gopher sites and other Internet resources.

Hotlist A personal list of favorite Web sites, kept on a special file in your Web browser to facilitate repeat visits.

HTML Hypertext Markup Language, the simple system of codes used to construct Web home pages. In Internet addresses, it is always all lowercase.

http (or HTTP) Hypertext Transfer Protocol, the software standards that make the World Wide Web work. In Internet addresses, it is always all lowercase.

Hypertext A marked section of text linked to another Web document. Hypertext links are typically identified by special underlined type. To retrieve the linked document, simply click on the hypertext.

Log A transcript of an online session, often used to record the exchanges of a real-time meeting. The software for some commercial services includes a Log function that enables users to keep a copy of all their online transactions. Sysops can sometimes supply a log for past meetings of a regularly scheduled online group you weren't able to attend. Sometimes, logs of past meetings are available in the group archives.

Lurking Logging on to a self-help forum or chat group as an observer and reading the messages without responding. This procedure is recommended for new group members. When a former lurker begins to take an active role, it's called "delurking."

Mailing list   A list of the e-mail addresses of individuals interested in a common subject. The list owner can receive and send shared messages to and from group members, creating an online discussion of the central topic. Mailing-list software, called a mail server, automates the handling of mail to and from such a list.

Modem   A device that allows your computer to send and receive digital data over a phone line or other channel. The modem got its name from its function as a *mo*dulator and *dem*odulator.

Moderated   A forum, mailing list, bulletin board, or newsgroup in which a human editor reviews and edits incoming postings and makes sure that only selected messages go out to other members. Commercial messages, off-topic postings, misdirected e-mail, flames, and other inappropriate messages are usually omitted.

Mosaic   The pioneering Web browser, still widely used.

Netscape   The most widely used Web browser. Technically the name of this software is Netscape Navigator.

Posting   A publicly accessible written message typed into a computer and sent via modem to a computer bulletin board, forum, mailing list, or newsgroup for others to read and respond to.

Real time   A general computer term indicating the actual time in which a physical process occurs. The "live" interactions of chat groups and similar types of communications are real-time.

Sysop   The host, organizer, or administrator of a forum, bulletin board, or other online group or network. The term had its origin as an abbreviated form of *sys*tem *op*erator.

Thread   A series of messages (or "postings") on a single topic, including the original message and all subsequent responses. One person starts the thread by establishing the subject heading and posting the first message. Later posters respond to the earlier messages, adding their own comments on the topic.

URL   Universal Resource Locator, the Internet "address" you need to find a given Web home page or other Internet resource. A typical URL might look like this: http://www.yahoo.com/health.

World Wide Web (WWW)   A hypertext-based protocol that provides access to various resources on the Internet. The Web makes it possible to create, access, and transfer online documents, e.g., Web sites or home pages, that contain a wide variety of multimedia resources, e.g., text, graphics, video, sound.

Part I

The Basics

This section provides a brief tour guide to the world of online self-help. And just to whet your appetite, here are twenty things you can do in self-help cyberspace:

1 Exchange private e-mail with existing friends.

2 Exchange private e-mail with new friends, e.g., self-helpers you meet online.

3 Search for, read, and download health-related information on a particular topic of concern from databases on your commercial service.

4 Find a support forum for your special area of concern on your commercial service.

5 Read the postings by other self-helpers on your chosen support forum.

6 Respond to postings by private e-mail or by a public message on the forum—or start a new topic.

7 Attend a scheduled online self-help meeting on your topic of choice in a virtual room on your commercial network.

8 Send a private instant message to another person attending the meeting—the equivalent of whispering in someone's ear.

9 Participate in a drop-in or ad-hoc online chat session—or set up a chat session of your own in a virtual room and invite others to come.

10 Search for health news on a given topic or set up a standing search that will automatically send you news items on your chosen topic.

11 Exchange real-time instant messages with another member of your commercial service who is logged on at the same time.

12 Attend a theater-style appearance in a virtual auditorium by an author, health expert, or other speaker.

13   Read the postings on an Internet newsgroup on a topic of interest to you—and add your own postings.

14   Subscribe to a self-help mailing list. Once you've subscribed, you'll receive all list messages by e-mail and may post your own by e-mailing to the list address.

15   Read current and past issues of a wide variety of magazines, newspapers, and medical journals.

16   Consult an online Web page directory that lists hundreds of health-related Web pages. You can then access any of the pages listed with a single click.

17   Jump to other health-related Web pages by simply clicking on the hot links you'll find on the first site you visit.

18   Use your Web browser to access a Gopher site, where you can read or download files.

19   Subscribe to an e-mail newsletter.

20   Set up your own informal e-mail mailing list.

Chapter 1

Going Online the Easy Way

You can't kiss anybody [online], and nobody can punch you in the nose, but a lot can happen within those boundaries.

Howard Rheingold
The Virtual Community

YOU'RE PROBABLY READING THIS BOOK right now because you're curious about the positive potential of cyberspace. Perhaps you have a sense there's something interesting going on in the world of online self-help and you want to be a part of it. Maybe you're already a part of it, and you'd like to become more involved. Or maybe you're an experienced self-helper in the face-to-face world and are curious about what you might be able to do online. Perhaps you picked up this book because you still don't really understand why people could get so excited about online self-help networks.

You get excited when you realize that there are special-interest support networks on *your* top-priority concerns just a few mouse clicks away. You get excited because you get a whole new opportunity to make like-minded friends, to give and receive support, and to become a regular in one or more virtual support communities. For many people, the online friends they make in cyberspace can become as important as the real-world friends they already have. And online communications can help broaden and deepen existing friendships and family links—both with locals and with friends and family who live far away.

There are other benefits as well: Many self-helpers can use online discussion groups to "talk" to experts on their particular area of concern (e.g., anxiety, toilet training, breast cancer, Crohn's disease, obsessive-compulsive disorder, or parenting a teenager). You can trade e-mail with researchers who are developing new treatments for a medical or psychological condition that affects your child (e.g., attention deficit disorder, childhood diabetes, or Down's syndrome). You can join an online self-help group for those who share your specific concerns (e.g., adoption, alcoholism, AIDS, stuttering, or recovery from a heart attack). You can use your online communications as a form of psychotherapy. You can chat, argue, flirt, lecture, share information, give and get emotional support, and much, much more. But above all you can make new friends and deepen existing friendships.

On Keypals and Cyberfriendships

When I first went online, I had my doubts that I would really be able to become friends with someone I'd never met, never even seen a picture of, after communicating only by computer. The idea that you can make friends around the country and around the world while sitting at your keyboard is a big stretch for most of us. When online friends first tried to convince me of the possibility, I thought it was the craziest idea I'd ever heard.

Now that I've spent some time on the computer networks, I have to say that being online has become a very important part of my life, both personally and professionally.

I've learned to communicate more conveniently and effectively with a number of people I already knew. I've had satisfying and enjoyable face-to-face meetings with a variety of friends I first met online. And I continue to have valuable interactions with many online friends I've never met—and probably never will.

I look forward to checking my e-mail because I know that there are people out there who care about me and share my interests and concerns and passions. It has become a nurturing and sustaining part of my life. I feel that I have my own informal online support community. And I know that I am an important source of online support for others.

Why Going Online Seems So Scary

I can also understand that you may have some fears about joining the online revolution. If so, you're not alone. According to a recent Gallup poll, roughly half of those surveyed admitted that they had similar concerns. The reasons given for cyberphobia included:

- Anxiety about the constant need to learn new skills
- Fear of losing privacy
- Information overload
- Fear of losing face-to-face contacts

I can well remember how anxious *I* felt venturing into this unknown realm. *Everyone* experiences some uncertainty at first. You wouldn't be fully human if you didn't. I still experience those feelings when logging on to a new system—or on those (happily quite rare) occasions when I encounter technical difficulties.

I can assure you that most cyberphobia is simply fear of the unfamiliar. Once you get there, the real thing feels quite safe. Indeed, once you've made the leap, the biggest problem may be liking your online connection so much you're tempted to run up big online bills. But as we'll see, there are ways to manage this problem too.

Going online used to be quite a hassle. But if you follow the guidelines in the following chapters, you'll see that going online is just not all that difficult these days. Help is almost always close at hand. And the people you meet and the other online discoveries you make will draw you on.

By the time you finish this book, you'll know everything you need to know to log on and begin using your service of choice. And we'll show you how to pick up the rest online.

So hang in there. You can do it. While it may feel a bit strange at first, before you know it you'll be logging on with hardly a second thought. It won't be long before your regular online sessions will become as much a part of your life as brushing your teeth or talking on the telephone.

What You'll Need to Go Online

To go online you'll need four key pieces of equipment: a computer, a modem, a phone line, and the software that will connect you to your online service provider.

- **Computer** Just about any kind of a personal computer will do the trick. While most of the advice in this book applies to computers that run the DOS, Windows, or Macintosh operating system, a variety of other operating systems also can be used.

- **Modem** Pick your computer first, then choose a modem that's compatible. (Some computers come with a modem already installed.) Get the fastest modem you can afford—it will mean less waiting while accessing graphics-intensive resources. If you don't currently own a computer, you'll probably want to get your computer and modem as a package from the same dealer.

- **Phone line** You can use your existing phone line to log on to your online service. But if you do, people trying to call you while you're online will get a busy signal. (Signing up for a voice mail service will keep you from missing calls while you're online.) If you end up spending a good deal of time online, you may want to consider getting a second phone line.
- **Software** All the major commercial services will send you a free software package (available in DOS, Windows, or Macintosh format—be sure to specify which) that will allow you to connect to their host computer. For tips on choosing a commercial service provider, see Part II.

Identifying the Friends Who Will Help You Go Online

When it gets right down to it, the process of going online is itself almost always a self-help phenomenon: People learn to do it from other people—from friends, neighbors, and colleagues, online and off—as well as from books like this one.

Most of us get our first online experience by looking over a friend's shoulder, and most online "net bunnies" will be only too happy to give you a demonstration of their favorite online haunts. When you get ready to take the big step, you may want to ask one of your experienced online friends to come over and walk you through your first few sessions.

If possible, seek advice from several friends who're familiar with the online universe. Suppose you have a good friend who's active on CompuServe, and she's dying to show you how to surf the net. That's a strong argument for choosing the same network for your first step into cyberspace.

There are a number of other advantages to joining the same commercial network your friends belong to. While you can send e-mail to friends on other services, on some services there's an extra charge for receiving such e-mail. And to attend a real-time online meeting or lecture or to participate in a support forum, you must be a member of the same service. If you have other friends who're ready to make the leap into the online world, you all may want to pick the same provider and log on together.

Mark my words, a few months from now, you'll be laughing about your reluctance to take this giant step into the future, and you'll wonder how you were ever able to get by in the days before e-mail. Also, if you're like me, once you've made the leap into the online world, you'll immediately start nagging your closest friends to do likewise. You'll be dying to exchange e-mail and e-clips and news of your latest online discoveries.

Remember too that you are something of a pioneer. Cyberspace is a young, rapidly growing world, and you're getting into it quite a bit ahead of the pack. There'll be many others coming along later.

By the time you're feeling totally at home on the net, there'll be hundreds of thousands of new online explorers, clueless "newbies" who will need *your* help to learn how to get around.

Be patient with them. Remember: Going online *can* be a little intimidating at first.

Q *How much will the hardware cost?*

A As we go to press, you can find a bare-bones system that will let you go online for less than $1,000. Systems with extra features will cost more. And although it may be a bit more hassle, you may be able to find a used system for considerably less.

Q *OK, I have a computer and a modem. What do I do now?*

A Decide which of the commercial computer networks you want to join. (We'll devote Chapters 5 through 8 to helping you figure out which will be best for you.) Then call the 800 number for your chosen service. They'll send you a disk with their free software by first-class mail. It should arrive within a week or so.

When your software package arrives, simply put the disk in your machine, follow the easy step-by-step directions on your computer screen, and within ten to fifteen minutes, you'll be online.

Q *Can I use the software my commercial service sends me to log on to other networks? to computer bulletin boards? to the Internet?*

A The software you'll receive from your commercial computer network is a proprietary telecommunications program that will allow you to connect only to the service that sent it. To log on to a computer bulletin board, you'll need to obtain a general-purpose telecommunications program. (You can buy a commercial package or use freeware or shareware.) And while you can't use the software your commercial service provides to connect *directly* to the Internet, you can access most of the features of the Internet *through* most commercial services.

Q *Can I really use America Online, CompuServe, or Prodigy to access the Internet?*

A Yes. All these services now provide access to a wide range of Internet resources. Accessing the Internet through a commercial service is often easier than setting up a direct Internet account.

Q *How much is all this going to cost?*

A The basic monthly charge for the Big Three commercial services runs about $9 to $10 a month minimum. This generally covers the first five hours of online use. After that, it's about $2 to $3 per additional hour. If you read and write your e-mail offline and don't spend too much time exploring the boards, your online bill should run between $10 and $20 per month.

On the other hand, it's not completely unheard of for people to run up bills of $100 to $200 per month or even more if they attend a lot of online meetings or spend hours searching for information. Some of the services described in the chapters that follow offer special low rates for heavy users.

Q *What is a users' group and how can I find one?*

A A users' group is like a club that gets together to discuss a common computer interest. There are hundreds of local users' groups for DOS, Windows, and Macintosh computers—as well as for many other specific computer-related topics. One good way to begin learning more about going online is to find out if there's a local users' group in your community for your type of computer, and then attend a meeting (especially if they have a special meeting or subgroup devoted to going online, the Internet, or the commercial networks).

These meetings are generally both interesting and fun. You'll find people who are at all levels of knowledge and experience in terms of using their computers, including a lot of people who are interested in doing things online. You may find a formal or informal consultant who'll help you get up and running online. To find a local users' group, consult the following:

- The business pages of your local paper
- The computer writer or columnist at your local paper
- Local computer dealers
- Computer science teachers at a local high school or college
- Computer-savvy friends and colleagues, especially those with some online experience

Q *I have some serious hesitations about getting involved in the online world. My boyfriend is a real net bunny. He logs on at least two or three times a day. When he does, I notice that he goes into a strange sort of trance. It's as though* *his brain were physically connected to that computer and modem. I've given up trying to talk to him when he's online. It really seems like an altered state, to the point where it sometimes scares me. I don't want to become a zombie linked to my computer to the point of ignoring everything around me. Do you think will happen to me if I log on?*

A You're right, online services can be so interesting and so attractive that people sometimes get totally absorbed in them. It's all too easy to get distracted from your main purpose in going online and end up hours later with the realization that you've been traipsing around on some new section of your commercial computer network or the Internet. Your eyes are bloodshot, your mind is numb, and you hardly know where you've been.

But let me assure you that there *are* people who can deal with being online and also be very aware of a crying baby, a family member, or others in their environment. This ability varies a great deal from person to person. If, when you go online, you tend to "space out" like your boyfriend, it may be a good idea to set a timer and limit yourself to 30 minutes or so per session.

Q *I'm a busy woman, with a job, a family, and a busy social life. I barely have a spare moment in my life right now. I'm worried that if I go online, it may suck up more time than I can afford.*

A You're completely in control of your own level of involvement in the online world. You can spend as much or as little time online as you like. Your phone will never ring. Your beeper will never go off. And unless you set it up otherwise, checking your e-mail is never an emergency.

The problem, if you want to call it that, is that you may *want* to spend more time on the Net—because you find it so much fun.

The best way to keep your time commitment to a minimum is to confine yourself to certain times of the day or to a certain length of time per session, or to both. (Most people end up using online services most heavily in the evening.) The best way to keep your e-mail sessions short is to prioritize: Answer the important messages first and, if necessary, simply postpone or ignore the rest.

Q *I still have some serious reservations about going online. First, I don't have any free time as it is. Second, I'm on a tight budget and I'm afraid it will cost a lot. And third, I'm a computer moron and I don't look forward to the technical hassles. On the other hand, I'm half afraid that if I don't go online pretty soon,*

I'll label myself as hopelessly out of date, lose touch with my friends, and deprive myself of the most useful tool since the telephone. Are my fears realistic? Or should I just go ahead and take the plunge and not worry about it?

A Great question! This is exactly how many people feel before they make the jump.

Your fears about losing touch with your friends if you don't go online may be well grounded. Many of the people who have made the jump to the online world now regard the U.S. mail—almost always derisively termed "snail mail" on the Net—as something close to a prehistoric relic. This view reflects the fact that communicating by e-mail is so convenient and so easy for people who have learned to do it that they prefer that medium to all others.

In the days before I went online, there were certain people I just couldn't get through to because they were spending all their time in the online world. There are growing numbers of such people.

My suggestion: Try it for two or three months. If it's not working for you by then, let it go—or limit your use to occasional e-mail to friends and family.

Chapter 2

What You'll Find
When You Get There

One cannot travel very far on the data networks without coming across new communities, new friendships, and spontaneous acts of kindness among strangers, a phenomenon that sometimes seems to be all too rare 'in the real world.'

Peter H. Lewis
The New York Times

———— ◆ ————

BEFORE YOU GO ONLINE, the idea that you might be able to connect with others in any intimate or meaningful way by exchanging typed messages on a computer bulletin board may sound extremely farfetched. Let me assure you that online self-help forums can be genuine, meaningful communities. Think of them as support groups in slow motion.

The participants in support forums are much more than random assortments of online strangers. By their very presence, they've already demonstrated their special concern for the topic—be it AIDS, depression, or a desire to lose weight. Knowing that others in your online community are walking the same path, understanding that they've come to give and receive support, seeing the remarkable candor and empathy of their online interactions, you'll soon feel comfortable sharing even the most personal, frank, and difficult feelings. Online self-helpers often say they can share feelings on their favorite self-help forums they could never discuss at home—even with their closest friends and family members.

Even in the most extreme difficulties, online forums can help. Here's one of several dozen deeply sympathetic replies to a self-helper whose young son had just been killed in a freak accident:

```
Dear Jack,
    There're no words to express the sympathy we all feel--for
you, for your wife, and for everyone who shared in the loss of
your son. I've been there too--several years ago, I lost my
dear sister to murder. For awhile, I didn't think I could go
on. Here are the four most important things I learned from my
own experience of healing:
    1. Don't drink or use drugs--and I mean not at all. (I'm
not talking about medicines prescribed by a doctor.) Remember
that alcohol is a depressant--something you don't need even one
drink of right now.
    2. Continue with your therapist, even though your sessions
are painful. If she suggests an antidepressant medication, you
should seriously consider it. If you have other children, be
sure they get help too.
    3. If you're involved in a church or other faith community,
see if they have a grief support group. And if your tradition
includes healing prayer or services for the dead, use them to
help heal your grief.
    4. Above all, make a pact with your wife to be extra kind
to each other. Never, never blame each other for your son's
death. For the next few months, your relationship will be under
the worst imaginable stress. Sometimes people are so desperate
to stop the pain that they'll do anything--even divorce. But
even that doesn't stop it. It just adds more problems. So be
kind to each other. You've both lost so much.
    Wish I had the magic words.
    P.S. There's a wonderful support group called Compassionate
Friends for parents who've lost a child. To find the nearest
chapter, call (708) 990-0010.
```

In the course of researching this book, I put out online requests for personal stories that showed how online links could be a valuable resource for anyone going through a health-related crisis. Here's one of the many responses I received:

```
Subj: Cyberspace Love and Other Strangers
From: Linda A. Kerwin
    I live in Atlanta, but I'm currently here in Cincinnati,
caring for my mother, who has inoperable cancer. I arrived
here several months ago and have yet to go home.
    The day I arrived, the cancer ruptured through my mother's
intestines and out the abdominal wall. A few days later, it
ruptured again. The doctors gave her less than a week to live.
But here it is months later and, happily, she's still hanging
in there. I've been her primary caregiver 24 hours a day.
```

```
      I arrived with four days worth of clothes. After the first
month, a friend brought me my car, my dog, and my computer.
Luckily, I'd just joined CompuServe a few weeks before.
      Once I had my computer, I began doing my own online
research. I first posted on MedSig [Medical Special Interest
Group], then on the Cancer Forum. During the early and most
confusing days, I received the most helpful responses from
physicians, most of them oncologists, on MedSig.
      Responses from the Cancer Forum didn't start to kick in
till later. (I'd recommend posting frantic 'Help!' type mes-
sages on both Forums for the quickest and most helpful
responses.) I've also been participating a lot on the Cancer
Support and Gyn.Onc. sections and also the Hospice section.
      I can't tell you what it meant to have help, advice, sup-
port and encouragement available literally overnight. These
people are wonderful to give so freely of their time and
knowledge. And much of the advice I've received online is
more complete and more useful than what I get face-to-face
from our attending physician. More than once, the kindness of
strangers has brought tears to my eyes.
      I use e-mail to stay in touch with my friends back home
too--I keep everyone up to date by preparing one main letter
and customizing copies for everyone. I've more than once
referred to the network as my "lifeline." When people say
they don't know how I keep going, I tell them I actually have
plenty of friends and a lot of support--I'm referring to my
friends on CompuServe. I know I can log on whenever I need
to, so I don't feel so alone.
```

As Linda's story shows, when people go online to find health information, what they end up getting is not just the kind of information you might find in a reference book. They connect with people, not just data. And so they receive—and give—something much more personalized and interactive.

"Information-plus-Involvement"

A recent Louis Harris poll showed that Americans listed "obtaining information on staying healthy, on diseases or related topics" as their number one choice when asked what they'd most like to see on our emerging online systems. And when self-helpers do go online, most, like Linda, find it even more valuable than they'd expected.

People new to the Net often expect to find a sort of giant electronic health encyclopedia, containing the same kind of polished, impersonal prose you might find in a medical reference book. While this kind of material *is* available, most self-helpers prefer to get what they need not from such impersonal sources, but from online support communities, which offer a combination of sympathetic listening, shared experiences, information, support, expert advice, advocacy, and the companionship of fellow self-helpers.

The kind of information online self-helpers value most is not the traditional professionally prepared patient education material you might find in a clinic handout. Rather, it is the kind of *information-plus-involvement* you can only find within a caring self-help community. And if you choose to become involved, you, like Linda, will undoubtedly have an opportunity to give, as well as receive, advice and support.

Don't get me wrong. In some cases the traditional kind of "canned" information is just what the doctor ordered. You may want to look up the side effects of a new drug or read a description of a particular diagnostic test, and you can certainly do so. In the chapters that follow, I'll describe a variety of excellent online health databases.

But even if you choose to use one, you'll probably want to discuss what you've found with fellow members of your favorite self-help forum, bulletin board, or discussion group. These communities can provide much more than just the traditional patient education information:

- A chance to meet experienced self-helpers who share your interests
- A chance to benefit from the experiences of others who have dealt with the same or similar problems
- A chance to discuss your problem with a variety of knowledgeable health professionals
- The opportunity to receive support and understanding from a caring, supportive community
- And, possibly, the beginnings of new online friendships

Most online self-help thus involves two-way, not just one-way, communication. That's why going online may feel more like getting to know a new community than like visiting your local library. The process you'll go through is much like venturing out into a new neighborhood, walking around the streets, meeting people, getting to know the neighbors. Before long you find you're getting into conversations, being invited into people's houses, and attending neighborhood social events. And before you know it, you'll start to feel that you're a vital member of the community.

Doing Your Own Editing

Whether we realize it or not, most of what we read in magazines, newspapers, and books, including this one, is highly processed, polished, and proofread. This chapter went through more than twenty-five drafts, was reviewed by nearly a dozen people, and was run through spelling and grammar checkers several times. But while the resulting product may be nicely polished, it is inevitably shaped and "sanitized" by the preferences and sensibilities of those doing the writing and the editing. To cite just one example: In an earlier draft of this chapter I had included the original message by the self-helper whose son died in an accident. In his e-mail comments on that draft, my editor commented:

```
The message describing the death of Jack's son feels too
strong to me. The later quote by Linda explains how support
flows in times of crisis, but the death of Jack's son is so
sad...that I fear it may flood your readers' minds with ques-
tions and emotions, distracting them from your message
instead of reinforcing it.
```

After some consideration, I decided that he was right and cut the section. I think that on the whole this makes the chapter more readable—and certainly more professional—but at a price. The current draft lacks some of the raw human drama of the earlier draft.

In contrast, much of the information you'll find on the Net is unprocessed, unpolished, and uncensored. It may therefore sometimes come across as raw, sloppy, and "unprofessional," with frequent typos and misspellings. You may come across postings or receive e-mail messages that are highly emotional. An occasional posting may even strike you as ill mannered. Although this is relatively rare in self-help cyberspace, online bad manners are quite common in other online neighborhoods.

Netters sometimes refer to the "signal-to-noise ratio," often abbreviated as the S2N ratio. In some newsgroups there may be only one interesting posting (signal) for every three or four messages that, for your purposes, are a near or total waste of time (noise). These messages may include off-topic comments, flames, requests to unsubscribe, and comments that quote so many previous messages that you lose all interest before getting anywhere near the end. Such groups are said to have a low S2N ratio. Unmoderated newsgroups and mailing lists are frequently the worst in this respect. The forums on the commercial services and the moderated (i.e., edited) mailing lists and newsgroups are usually much better.

Don't be put off by the presence of such "unprofessional" content on the Net. This is not supposed to be *Time* magazine, after all. The other side of the coin is that you get a wonderful variety of points of view, something unequaled in the mass media. An important part of the online revolution is realizing that we have become accustomed to letting others do our editing for us. On online networks, we get to do our own.

Finding low-quality, off-topic, or misdirected material is irritating to everyone at first. But in the end it is a reasonable price to pay for the privilege of participating in this brave new medium. You'll soon learn to skim through the chaff and focus on the good stuff.

How a Forum Works

When you first venture onto a self-help forum, bulletin board, or discussion group, a good place to start is the message area, where you'll find postings on many topics by a variety of members. On many systems, these messages are organized by folders or by thread (a sequence of postings on the same topic).

A message area of a forum is basically very simple:

1. One person posts a message.
2. Others respond with messages on the same topic.

In their first visits to a given forum, most self-helpers will engage in the following activities—although not necessarily in this order:

1. **"Lurking."** Reading without posting is a good way to check out a new forum. Just browse through the list of subject headings, reading the messages that interest you. This should help give you a sense of whether the forum is for you. And you may begin to notice one or more particularly interesting "voices" among the regular participants.

2. **Private Introductions**. Introduce yourself to the sysop (host) or other active forum members by private e-mail. This is a good way to get additional information about the forum, forum archives and files, and real-time meetings. It's also a comfortable, low-level way to "get your toe in the water" of forum participation.

3. **Public Introductions**. If you decide you'd like to become a more active forum member, you may want to introduce yourself to the group at large by posting a public message telling other forum members a little about yourself. Some forums have a special section or format for self-introductions. As customs vary from forum to forum, you may want to read other members' self-introductions first to get an idea of how to introduce yourself.

4. **Posting to an Ongoing Thread**. Contribute to one or more of the ongoing discussions, or threads, by posting public messages that respond to earlier messages.

5 **Starting a New Thread**. Post your own question or comment on a new topic to start a new thread.

6. **Real-Time Meetings**. Attend a real-time get-together in a virtual meeting room.

Your First Trip Online

Let's say you're a 43-year-old leukemia survivor named Lois, and you're just logging on to your commercial service for the first time. You click into the message section on the health forum you've chosen and are offered a menu that includes the following choices:

General Health Discussions	Alternative Healing Approaches
Self-Help & Support Groups	For Men or Women Only
Mental Health Issues & Concerns	Running, Exercise & Fitness
Health Professionals' Networks	Cerebral Palsy/Related Concerns
Health Reform & Consumerism	Multiple Sclerosis

You click on "Self-Help & Support Groups" and find yourself offered the following options. (This list is edited. The real list is considerably longer.)

12-Steppers & Recovery	Hepatitis
AIDS/HIV	Herpes Support
Alopecia Areata	HIV+ Mates
ALS [Lou Gehrig's disease]	Incontinence
Arthritis & Lupus Support	Living With Cancer
Attention Deficit Disorder	Lupus
Breast Cancer Support Group	Menopause Support
Chronic Fatigue Syndrome	Neurofibromatosis
Chronic Illnesses Support	Overcoming Eating Disorders
Crohn's, Colitis & IBD Support	Parents of Children w/Disorders
Death & Dying Support	Parkinson's Disease
Diabetes Support	Rare Disorders Info & Support
Dieters Unite!	Sexual Abuse Support Group
Diverticulitis	Suicide Prevention
Headaches	Thyroid Problems
Heart Disease Survivors	Transplant Survivors

You click on "Living With Cancer" and are presented with yet another long list of message titles, accompanied by the screen names of the authors. As you read through the messages in the folder, you find many discussions of problems and experiences, ranging from chemotherapy, remission, and recurrence to the shock of diagnosis and difficulties in dealing with doctors and family members.

You come across several messages from "GlennaT" and notice that Glenna is very active on the board, answering lots of people's questions, providing resources. She's courteous, attentive, and knowledgeable and seems to be acting as a kind of hostess for the group. One of her messages reads as follows:

> Hi, everyone. I'd like to invite you to meet with us in the LIVING With Cancer Support Group. We meet each Sunday evening at 7 p.m. EST in the Better Health & Medical Forum Chat Room. Each Sunday there's a different subject for discussion, and there's never a shortage of friendly and sympathetic self-helpers eager to help you and hear what's happening in your life.

Her sign-off quote is "Life is a dance if you take all the steps."

You now have the option of posting a message on the public message board, for public access. But you're still feeling a little nervous and don't feel ready to do that. Instead, you decide to send GlennaT the following e-mail message:

> Hi, Glenna. I saw your message about the LIVING With Cancer Support Group and wanted to see how I might participate. My name is Lois. I'm 43. I was diagnosed with leukemia four years ago, had many sessions of chemotherapy, and am currently in remission...

You go on to give her some of the details of your own situation. Within a matter of hours, she e-mails back:

> Hi, Lois! Of course, you're welcome to come to the LIVING With Cancer support group! There aren't any qualifications to meet before you can come. Some of our members don't have cancer and never have, some of us have HIV/AIDS, some have cancer, and some, like you, are in remission. I have both AIDS and spinal cancer. I'm sorry to hear about the lack of a local cancer support group that feels right for you. It was the same for me until we got this online group going.
> Your news about being in remission from your leukemia is just great! I always like hearing about folks who are winners against cancer. I think you'll have much to offer the group. As a survivor you will be a walking, breathing symbol of hope for a lot of us. And, perhaps, we can be there for you to help with the fear of a relapse and any other feelings or problems you're having...

Our current schedule is to meet every Sunday at 7PM EST in the Better Health & Medical Forum Chat Room. We usually have an announced topic for discussion--though we follow the topic very loosely. If a member comes with a need to talk about something else we usually scrap the topic and all try to be there for them. The meeting is usually logged, so if you miss a meeting and would like to have a log of it, I can send you one.

In a few days, I'll be sending out a ballot to vote on the next 8 weeks of topics and I'd love to add your name to the mailing list. Would you like to participate in the voting?

In answer to your question, the best way to make friends online is to participate in the real-time meetings or live chats. Second to that, the message area of the forum is a real gold mine. Many of my dearest friends today are people I first met through the forum.

You decide to take GlennaT's advice. You log in at the appointed time and attend your first online support group meeting. You meet lots of other people who are dealing with cancer—you recognize many of the names from the postings you read in the "LIVING With Cancer" folder. The two-hour meeting goes by very quickly. You selected the "Log" command before you joined the meeting, so after you sign off, you open the log and read over the transcript of the meeting you've just attended.

You're amazed at how much happened in so short a time. You realize that you picked up a great deal of useful information and met several people you'd like to talk to again.

As you continue to attend the group and read and respond to the forum's postings, you gradually get to know your online friends better and better, and they gradually get to know you. As these relationships deepen, you'll begin to care more and more about them. You find yourself looking forward to your next meeting, to your next batch of e-mail.

It feels as if a whole new realm has opened up in your life, a place where you can always go, twenty-four hours a day. And there will always be somebody there who knows you, somebody interested in what's happening with you, someone who'd like to hear what's going on. In a surprisingly short time, it begins to feel like a real community.

Basketball, Butterflies, Barbie Dolls, and Other Online Forums

One final note on getting the most from online forums: A great deal of support takes place on special-interest boards devoted to topics that are not explicitly listed as health or support groups (e.g., computer forums, hobby boards, professional discussion groups).

You might not think that an online group for collectors of Barbie dolls could be a major source of mutual support, but in fact it is. A group of Barbie doll collectors on GEnie (see Chapter 8) has "become a support group for any one of us who may be having a rough time with life in general." If you're a Barbie doll collector, you can join with others who share your passion by logging on to the Collecting Roundtable and selecting Category 26, where you can receive your social support and make pals while discussing your Barbie doll collection.

There are online forums for almost every conceivable topic. So in addition to checking out online resources for your health-related interests, I'd strongly recommend that you choose at least one other non-health-related online community to be a part of. The best guideline is simply to choose a topic or topics (e.g., books, figure skating, hunting, archeology, basketball, a favorite music group or TV show) that would be the most fun.

Q *Talking with other self-helpers is well and good, but suppose I just want to track down a specific piece of health information, without posting my message on a forum or bulletin board or talking to anybody? Are there some good general health databases I could use to find a specific piece of health information?*

A All of the commercial services have searchable or browsable health encyclopedias and databases; see Chapters 5, 6, and 7 for descriptions of the such resources available on America Online, CompuServe, and Prodigy. My personal favorites are the Health Reference Center on CompuServe (includes full-text articles from both popular and professional sources) and MEDLINE on America Online (provides abstract-only searches of the professional medical literature). You'll find more on both in Chapters 5 and 6.

Q *I've heard that women online may be subject to come-ons, rudeness, flaming, and downright harassment. Is this something I need to be worried about?*

A For the most part, members of online self-help communities are well-behaved. However, you may encounter bad online behavior on any part of the Net. You may also run into people who are less than honest, so it pays to be cautious about meeting people online.

In some online areas, women, especially those with female-sounding screen names, may have to deal with tasteless or flirtatious messages. The best response is to block further transmissions from offenders (on forums that allow this option) or to simply ignore them.

If you plan to spend much time on the forums, it may be wise to choose a screen name that is not provocative or inflammatory in any way. One's screen name, like a person's appearance, is a real trigger for first impressions. If you don't want to be immediately identified by gender, you can give yourself a non-gender-specific screen name that will eliminate some of these potential difficulties.

As one self-helper wrote of her experiences in singles' chat groups:

> "Andreanna usually gets immediate attention from many of the males in any onscreen room I go into, and I sometimes get more Instant Messages [IMs] than I can answer. Happy2B gets very few IMs and little response from the people in the chat rooms because no one is sure whether I am male or female. Annie12345 gives me a positive identity as a woman, but evidently is not as intriguing as Andreanna, so that I am not bombarded with IMs."

Q *I've noticed that many self-helpers first go online to meet their own needs, then become much more interested in helping others. Why is that?*

A I've noticed the same thing. People online seem unusually willing to go out of their way to help others in their electronic network. There are many tales of unexpected levels of online altruism on the self-help networks. Here's just one:

When Brendan Keho, the 24-year-old author of the legendary *Zen and the Art of the Internet*, a popular guide to cyberspace, was severely hurt in an auto accident, the word spread throughout the Internet within hours, in a pattern *New York Times* writer Peter H. Lewis described as "the cyberspace equivalent of jungle drums."

Friends posted regular online updates on his condition. Dozens of cyberbuddies offered financial help. Others sent current state-of-the-art medical information gleaned from medical journals and medical databases. When Keho regained consciousness, online friends who'd had similar experiences offered advice on what to expect in the days ahead.

In the days before online links, none of that would have happened. Readers of Keho's book might never have heard of his misfortune. And if they did, it would not have been nearly as easy to join together to provide that kind of encouragement and support. One reason online self-helpers exhibit such a notable level of altruistic behavior is that online networks provide an almost effortless way to show our innate concern for others.

Chapter 3

The Human Side of E-Mail

E-mail is sooo easy—it's always a lot more fun than working on what I should really be doing.

Julia Karet
Health Educator

ONCE YOU GO ONLINE, you can send e-mail to anyone else who has an e-mail address, and all your friends who have online connections will be able to send e-mail to you, twenty-four hours a day, no matter where in the world they may live. Little wonder that most Net users find that sending and receiving e-mail is their primary online activity.

But what is e-mail, anyway? What does a piece of e-mail look like? And why in the world would anyone be interested in communicating with others by typing into a computer? These are some questions I was asking myself not long ago. Frankly, I had my doubts. It seemed like such a strange thing to do.

How do I feel a year later? Let me just say that at the moment I have more than two hundred messages in my electronic mailbox.

E-mail is such a powerful, easy, and fun way to communicate that it can easily become addictive. When I first started using e-mail, I would eagerly rush to read my messages first thing each morning. But I soon had to stop. I found myself spending so much time on e-mail I didn't get much else done.

I currently use e-mail as a reward. After I finish my other essential tasks (like writing this chapter), I get to read my e-mail.

E-Mail: The Benefits

First of all, e-mail can handle many of your current communications needs—contacts that formerly required a letter, a phone call, or an in-person interaction—more conveniently and effectively:

- No more phone tag. Your correspondent is in a meeting, in the bathroom, or out to lunch? No problem. Your e-mail message will be there whenever he or she is ready to receive it.

- No more interruptions. If you stop by or phone, your friends are forced to drop everything to accommodate you. With e-mail, they can respond when the time is right for them.

- No more catching people at a bad time. You'll never have to worry that your correspondent is in the middle of an argument or in a bad mood. People log on only when they're ready to handle your message.

- No more wasting fifteen minutes on a phone call or half an hour getting a letter just right—unless you want to. I can often compose and send a satisfactory e-mail message in just a minute or two.

- No more unintentionally leaving friends or colleagues "out of the loop." With e-mail, it's always easy to send a copy of any message to a friend—or a whole list of friends.

- No more distractions that prevent you from saying what you really want to say. When you're sending e-mail, no one can act preoccupied, sound uncomfortable, change the subject, or put you on hold. And when they read your message, you'll most likely have your correspondent's complete attention.

- No more holding back on the topics that are most important to *you*. Online discussions are often more frank and open than face-to-face interactions. Once they get used to it, most people feel more comfortable being candid via e-mail than with in-person interactions.

- No more feeling you can't talk to your boss, your elected officials, or other "important" people. E-mail levels hierarchies by giving everyone the same access to everyone on the network.

- No more unconscious prejudices about things like looks, age, ethnic background, or disabilities. When you send e-mail, these potential communication barriers simply disappear. You will, however, be judged by the quality of your thinking, your feelings, your prose style, your typing accuracy, and (unfortunately for people like me) your spelling.

- With e-mail, it's always easy to keep a record of your online conversations.

- E-mail allows you to connect with many new friends you'd never have met without it.

Twenty-Five Essential E-Mail Tips

Using e-mail is much easier than it may first appear. Most people take to it like a duck to water. Here are some guidelines for getting the most from this powerful new medium:

1. When you're composing a new piece of e-mail, you'll see a special blank for "subject." Take this opportunity to enter a short, well-chosen title for each piece of e-mail you write. This will help your correspondents sort and file your message quickly.

2. Keep messages brief. Use short sentences.

3. E-mail is not a business letter. You're not expected to use any particular format. Feel free to develop your own e-mail style, using any form you like. Just focus on what you want to say.

4. Don't bother with fancy formatting (bold type, italics, etc.) on your e-mail messages. Except for e-mail sent within some commercial networks, only basic characters are sent. Colored letters, fancy display type, curly quotation marks, em-dashes, tab marks, bullets, and other fancy characters will be lost.

5. You can't boldface or underline when sending e-mail, but you can emphasize a word by using CAPITALS or by using an _underline_ or an *asterisk* before and after the word.

6. Use all caps sparingly. WRITING IN ALL CAPS for more than a word or two is considered shouting and is considered rude. Use an asterisk or an underscore at the beginning or end of a phrase to give it special emphasis.

7. Since e-mail messages can be written and sent so quickly, it's easy to make mistakes. Take time to proofread your messages. Consult the dictionary when necessary. Some spell checkers work on e-mail. Or you can check your spelling in your word processor, then transfer the completed message to your e-mail program. Your message may be seen by many more people than you originally intended, so you can spare yourself embarrassment by checking it over for typos, misspellings, and other errors.

8. You may want to compose a regular "signature" for your e-mail messages, especially those used for professional or business communications. Your signature should include your name, position, affiliation, and Internet address. You may also wish to include your phone number, fax number, and mailing address. Some netters also include a favorite quote. Save your signature in a special file so you won't have to retype it each time.

9. It's a common practice to copy and paste selected portions of the note to which you are responding into your e-mail response. When that is done, the copied note is usually set off by one or more copies of the "greater than" sign (also called an angle bracket or chevron), e.g.,">>". For example:

```
>>I hope you can send me the list of self-help groups for
>>Parkinsonism you mentioned...


No problem. Here they are:
```

10. When writing to people you don't know well, especially those who get lots of e-mail:

    • Keep messages extremely short.
    • Focus on one subject per message.
    • Invite the person to e-mail you back for further details.

11. Don't post anything you'd be uncomfortable having others see. Remember that your e-mail can easily be forwarded to others or even posted to a newsgroup or mailing list where it might be read by thousands of people you've never met.

12. It's easy to write a single piece of e-mail (like a family letter) and send copies to many correspondents—or to do an informal e-mail newsletter, or send e-mail "clippings" to a list of friends or colleagues.

13. Be sure to save important e-mail addresses in the Address Book that comes with your e-mail software.

14. If you're going away on vacation, let your regular e-mail correspondents know you'll be gone so they'll understand why you're not responding to their messages. With some e-mail programs, you can leave an automatic "on vacation" message.

15. It's usually better to respond to e-mail quickly and briefly than to put it off till later, even if this means only a short and tentative reply. People are accustomed to short, quick e-mail. They can e-mail you back with any unfinished business.

16. Empty your mailbox regularly. Don't use your mailbox to store old messages. Delete completed or unwanted messages immediately and transfer those you wish to save to another folder (e.g., by subject, person, week, or month). Don't let your messages stack up. If you exceed your mailbox's capacity, you may lose messages.

17. Ask your friends and business associates if they have an e-mail address.

18. Put your e-mail address on your stationery and your business card.

19. People have very different e-mail styles. Some "Type A" e-mail regulars will reliably respond to your messages within a few hours. Others don't check their e-mail for weeks at a time. You may need to leave them a phone message to let them know they have an important piece of e-mail in their mailbox.

20. You may be able to save time by automating your e-mail. I have my software set to automatically go online at 6 A.M. to send any e-mail I've written and download any I've received so I don't have to tie up my computer by logging on manually. This setup also allows me to log on when the system is less crowded and the phone rates are lower.

21. Remember, you can send and read e-mail around the clock without disturbing your correspondents. In fact, reading and sending e-mail may soon replace counting sheep as the most popular activity for insomniacs.

22. Whenever you send e-mail, consider sending a copy of your message to one or more other e-mail correspondents. It's a wonderfully convenient way to keep others informed.

23. Some e-mail addresses connect you to a computer, not a person. Such computers are called mail servers. They run a program that automatically sends you certain kinds of information and performs related functions, e.g., adding your name to a mailing list or forwarding your message to all the members of a list. LISTSERV, a popular mailing list manager, is one frequently encountered mail server program.

24. Most commercial systems come with an off-line e-mail reader that enables you to go online just long enough to send or receive e-mail and then log off. You can thus read your e-mail and compose your responses without incurring an online charge.

25. How do you find your friends' and associates' e-mail addresses? The commercial services have directories so that members can look up other members of the same service, but in the wild and woolly world of the Internet, the best "directory" is to call up and ask.

Common E-Mail Mistakes

- Sending "private" e-mail containing personal or confidential information that ends up getting forwarded to the wrong person (like your boss or your spouse). Remember that your e-mail can be easily forwarded to anyone on the Net.

- Addressing private e-mail to a mailing list address—and having it appear in hundreds or thousands of list members' mailboxes. This is a minor annoyance to other list members.

- Online irony or sarcasm that is misunderstood. Sarcasm should be used sparingly, if at all, for it is rarely successful. In the online world, there's no body language or tone of voice to let people know you're not serious.

Anatomy of an E-mail Message

Just as letters come in envelopes, e-mail messages come, in effect, in electronic "envelopes" that contain various types of information technically called "fields." The information varies greatly, depending on the software used to compose and send the message. Here are a few examples of common fields you'll sometimes see in the footers and address areas of your e-mail messages:

To: Name of the recipient, with his or her e-mail address

Date: Date the message was created

From: Name of the sender, with his or her e-mail address

Subject: What the message is about

Mail Reply To: Used when the sender wants you to reply to a different e-mail address

Keywords: Words that indicate the content of the message. In some systems e-mail is stored in a database, and keywords can be used to conduct searches

Comment: An alternative way of adding one or more keywords or describing the general nature of the discussion

Cc: The names of people receiving copies of the message in addition to the principal recipient. The original recipient will know that the copies were sent and will see the e-mail addresses of those who received them.

Bcc: The names of people receiving a "blind copy" of the message. The principal recipient and those receiving normal cc's won't know that any blind copies were sent.

E-Mail Examples

Here are some examples of actual everyday e-mail. They were randomly chosen from those I sent and received on the days I was working on this chapter. The first, wouldn't you know it, is from my mom:

```
From: HennyMay
Subj: Logs
To: DrTomHO
Dear Tom,
    Tonight after sending you that last note, I pulled down
the FILE, menu clicked on 'Logs' then clicked on 'System"...
and ended up with a blank screen. What happened?
    How about walking me through this on the phone one night
this week? I'd really like to be able to use it. Any evening
but Wednesday would be fine, if you can do it.
Love,
Mother
```

Comment: My mom recently signed up for America Online (at age 80) and was having some trouble with the "Log" function (which allows you to automatically make a complete record of your online sessions). I called her and walked her through it and everything worked out just fine.

Because both my mom and I have accounts on America Online, the system used only our screen names (DrTomHO, HennyMay) not our full Internet addresses (DrTomHO@aol.com, HennyMay@aol.com).

Here's one from a good friend from another city who only recently came online:

```
From: QLVJ97M@prodigy.com
Subj: News from the Seattle Robertsons
To: DrTomHO@aol.com
Hi Buddy,
    I've been reading the various goodies you've been e-mailing
me. Thanks so much for sending them along. Keep it up! I'll
become a regular on the e-mail circuit yet!
    Been thinking a lot about you, buddy. Hope you are feeling
good & things are going well.
    Things are coming along pretty well here. I'm almost com-
pletely healed up from my recent skiing accident. My broken
bones seem nearly as good as new. I've been back at the gym,
working out. Doing some skiing (not so fast this time) and
even mountain biking a bit.
    Our daughter Sarah is still just barely scraping along in
school. We've tentatively diagnosed her as suffering from
Attention Deficit Disorder (ADD) and are trying an experimen-
tal treatment--a form of biofeedback training. We're very
hopeful that it will help. A colleague of mine is now into
this professionally. They claim to have some success in treat-
ing a variety of problems, e.g., attention deficit disorder,
depression, anxiety, bulimia, drug abuse, closed head injury,
trauma and stroke. But in addition to her ADD, I definitely
think Sarah is depressed. If the biofeedback doesn't work, I
would like to try her on a course of Ritalin or anti-depres-
sants. Lots of love to you buddy. Keep the e-mail coming.
    --Hank
```

Comment: As you can see, just staying in touch with good friends like Hank entails a good deal of supportive listening and self-help. Hank and I had been keeping in touch by phone and occasional visits for years, frequently sharing our experiences and giving each other support. I have to admit that I was guilty of several months of intensive nagging to get Hank to become a more regular online correspondent. But it was worth it. It's so great to be able to exchange e-mail regularly with my good buddy.

Although much of this book will be devoted to connecting with new online resources for health and support, don't forget that your biggest and most important single resource for building your own online support network will most likely be your existing friendships.

The next e-mail message is from my friend David Stansbury. David and his brother John are multimedia designers and producers. During this interaction, David had an office two floors down from mine in the same building.

```
From: 25315.8345@compuserve.com
Subj: Re: Lunch
To: Dr Tom HO@aol.com

Brother John is doing well & is recovering nicely from his
heart surgery. You can hear a gentle click-click-click from
his new valve if things are quiet enough. He is looking for-
ward to asking you a couple of medical questions.

How about an early lunch at Manuel's at 11:30, this Thursday?
Can't wait to tell you our big news. I've put it in our
calendar, so let me know if that date still works for you.
Looking forward to it,
David & John
```

Here's my reply:

```
From: DrTomHO@aol.com
Subj: Re: Lunch
To: 25315.8345@compuserve.com

Dear Dave,
Thursday at 11:30 AM at Manuel's looks fine. Will look for-
ward to seeing you & John hearing the news. What ever became
of the plan to run a T-1 line (or other high-bandwidth line)
into the Scarbourough Building? Warm wishes,
Tom

>From: 25315.8345@compuserve.com
>Subj: Re: Lunch
>To: DrTomHO@aol.com

>How about an early lunch at Manuel's at 11:30, this Thursday?
>Can't wait to tell you our big news. I've put it in our
>calendar, so let me know if that date still works for you.
>Looking forward to it,
>David & John
```

Comment: You may think it odd that I would use e-mail to communicate with friends who had their office in the same building, but sending and receiving this sequence of e-mail was much more convenient than calling on the phone (no phone tag) and *much* quicker than actually going downstairs (especially with our elevators). Using e-mail also meant that I didn't have to interrupt them. Note that I copied and pasted a copy of their original message at the end of my note. Their big news was that they'd both been offered exciting new jobs at Human Code, a fast-growing Austin, Texas, software company that produces interactive electronic games on CD.

The next piece of e-mail is a message from a depression mailing list I currently subscribe to. Like many messages that come in via the Internet, it was accompanied by an extensive header (most of which is intelligible only to those with pocket protectors) containing information about the message and the path that it traveled to get to my mailbox. With all the other e-mail messages in this book, I've edited out the gobbledygook-filled headers. But in this message and the next, I'll include the full headers so that you'll know what to expect:

```
Subj: Re: Dysthymia or depression?
Date: Mon, Dec 19, 1:19 PM CST
From: paulachu@netcom.com (Paula Chu)
Sender: depress@soundprint.brandywine.american.edu
Reply-to: paulachu@netcom.com (Paula Chu)
To: depress@soundprint.brandywine.american.edu (Multiple
recipients of list)

Dear Janey

Dysthymia is simply technical jargon for mild or subclinical
depression. Your symptoms, however, sound much more like a
case of full-blown clinical depression. The key clues here
are your suicidal thinking and the way you describe feeling
worse as the day goes on. From what you've told me so far,
this could be a case of so-called "atypical" depression--which
is actually much more common than we used to think.

If I were you, I'd seek immediate help from a psychiatrist with
extensive training and experience in psychopharmacology. In my
experience, such docs do the best job of diagnosing and treat-
ing mood disorders like the one you seem to be dealing with.

Please feel free to write me back if you like. Although I
don't suffer from depression myself, I have several family
```

```
members who are bipolar (manic-depressive), and I have
learned "more than I ever wanted to know" about this illness.
Hugs & hope,
Paula
paulachu@netcom.com
---------------------- Headers --------------------------------

From depress@soundprint.brandywine.american.edu Mon Dec
19 14:17:36
Received: from soundprint.brandywine.american.edu by
mailgate.prod.aol.net with SMTP
(1.37.109.11/16.2) id AA274864656; Mon, 19 Dec 14:17:36 -0500
Return-Path: <depress@soundprint.brandywine.american.edu>
Received: from Listserv ([127.0.0.1]) by
soundprint.brandywine.american.edu with SMTP id <10445-5>;
Mon, 19 Dec 13:51:39 -0500
Message-Id: <Pine.3.89.9412191025.A26455-
0100000@netcom17>
X-Archive-Key: DEPRESS
Comment: Depression Discussion
Precedence: junk
Originator: depress@soundprint.brandywine.american.edu
Errors-To: depress@soundprint.brandywine.american.edu
Reply-To: "Paula Chu" <paulachu@netcom.com>
Sender: depress@soundprint.brandywine.american.edu
Version: 5.5.JHU3
From: "Paula Chu" <paulachu@netcom.com>
To: Multiple recipients of list
<depress@soundprint.brandywine.american.edu>
Subject: Re: dysthymia
Date: Mon, 19 Dec 13:51:36 -0500
```

Comment: This message is a typical posting on a support-oriented Internet mailing list. Once you subscribe to such a list, you'll receive all the messages sent to the list address. So although it operates like a forum or bulletin board, with different people posting and responding, instead of your going to the forum, the postings on a mailing list automatically appear in your electronic mailbox. (For more on Internet mailing lists, see Chapter 9.)

The header information varies from system to system but typically includes the e-mail addresses for both sender and receiver and an assortment of other information, most of which can be safely ignored. (See "Anatomy of an E-Mail Message," p. 28).

The next e-mail message is from Larry Green, an old friend and professional colleague. Our paths had crossed at scholarly self-help meetings years before and I hadn't seen him for nearly a decade. We "met" again with this message—when he responded to my posting on the Internet mailing list called the Self-Help List (see p. 193).

```
Subj: Re: Online Self-Help
Date: Fri, Dec 16, 11:15 PM CST
From: lgreen@unixg.ubc.ca
X-From: lgreen@unixg.ubc.ca (Lawrence Green)
To: DrTomHO@aol.com

Dear Tom: Good to be back in communication with you after all
these years. What are your Harvard vs. Texas responsibili-
ties? I did that loop myself a few years back after I left
Hopkins and the Federal Government. My leave of absence was
up at Hopkins and I needed a sabbatical (the Fed. Govt. role
was anything but a sabbatical). Univ. of Texas offered me an
up-front sabbatical year to take advantage of an offer to
come to Harvard as a Visiting Lecturer for a year in the
Health Policy Center, then to settle into starting up the
Center for Health Promotion Research and Development at UT
Health Science Center in Houston. After 6 years there, I
wormed my way back to California with the Kaiser Family
Foundation, then up the coast to U.B.C. to start another
Institute of Health Promotion Research. But enough of my
odyssey.

You asked for addresses: Natl. Health Information Center is
<nmpinfor@hp2k.health.org>

Nancy Milio is at the School of Nursing at University of N.
Carolina, but I don't have phone or e-mail at hand.

--Larry
```

```
--------------------- Headers ------------------------------
From lgreen@unixg.ubc.ca Fri, Dec 16 23:32:37
Received: from unixg.ubc.ca by mailgate.prod.aol.net with
SMTP
     (1.37.109.11/16.2) id AA114178757; Fri, 16 Dec
23:32:37 -0500
Return-Path: <lgreen@unixg.ubc.ca>
Received: by unixg.ubc.ca (4.1/1.14)
     id AA09168; Fri, 16 Dec 17:20:32 PST
Date: Fri, 16 Dec 17:20:31 -0800 (PST)
From: Lawrence Green <lgreen@unixg.ubc.ca>
To: DrTomHO@aol.com
Subject: Re: Online Self-Help
In-Reply-To: <941215111915_6794166@aol.com>
Message-Id: <Pine.SUN.3.91.941216171336.27892K-
100000@unixg.ubc.ca>
Mime-Version: 1.0
Content-Type: TEXT/PLAIN; charset=US-ASCII
```

How to Read an E-Mail Address

The "@" ("at" sign) in your Internet e-mail address is always read as "at." All periods are read as "dot." So if you were reading my e-mail address aloud, you would say, "Doctor Tom Ho at A-O-L dot com."(The "HO" stands for *Health Online*.)

An Internet address can contain clues about the person who uses it. An ".edu" domain name indicates that the user is probably a staff member or student at a university or other educational institution, ".mil" means military, ".org" means nonprofit institution, ".uk" means Great Britain, ".ca" means Canada, and so on.

Some home system names can be deciphered from the available clues: "@umkc.edu" probably means that the sender is at the University of Missouri at Kansas City, "@stanford.edu" is the address for Stanford University, and the address for The Health Commons Institute is "@hc.org."

Internet addresses usually follow certain rules: no spaces; capitals don't count; no commas, question marks, or other special characters; and only one "@" is allowed per address.

Understanding Internet Addresses

You can think of the general form of an e-mail address as:

Your-personal-identifier@Your-home-system.Your-domain-name.

You can visualize it this way:

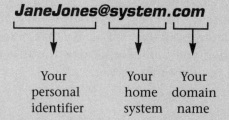

JaneJones@system.com

| Your personal identifier | Your home system | Your domain name |

So if we look at my e-mail address, DrTomHO@aol.com, we see that my personal identifier (or screen name) is "DrTomHO," my system is "aol," or America Online, and my top-level domain is "com," for "commercial system."

Emoticons

You'll probably find some of your e-mail correspondents using "emoticons" or "smileys" — onscreen symbols made up of punctuation marks, each with its own meaning. The most common is the smiley face, which is frequently written:

:-)   or just   **:)**

Turn the page ninety degrees clockwise to see the "faces." Here are some other common smileys:

:-D	Big smile
;-)	Wink or "just joking"
:-p	Sticking out tongue
:-(	Feeling sad
<:-(	Feeling like a dunce
{{{{{}}}}}	Sending a hug
{{{{Moe}}}}	Sending a hug to Moe
{{{{Moe}}}}{{{{Larry}}}}{{{{Curly}}}}	Sending a group hug

Managing Your E-Mail

It's not unusual for Internet mailing lists to generate large quantities of mail—in some cases ten, twenty, or even more pieces of e-mail per day per list. An active news service can produce two to three times that number. And that doesn't include your personal and professional correspondences.

I currently receive at least thirty to sixty messages a day. After this book comes out, that number will probably double. So I can tell you from hard-earned personal experience that you must manage your e-mail effectively to keep yourself from being overwhelmed—and to avoid losing messages.

The capacity of electronic mailboxes varies from system to system. On America Online, for instance, mailboxes will hold a maximum of five hundred and fifty pieces of e-mail. If you don't keep it down to that number, the system will—by deleting your oldest messages.

From Phone Calls to Fax to Voice Mail to E-Mail

As more and more people log on to the Net, those without e-mail may find themselves at a distinct disadvantage. For many online regulars, the U.S mail is spoken of as something akin to cave paintings or scratching on clay tablets. In some circles, even live phone calls are now perceived as mildly intrusive, even slightly rude (except in real emergencies). Many telephones, my own included, are now kept on voice mail a good part of the time or even permanently. (Sorry if you're one of the people who tried to call, but otherwise, I would never have finished this book.)

It's increasingly the case that if you want someone's attention, the best way to get it is to send him or her e-mail. It may not be long before the e-mail–challenged may have difficulty connecting with the people they most want to reach. Or as Peter H. Lewis recently wrote in the *New York Times:* "electronic mail is the killer app [an application so good it makes people go out and buy a computer] for the 1990's. . . [It] is so clearly superior to paper mail for so many purposes that most people who try it cannot imagine going back to working without it."

Your E-Mail Address Book

Here's one of the very first things to do when you initially go online: Learn to use your e-mail address book.

I can't believe how many people either don't know they have one or never use it, saving my old messages rather than entering my name and e-mail address in an easy-to-find spot just a mouse click away. Many address books also allow you to create personalized mailing lists (e.g., relatives, neighbors, professional colleagues, people with muscular sclerosis). This makes sending group messages much easier.

If you encounter an interesting person online and don't keep a copy of his or her address, you may never be able to get back in touch. Unfortunately, there is no universal phone book for cyberspace.

Here's one entry in my online address book:

```
                    Petersen, Julie (HotWired)
```

Julie is an editor at Wired magazine. When I click on her name, it brings up Julie's complete listing:

```
julie@wired.com (Julie Petersen)

Work homepage: http://www.hotwired.com/

Home homepage: http://www.awaken.org/

(415) 222.MEME
```

The listings refer to Julie's e-mail address, at-work Web site home page, at-home Web site home page, and phone number. Note that like many net bunnies, Julie does not even bother to list a U.S. snail mail address.

Q *When choosing an e-mail address, is it best to remain anonymous or to be up-front with your real identity?*

A The decision depends on your system's requirements and your personal preference (whether you wish to remain anonymous). Systems like CompuServe issue you a number, something like "70731,7722," although you can select a more personable screen name to use on the message boards. America Online and Prodigy allow you to choose your own personal screen name, which also serves as your ID.

Remaining anonymous may make you feel more comfortable discussing sensitive topics with people you don't know well. Many self-helpers find that being anonymous makes it easier to communicate honestly. On the other hand, if you want to make it easy for people to contact you, you may want to use a full or abbreviated version of your real name.

In some cases I've found that the principal screen name I've used while researching this book—"DrTomHO"—poses certain problems. For better or worse, in some self-help chat groups and forums people sometimes see me only as a "doctor" and project onto me their positive or negative feelings (or sometimes both) about doctors in general. In some cases, their perception leads to a useful discussion. In others, I feel that I am being uncomfortably stereotyped. Also, having a "doctor" in some self-help groups can keep participants from dealing with their concerns from a position of empowerment. So I sometimes use another screen name for visiting self-help forums or attending real-time support meetings. Many systems allow you to use more than one screen name.

Q *What would Miss Manners say about the acceptability of e-mail for highly personal and family messages, thank-you notes, etc? Are they considered acceptable? It would seem almost too easy.*

A Traditionalists notwithstanding, I think that for those who choose to use them, e-mail messages are just fine for all kinds of personal or professional messages. On the other hand, I'm also a big fan of written notes and cards and send them frequently. Having access to e-mail doesn't prevent you from using other media. It's all a matter of personal style.

Although such questions will doubtless keep future generations of "Miss Online Manners" busy for many years, the important point here is that e-mail can eliminate some of the barriers that can keep people from communicating. The easier it is to communicate, the more likely we are to send all kinds of authentic, useful, and positive messages of appreciation and support to all the people we care about.

Chapter 4

Cyberspace Friends and Online Angels

Discussing your personal problems online turns out to be surprisingly comfortable... There's no need to travel or dress up. No one need know who you are. And it feels so safe to have complete privacy while participating in a supportive group interaction.

> *"KOGen"*
> *Forum coordinator*
> *Parents Information Network*
> *America Online*

——————◆——————

YOUR INVOLVEMENT IN ONLINE SELF-HELP can develop gradually or quickly. You can begin by reaching out to family and friends and exchanging social and emotional support with people you already know. You can reach out to the online self-help communities listed in the chapters that follow in response to a pressing need, plugging into a powerful network of proactive people with similar concerns. Or you can simply start exploring, collecting your own list of online friends and resources at a pace that feels right to you.

Whichever way you choose, one of the nicest things about self-help cyberspace is this: Just by virtue of being a member of the same service, a participant in the same forum, or a member of the same mailing list or newsgroup, you'll have hundreds of new online "neighbors." From the very first time you log on, you'll find lots of people who'll be glad to hear from you and happy to help you find what you're looking for.

HOT

TIP

All the commercial services have a member registry where you can search the membership roster for characteristics, e.g., to see who else is from your home town, has fibromyalgia, or collects first editions of Dr. Seuss. Looking through the registry is a great way to find the people you'd like to connect with. On America Online, click on "Get a Member's Profile" in the Members menu. On CompuServe, use "Go dir" (for "directory"). On Prodigy, use the jumpword "member list".

Some of the people you'll meet will be forum hosts (sometimes called "sysops") who make their living running a self-help forum. Some will be volunteer group coordinators or discussion leaders who get free online time in exchange for coordinating their forums. Others will be list keepers, newsgroup participants, or volunteer self-helpers. And although most self-helpers on commercial networks like CompuServe work primarily with members of their own networks, most will gladly respond to e-mail from those on other systems.

Getting Started

The first person I met online was Elin Silveous (screen name "ESilveous"), the forum host of the Better Health & Medical Forum on America Online (AOL). She was gracious, upbeat, and forgiving of my near total ignorance of online matters. When she responded kindly to my first e-mail effort, I let out a long sigh of relief. I'd made my first virtual friend. Now I had someone I could ask for help.

Sometime later I invited Elin and her husband, physician Allan Douma, a medical writer who edits many of the health databases on AOL, to speak at a professional meeting on online self-help and was able to meet them face to face. Elin and Allan reviewed sections of the manuscript for this book, making many helpful suggestions.

Elin is the forum host for both the Better Health & Medical Forum and the disABILITIES Forum on America Online. A forum host is a sort of virtual den mother who spends a lot of time online greeting new users and making sure that everyone finds the people and resources they're looking for. (Most net bunnies would consider the role of forum host the ultimate dream job.)

Elin has her counterparts on CompuServe, Prodigy, eWorld, and many other networks and bulletin boards. You'll find many of these online helpers listed throughout this book.

Online Angels

One of the next people I met online was Glenna Tallman, universally known to AOL self-helpers as "GlennaT"—to whom this book is dedicated. Glenna, who died while the book was being written, was an exemplary online self-helper, the first and still one of the most impressive of the "online angels" it has been my privilege to meet. She shared her wisdom, courage, and caring in a way that inspired us all. Reading through the final drafts of this book, I was impressed by how many of the wisest nuggets of advice can be traced back to Glenna.

It was only after we'd been corresponding for some time that I discovered that Glenna was battling two serious medical problems of her own. Yet in her online communications she was so caring and upbeat, so involved and funny and wise, that I sometimes found it hard to believe that she could be seriously ill.

Glenna knew she hadn't much time left. She was determined to spend all the time and energy she could in helping other people. Yet she received as much love and care as she gave. Glenna's online life brought her into a world where she was valued, loved, and very much appreciated.

I first learned from Glenna something that I've seen many times since: In the online world, the wisest and most generous self-helper is often the one with the gravest problem or the worst prognosis.

The online memorial service for Glenna extremely moving. My wife was startled to find me sitting in front of my computer with tears running down my cheeks. Dozens of self-helpers whose lives had been affected by Glenna's caring, humorous, and witty ways paid tribute to a woman who will always remain a legend of online self-help.

Luckily for us who remain, many others are still carrying out her work. They are out there, waiting for you, just a few mouse clicks away.

Self-Help Communities in Cyberspace

Online self-help networks are like surrogate families: Members share common problems, help each other toward mutual goals, and support each other through good times and bad. The support they provide is available for free and, in most cases, around the clock, as needed.

These new online "families of choice" can help provide life-saving information and advice and can serve as a life-preserving buffer against the stresses and challenges of life. We can log on when we need advice with a specific problem; when we are struggling and want sympathy, comfort, and support; or when we have come through a hard time and want to share our victory with others.

The tips and personal experiences we share as group members can help us build our self-confidence and develop the coping skills we need to manage our own health problems. The advice we get from other self-helpers on our online networks can help us face our challenges and make realistic, hopeful, and uniquely personal choices about managing our own care.

Nighttime Is the Right Time

Unlike professional medical care, which typically occurs during normal business hours, a surprisingly large proportion of online self-help activity takes place between 7 P.M. and 1 A.M.

Understanding Online Self-Help

The kind of information and support provided by self-helpers is subtle and complex. It often includes, but is not limited to, the kind of academic and clinical knowledge that until recently was the near exclusive domain of health professionals. Unlike academic book-learning, self-help wisdom is based on practical, real-world experience that comes only from living with a problem twenty-four hours a day.

Like other types of health care, online self-help is far from perfect. Self-helpers sometimes lack a personal knowledge of many similar cases and generalize too widely from their own experiences. Not all self-helpers are well informed about the latest research in their field of interest. On the other hand, sometimes these very features—a breadth of personal experience and an up-to-date knowledge of the latest research—are more advanced on certain self-help networks than in many doctors' offices or hospitals.

I am continually impressed by the high level of discourse that takes place on some self-help networks, from computerized searches of the medical literature, to shared wisdom from visiting researchers and clinicians, to the insightful perspectives expressed by experienced self-helpers.

No one would deny that there are dramatic variations among self-help groups. Some groups provide great support and friendship but lack sophisticated technical resources. Others may provide in-depth scientific information at the price of putting up with doctrinaire self-helpers or arrogant health professionals.

The most impressive thing about self-help cyberspace is that, by and large, online self-helpers can, at least in some cases, supply almost everything that health professionals can, and much that they cannot:

1. Many self-help networks can supply technical medical information of the kind that until recently was available only from medical professionals (e.g., details of diagnosis and treatment).
2. Self-helpers who share your condition or concern can critique the care provided and the information supplied by your clinician.
3. Your self-help support group can listen sympathetically to your experience, offering emotional aid as only those who have walked the same path can do.
4. Self-helpers routinely share much practical advice that health professionals may not know (e.g., "the X-ray table is cold—take a blanket.").
5. The supportive social interactions that take place on self-help networks may themselves have a beneficial effect. Research studies are beginning to show dramatic links between participation in support networks and improvements in both physical and mental health.
6. Unlike many health professionals and institutions, which are often unintentionally disempowering, self-help networks encourage members to build their competence and to hold on to their power.

Indeed, there are only two things that self-help networks will not do:

1. Take on the august mantle of the health professional and tell you what to do.
2. Charge you a fee for their advice.

How to Make Friends and Influence People by Computer

The best way to find a friend is to be a friend. Here are some tips for being a responsible and desirable cyberchum:

- Online friendships don't just happen. You have to create them, just as in real life. The best way to do that is to keep in touch regularly with the online people you care about. Just as in real life, regularly receiving a "how're you doing?" message with your latest news on a regular basis will make people realize that you care.

- When you come across a posting by somebody with something interesting or useful to say (e.g., on a forum, mailing list, or newsgroup), send them an appreciative e-mail thank-you. There's nothing like honest admiration to start a promising friendship.

- Chat groups are a great way to "meet" new people. Attend an online meeting on your commercial service. Identify the people you'd like to connect with. Beam them private Instant Messages while the meeting is in progress or send them e-mail later.

- If you find yourself becoming involved with a network of people interested in the same topic, consider doing an informal newsletter or mailing list for everyone in the group. A group letter might contain brief pieces you've written, copies of items you've found on the Net, copies of e-mail you've sent and received, or other items you've copied or created.

- Keep an eye out for messages that will be of interest to your online buddies. When you come across something interesting, send them a copy.

- Whenever possible, respond to e-mail quickly. There's nothing like getting a fast response to make you want to keep up a correspondence.

- Be generous and funny, understanding, warm, and supportive. In short, be someone who cares—a person others will want to connect with.

Meeting New People Online

Making friends in cyberspace is much easier and more natural than it sounds. In the real world, you normally meet new people by geographical accident, then by chance you find a few who share your interests. Let's say that, like me, you collect antique poker chips. What's the chance that your next-door neighbor does likewise? Not too great. But suppose that you and I went to a gathering of antique poker-chip collectors: We would automatically share a common interest with everyone in the room.

That's exactly what happens with online special-interest groups. So when you join a self-help network, you'll be starting each new potential online friendship with a built-in bond.

Here's another unique thing about making online friends: When you meet people online, you're no longer dealing with all the automatic prejudgments one might apply in the real world—those based on age, size, looks, physical characteristics, dress, hygiene, state of health, geographic location, or economic or social status. None of those factors comes across in cyberspace. You may even find yourself unsure of the gender of the person you're talking to, a startling experience for most new netters. (A routine query on the teen boards is "BoG?" which means "boy or girl?")

Young people find themselves treated as adults. People with disabilities and people of color find themselves treated without prejudice. As all the normal clues are missing, you're obliged to judge people on their prose style and on the quality of their feelings and their thinking. It sometimes feels as if you're communicating directly with your correspondent's heart and mind.

To Be Anonymous or Not? That Is the Question.

Before you log on to your network of choice, you'll need to decide whether you want to be anonymous or to use your real name. In the academic and business worlds, online users traditionally use an abbreviated version of their real names (e.g., "BGates" for Bill Gates). But many self-helpers, like Lucinda L., quoted below, find that using an anonymous screen name makes them feel safer:

```
I'm still pretty embarrassed about the condition I'm dealing with [sex-
ual abuse by a family member]. I didn't want everyone to know who I was
or where I lived, so I felt more comfortable using a pseudonym. Then,
gradually, as I began to feel more comfortable, I'd let a few select
people know where I lived and, sometimes, my real name. I felt that I
was totally in control of the whole process.
```

Your choices may depend in part on your home system. While America Online and Prodigy permit anonymity, on CompuServe anonymous names are encouraged on some forums and forbidden on others. On the Well, it's a key policy that anonymity is *not* permitted.

Finding Your Preferred Self-Help Neighborhoods of Cyberspace

In the final analysis, there's only one way to tell if a particular forum or group will feel right to you: You must go there and experience it. Different self-help networks on the same or similar topics may have completely different attitudes, beliefs, styles, and personalities. Choosing a self-help network is much like choosing a potential romantic partner: You just have to try it and see how it feels. If the first one you try doesn't seem right, try another.

Eventually you'll find a few that seem exactly right to you. You'll then want to return to those haunts again and again. Online self-helper Patrick L. catches this feeling nicely:

> When I took my first steps into cyberspace, I was frightened, uncertain and unsure. I'd recently been diagnosed with a fairly serious form of cancer, and I felt isolated and powerless. Then, to my horror, I become so depressed that it was hard to drag myself out of bed in the morning. I was feeling desperate and afraid, alone and suicidal. I felt a great need to reach out, to find other people who were facing similar challenges.
>
> From my first online sessions I began finding people with similar difficulties, wonderful people, including some whose problems were ever so much worse than mine. Yet there they were, laughing and crying and enjoying their lives to the fullest and giving lots of support to others--myself included. It really helped me to stop feeling so sorry for myself.
>
> Everyone went out of their way to make me feel at home. Suddenly I'd found a place where I could talk openly about everything I was going through. I realized that I hadn't been able to do that before. I hadn't felt comfortable expressing my pain, even to friends and family, because it freaked other people out. So I had to be strong to protect them.
>
> My doctors are devoted and well-meaning people, and I'm grateful for their help. But in the end I'm ultimately just a 'case' to them. To my friends online, I'm a person.

Keep Exploring

One final piece of advice: Don't think of online self-help as a closed, fixed system. As you begin exploring the neighborhoods of self-help cyberspace, be on the lookout for newer, smaller, and less formal support groups and networks that may not be listed in this or any directory. As you'll see, the world of online self-help is ever changing, growing like a living thing. Use your networking skills. Post messages in the appropriate special-interest forums. And be sure to let your new online friends know what you're looking for. You'll end up finding or creating self-help links you won't find in any book.

Once you're comfortable with the online world, it will be there for you whenever you need it—as it was for writer John Perry Barlow when he recently found himself facing one of the most difficult life situations imaginable:

> Some months ago, the great love of my life, a vivid young woman with whom I intended to spend the rest of it, dropped dead of undiagnosed viral cardiomyopathy two days short of her 30th birthday. I felt as if my own heart had been as shredded as hers.
>
> We had lived together in New York City. Except for my daughters, no one from Pinedale had met her. I needed a community to wrap around myself against colder winds than fortune had ever blown at me before.... I found I had one in the virtual world.
>
> On the WELL, there was a topic announcing her death in one of the conferences to which I posted the eulogy I had read over her before burying her in her own small town of Nanaimo, British Columbia. It seemed to strike a chord among the disembodied living on the Net. People copied it and sent it to one another. Over the next several months I received almost a megabyte of electronic mail from all over the planet, mostly from folks whose faces I have never seen and probably never will.
>
> They told me of their own tragedies and what they had done to survive them. As humans have since words were first uttered, we shared the second most common human experience, death, with an openheartedness that would have caused grave uneasiness in physical America, where the whole topic is so cloaked in denial as to be considered obscene. Those strangers, who had no arms to put around my shoulders, no eyes to weep with mine, nevertheless saw me through. As neighbors do.

May the online angels be there for you, too, when you need them.

Part II

The Commercial Computer Networks

Think of a commercial computer network (e.g., America Online, CompuServe, Prodigy, or the Microsoft Network) as a giant computer mothership hovering somewhere in cyberspace. You can link your own personal computer into it via your modem and your telephone line. For most people, opening an account on a commercial network is the easiest way to connect to the InterNet.

When you sign up for an account on a commercial service, you'll receive your own unique e-mail address. In addition to sending and receiving e-mail, you'll be able to participate in your service's self-help (and other) forums, access health databases, participate in live chat and support groups, access the Internet, including the World Wide Web, and, if you wish, construct your own World Wide Web home page. In short, belonging to a commercial network lets you do just about anything you might want to do in the online world.

Commercial computer networks offer a simplified, one-stop connection to cyberspace. Indeed, many of the best online health resources, particularly the health forums and the live group meetings, are found *only* on the commercial systems.

How to Sign Up

Opening an account on a commercial service could hardly be easier. Here's all you need to do:

- Decide which of the services you want to join.
- Call the service's toll-free number. (You'll find it in one of the following chapters.)
- Ask the customer service representative to send you a free sign-up kit.
- A few days later, your software will arrive in the mail. Put the disk into your computer, follow the easy on-screen directions, and within ten to fifteen minutes, you'll be online.

As we go to press, all the major commercial services charge about $10 per month. This fee includes five hours per month of online use. Additional hours are charged at about $3 per hour. On America Online, the flat fee covers everything. On CompuServe and Prodigy, some "premium" services cost extra. On the other hand CompuServe and Prodigy offer a heavy-use discount. All the major services currently offer new members ten free hours, so you could easily explore two or more systems, then decide.

HOT

TIP

As soon as you choose a commercial service, be sure to buy one of the instruction manuals for your network. The $10 to $20 you'll spend will save you many hours of online floundering.

If you already have (or have access to) a direct Internet connection, you through your school, workplace, local Freenet, or other community connection, may be able to get along without a commercial service. But there may be certain advantages in signing up for a commercial service as well. If you're a beginning or intermediate user, You'll probably have a much easier time on a commercial service. Here's why:

- Commercial systems are better organized and easier to find your way around. The Internet is chaotic.
- In most cases it's easier to install and maintain the software required for a commercial service than for a direct Internet connection.
- On a commercial service someone always available to answer your questions, either online or via 800 number. On the Internet, you're on your own.
- Commercial services make it easy to access chat groups and support-group meetings. On the Internet, such groups are few and far between.

- On a commercial service, there's little risk of unintentionally encountering X-rated material. Parents can use special software on some commercial services to control their children's access to "adult" areas.

- People behave themselves better on the commercial services—because network staffers provide online monitoring, and those who misbehave may be thrown off the service.

The Big Three Computer Networks in a Nutshell

America Online

- Active, friendly self-help forums
- Most live chat and support groups
- Great forum for seniors (SeniorNet)
- Most graphically attractive interface
- Easiest to use, highly intuitive
- Limited selection of medical database materials

CompuServe

- Active, friendly self-help forums
- Most extensive medical databases
- Most medical professionals online
- Most medical professionals serving as sysops
- Most business-oriented
- Most expensive premium services

Prodigy

- Active, friendly self-help forums
- Great special membership rate for those with chronic illness
- Great kids' resources
- Great way to find information (Homework Helper)
- Clunky, childish graphics and interface
- Annoying unrequested ads flashed on your screen

Chapter 5

America Online

In my experience, AOL is much more community-oriented than CompuServe or Prodigy. It's easier to use, more fun, and much more intuitive. And you can't beat AOL's cheap, simple pricing structure.

"Dan Ash"
Depression Support Group host on AOL

——————— ◆ ———————

Signing Up

To sign up for America Online, call (800) 827-6364. You'll receive your free software (specify for DOS, Windows, or Mac) in the mail in about seven to ten days. Your first ten hours of online time are free. After that, the base rate is $9.98 per month, which includes up to five hours per month of connection time. Additional hours are billed at $2.95 per hour.

LET ME BEGIN THIS CHAPTER with a confession: It's no accident that this is one of the longest in the book. I learned a great deal about online self-help on America Online (AOL), and as this is a book about my experiences, this chapter is the best place to describe some of those lessons. So even if you plan to use another network, I hope you'll read on.

Over the last year, I've come to consider AOL my home online neighborhood. After hundreds of online hours, AOL has become as familiar a part of my everyday life as the front door of my house, the familiar clutter of my office, or the steering wheel of my trusty Isuzu Trooper. But the fact that I chose AOL as my home base doesn't necessarily mean that it's the best commercial network for you—or for health and self-help. There are great self-help resources on CompuServe, Prodigy, and the other commercial networks. (Indeed, both CompuServe and Prodigy have certain features that put AOL to shame.) But you probably *will* end up picking a "home network"—as I did— and spending a good deal of your online time there.

Two of the big things that attracted me to AOL were its *ease of use* and its extensive roster of *scheduled support group meetings*. AOL is the home of more regularly scheduled self-help support groups than any other network. According to one recent study, AOL had more than four times as many live chat groups as the next largest system.

HOT

TIP

One of the tricks to getting around in America Online is the use of keywords. You either click on "Keyword" in the Go To menu or press the Control (or Command) and **K** keys to open the keyword box. You then type in your keyword of choice, hit Return, and AOL will take you directly to your chosen area.

AOL's Interface and Graphics

**Health Online Distinguished
Achievement Award**

To: America Online

For: Best Interface

There's just one word for the AOL interface: superb. Using it seems effortless, automatic. In the language of interface design, it's highly transparent. When I'm cruising around AOL, I'm no more aware of the interface than I am of the wires and cables and switching networks that carry my voice when I use the phone. Transparency means less hassle and irritation in finding the resources I'm seeking and in going where I want to go. This ease of use is especially important for the new user.

Its state-of-the-art interface makes AOL an unmatched tool for connecting with other people. Reading and writing e-mail is a pleasure. Cruising the forums or sitting in on a support group are nearly effortless. The AOL software team deserves to be recognized as the Leonardos of online programmers.

A case in point: My 81-year-old mother recently decided to go online. When she asked me which service she should sign on to, I recommended

America Online. No one would ever mistake my dear mother for a highly wired hacker. When she wants to write me a letter, she still frequently reverts to her decades-old manual typewriter. So the whole idea of owning a computer was a bit of a stretch. But within a couple of months she became more and more comfortable with the service, and now she's a very competent regular AOL user. I doubt that she would have stuck it out on any other service.

HOT

TIP

- Use the keywords "Tour" or "Discover" to learn more about AOL. These two services provide a great overview of what America Online has to offer.
- On one of your first trips to AOL, be sure to stroll into the beginners forum (keyword: "Getting Started").

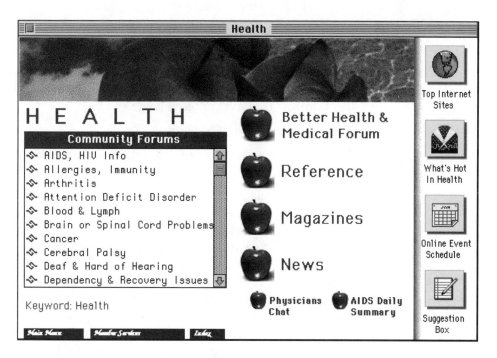

America Online looks easy to use, and it is. Click on one of the icons shown here to enter a forum, download a schedule, or send a message back to AOL.
(Design © America Online)

Support Group Meetings on America Online

Another great feature of AOL is the impressive number of self-help support groups. The list is so extensive that even in its abbreviated form, we've had to run it as a separate sidebar at the end of this chapter. In a minute I'll suggest that you flip ahead to take a look, but before you do, let's look at four representative listings on the schedule (all times are Eastern):

Cancer Survivors' Mutual Support

10 p.m. Sundays in the Better Health & Medical Forum's Health Conference Room. Keyword: "Health." Contact "KittyBa" or "JPLyons602"

SeniorNet Diet Club

11 a.m. Mondays in SeniorNet's Community Center. Keyword: "SeniorNet." Contact "JessieA2"

Mood Disorders Support Network

9 p.m. Mondays in the IMH Conference Room. Keyword: "IMH." For those new to a mood disorder, those still struggling, those recovered, and the friends and family of those with a mood disorder. Contact "Dan Ash" or "Jana Bike"

Chronic Conditions Chathouse

11 p.m. Wednesdays in the Equal Access Cafe. Keyword: "dis." Contact "DACLilly"

The first listing explains that the Cancer Survivors' Mutual Support Group meets at 10 P.M. each Sunday in the Better Health & Medical Forum's Health Conference Room. The keyword that will take you to this forum is "Health." The screen names for the two group facilitators are "KittyBa" and "JPLyons602."

The second listing tells us that the SeniorNet Diet Club meets every Monday morning at 11:00 A.M. The meeting location is in the SeniorNet Forum, in the room called "Community Center." The group coordinator's screen name is "JessieA2."

The third listing lets us know that the Mood Disorders Support Network meets every Monday evening at 9:00 P.M. The meeting takes place in the Issues in Mental Health Forum, in the Community Center room. The coordinators are "Dan Ash" and "Jana Bike."

The fourth listing announces that the Chronic Conditions Chathouse meets every Wednesday evening at 11:00 P.M. The meeting takes place in the disABILITIES Forum, in the room called "Equal Access Cafe." The group coordinator is "DACLilly."

Take a few minutes now to glance ahead at the AOL Self-Help Support Group Schedule on pages 87–90. Then come back to this point and continue.

Pretty impressive, isn't it? If you're like me, you probably found several groups you'd be interested in learning more about. If you have access to AOL, you can get more information about them by taking the following steps:

- These listings change frequently, so you might first want to consult the appropriate forum for current listings.

- Send an e-mail message to the contact person or persons listed for the group. Tell them about yourself, your situation, and your interests and ask the group leader to send you a copy of a recent meeting log—a transcript of all the messages exchanged during one online meeting—and any other available information about the group.

- Check for meeting logs in the software library of the group's home forum— some groups keep logs of recent meetings posted there.

- Read the leader's e-mail reply. If you decide you'd like to attend a meeting, e-mail the contact person again to let him or her know when you're planning to come. Make sure you understand the instructions for getting to the online "room" where the meeting will be held. (Don't worry, it's easy.) Ask the host to introduce you to other group members. Be sure to provide the host with whatever information about yourself you'd like the group to know.

- Be prepared to spend most of your time at the first few group meetings listening to and getting to know the other group participants. Feel free to comment, but—unless you're in the midst of a crisis—keep your initial comments short and on topic.

- Don't feel pressured to post messages of your own at first if it doesn't feel right. It's perfectly appropriate just to listen. (As we've noted before, listening passively online is called "lurking," a perfectly respectable thing to do.) Many new group members find that they prefer to simply observe for a meeting or two until they get to know the other group participants and become familiar with the customs of the group.

Let's say you decide to write to DACLilly, coordinator of the Chronic Conditions Chathouse, to ask her for the list of topics for upcoming meetings. When I did that, I got back the following message:

```
From: DACLilly
To: DrTomHO
Subj: CCC Starter Topics for upcoming meetings
Hi Dr Tom...
Thanks for your note. Here are some of the starter topics for
the weeks ahead:
** "The Bright Spots!" In darkest winter, lets look to the
bright spots of ourselves, our lives, and each other. What is
your bright spot, the thing you look forward to the most?
What is your funniest story? What is your funniest moment
online? off-line?
** "Drugs & emotions" Have you ever noticed a drug effecting
your emotional state? How did you know it was not just *you*?
Once you knew, were you able to be OK with that emotion,
because it wasn't *you*? If you were prescribed something you
knew changed emotions, did it work as you thought it would?
** "Expectations" Do you have expectations you try to "live
up to?" Are your set of expectations for yourself different
than for everyone else? Whose expectations are they? Are they
realistic? Are they impossible, and if so, why keep them?
** "Getting family to 'get it'" Does your family understand
your disability? How do they show that they do/don't? Is it
really possible to "get it" if a person hasn't lived it? What
can we do to help them understand?...
   Thanks for your votes that helped create this schedule.
The joking comments were so funny on some ballots I had to
sign off to finish laughing (especially all that growling
over discrimination) :) Your topic write-ins, as always, were
insightful! Keep 'em coming, your ideas are welcome anytime.
   All CCC meetings are in the Equal Access Cafe (keyword
"dis"). You are welcome at any & all meetings. We meet twice
a week, Wednesdays at 11 PM Eastern Time and Sunday evenings
at 6 P.M. DACSaj and I will be happy to see you by sunlight
and/or by moonlight!
Love & velvet roses, Lilly
(DACLilly)
```

Another way to use the support group list is to e-mail the host of a group on a given topic with a request for a specific piece of information. Consider the following listing from the schedule:

Attention Deficit Disorder (ADD)—Adults Only

12 midnight Eastern time Tuesdays in the IMH Conference Room. Keyword: "IMH." A group for adults with attention deficit disorder. Contact "Annie12345"

When I first saw this listing, I'd just spoken to a friend who was wondering if he might have attention deficit disorder, so I e-mailed Annie12345 to ask if she could send me a list of the diagnostic criteria for the condition. She answered as follows:

```
From: Annie12345
Subj: ADD Diagnostic Criteria
To: DrTomHO
   Hi Tom, A diagnosis of ADD can be made by a psychologist,
medical doctor or other therapist trained in identifying ADD.
Hallowell and Ratey's Diagnostic Checklist for ADD can be
found in their very useful book: Driven to Distraction (on
page 201). (Edward M Hallowell, M.D. and John J. Ratey, M.D.,
Pantheon Books, 1994. ISBN 0-679-42177-7)
   I must say that when I first read this list I was shocked
and amazed. It seemed as if they must have interviewed me
before making the list!
Best wishes,
Andrea Krapf Little (Annie12345)
```

She enclosed an abbreviated version of the diagnostic criteria for ADD, as excerpted from Drs. Hallowell and Ratey's book:

```
Attention Deficit Disorder is a chronic disturbance in which
A. At least fifteen of the following are present:
1. A sense of under-achievement, of not meeting one's goals,
   (regardless of how much one has actually accomplished).
2. Fast-paced mind, heading in different directions
   simultaneously.
3. Physical or mental restlessness.
4. Chronic procrastination or trouble getting started.
5. A tendency to have many projects going simultaneously, and
   trouble with follow-through.
6. A tendency to say what comes to mind without considering
   the timing or appropriateness of the remark.
7. A restive search for high stimulation, such as may be
   found in fast track careers, or risk taking, or gambling,
   or dangerous relationships or situations, or last-minute
   deadlines, a tendency to be easily bored.
8. Trouble focusing attention, tendency to tune out or drift
   away in the middle of a page or a conversation.
```

9. Tendency to change the subject, or the channel, or the project at hand without planning or preparation.
10. Often creative, intuitive, highly intelligent.
11. Trouble in going through established channels or in following "proper" procedures.
12. Impatient, low tolerance for frustration.
13. A tendency to worry needlessly, and ruminatively, tendency to scan the horizon looking for something to worry about, alternating with inattention to or disregard for actual dangers.
14. A sense of impending doom and insecurity, alternating with high risk taking.
15. Mood swings, depression, especially when disengaged from a person or project.
16. A tendency toward addictive behavior.
17. Family history of ADD or manic-depressive illness or depression, substance abuse or other disorders of impulse control or mood.
B. Childhood history of ADD (it may not have been formally diagnosed, but in reviewing the history the signs and symptoms were there).
C. Situation not explained by other medical or psychiatric condition.

As you can see, the combination of AOL's extensive roster of self-help groups, the easy availability of the screen names of the contact person for each group, and the willingness of most hosts to provide prompt and useful responses to direct e-mail inquiries makes AOL one of the best places in cyberspace to find (or form) the online support group of your dreams.

**Health Online Distinguished
Achievement Award**

To: Health ResponseAbility Systems and
America Online

For: Best Support Groups

America Online's Health and Health-Related Forums

As the self-help group listings indicate, each self-help mutual support group takes place in one of the forums listed below. The AOL forums with a major focus on health and support groups are:

- The Better Health & Medical Forum
- The disABILITIES Forum
- The Health Channel
- Personal Empowerment Network
- HealthZone
- The HIV/AIDS Positive Living Forum
- SeniorNet Online
- The National Alliance for the Mentally Ill Forum
- The National Multiple Sclerosis Society Forum
- The United Cerebral Palsy Association Forum
- The American Cancer Society Forum
- The Diabetes Forum (run by the American Diabetes Association)

In addition, there are a number of other AOL groups and forums in which health and support are included among other topics of discussion:

- Baby Boomers
- The Bicycle Network
- The Deaf Community
- The Gay & Lesbian Community Forum
- Longevity Online
- The Parents' Information Network

I'll describe the Better Health & Medical and disABILITIES forums first because they're the most active. I'll use them as examples to show how forums on AOL work, and then I'll describe the many other forums.

The Better Health & Medical Forum (Keyword: "Better Health")

The Better Health & Medical Forum is run by Health ResponseAbility Systems, Inc., and hosted by Elin Silveous (AOL screen name ESilveous) and her partner, physician Alan Douma (screen name AlDouma).

To go to the Better Health & Medical Forum, click on "Keyword" in the Go To menu, then enter "Better Health."

The main menu for the forum gives you a choice of the following:

Health Focus
Offers in-depth reports on special health topics, the day's top health-related news story, self-scoring quizzes, opinion polls on health-related issues, discussions and debates, and man-on-the-information-superhighway interviews

Organizations & disABILITIES
Takes you to five forums hosted by national nonprofit organizations and to the disABILITIES Forum

Message Center
Message boards organized by special-interest topics—see the listing below

Health & Medical Chat Room
Takes you to the virtual "room" where self-help group meetings and chat groups are held

Software Libraries
Software and longer text files you can download onto your computer

Search Health Forum
Allows you to search the forum databases for your topic of choice

Choices from the scroll box on the main forum menu include:

About the Forum
A general overview of the Forum

Online Chats, Self-Help Schedule
A complete listing of mutual-aid self-help chat groups that take place in the Better Health & Medical Forum, the disABILITIES Forum, and the Deaf Community Forum

Multimedia Self-Care Showcase
A graphics-intensive encyclopedia of lifestyle and wellness information

You'll also find a listing of the following searchable databases, each of which contains encyclopedia-like listings on the designated topic:

Lifestyles & Wellness	Men/Women/Children's Health
Mental Health & Addictions	Seniors' Health and Caregiving
Human Sexuality	Alternative Medicine
Informed Decisions	Home Medical Guide
Health Reform & Insurance	

Here are some of the things you can do in the Better Health & Medical Forum—and in other AOL forums as well:

- Read postings, participate in ongoing discussions, or start a new topic on the special-interest message boards. (Click on the Message Center icon to see a complete list of person-to-person bulletin board postings, arranged by topic.)
- Search for information (articles and encyclopedia-style listings) on your own special topic of interest by clicking on the Search Health Forum button in the forum's main menu.
- Join in scheduled weekly "live" mutual support group meetings on a variety of topics. (For a complete list of groups in the Better Health & Medical Forum, click on "Online Chats, Self-Help Schedule" in the main forum menu.)
- Browse through the table of contents for the forum databases and file libraries, looking at the selections that match your interests.
- Download health-related software and longer health articles by clicking on the Software Libraries button.
- Health professionals can join in professional forums or participate in "live" regularly scheduled health-professional networking meetings. (A schedule is included in the Health Professionals' Network and the Nurses Network sections of the Message Center.)

Special-Interest Message Boards in the Better Health & Medical Forum

Click on the Message Center icon in the Better Health & Medical Forum, then click on "List Categories," and you'll be able to browse through an extensive list of message boards devoted to a wide range of special-interest topics. Within each you'll find postings from AOL members who share that concern.

Here are the boards:

Alternative Healing Approaches	Health Professionals' Exchange
Cancer & Related Concerns	Health Reform & Consumerism
Cerebral Palsy/Related Concerns	Mental Health Issues & Concerns
Diabetes & Related Concerns	Multiple Sclerosis
Diet, Exercise & Fitness	Nurses' Network
For Men or Women Only	Self-Help & Support Groups
General Health Discussions	

Sample Topics on the Better Health & Medical Forum's Message Boards

General Health Discussions

Join In-Tell Us about Yourself, In Search Of..., Alzheimer's Disease, Arthritis, Asthma, Back Pain, Broken Bones, Carpal Tunnel-Repetitive Strain, Crohn's Disease, Ear-Nose-Throat, Fibromyalgia, Health Insurance Help!, Heart Health & Problems, Hepatitis C, High Blood Pressure, Irritable Bowel Syndrome, Knee Injuries, Lyme Disease, Migraines, Rheumatic Diseases & Lupus, Weight Loss, Women's Health

Self-Help and Support Groups

Alzheimer's Support, Parents of ADD/Gifted Children, Suicide Prevention, Menopause Support, HIV-Positive Mates, Polycystic Kidney Diseases, Parkinson's Disease, Kidney, Liver and Other Transplants, Death and Dying, Marfan's Syndrome, Hepatitis, ADD Support, Mitral Valve Prolapse Syndrome, Chronic Illness Support, Dieters Unite!, Thyroidism: Hypo-Hyper, Herpes Mutual Support, Overcoming Eating Disorders, Rare Disorders Information and Support, Chronic Fatigue Syndrome, Crohn's & Colitis, Irritable Bowel Syndrome Support, Arthritis and Lupus Support, Living with Cancer, Twelve-Steppers and Recovery

Mental Health Issues and Concerns

Panic Attacks, Manic-Depression, Paxil, Xanax, Zoloft, Schizophrenia, Adult Attention Deficit Disorder, Multiple Personality, Family Members' Mutual Support, Depression and Alcohol, Eating Disorders, Obsessive-Compulsive Disorder, Sexual Abuse, and Dyslexia

Health Professional's Exchange

Medical Software, Family Docs Network, Optometrists' Network, Occupational Therapists' Forum, Speech/Language Pathologists, Medical Help!

Alternative Healing Approaches

AIDS/HIV and Chronic Fatigue Syndrome, Alternative Health News, Chronic Conditions/Alternative, Anti-oxidants, Arthritis, Back Pain, Chelation Therapy, Diet and Nutrition, Eczema and Dry Skin, Fleas, Herbs, Supplements, Vitamins, Herpes, Holistic Health Centers, Homeopathic Remedies, Hot Flashes, Massage, Chiropractic, Midwifery and Natural Childbirth, Cancer "Cures" and Treatments, Shark Cartilage

The disABILITIES Forum (Keyword: "dis")

Like the Better Health & Medical Forum, the disABILITIES Forum is run by Health ResponseAbility Systems, Inc., and hosted by Elin Silveous (ESilveous) and Alan Douma, M.D. (AlDouma). While there is much overlap of content between the two forums, the focus here is on chronic illnesses and disabilities. The choices on the main menu are:

About the Forum

Employment & Empowerment
A searchable database

Assistive Technology Forum

disABILITIES Message Center
People-to-people message boards organized by special-interest topics

Software Libraries
Software and longer text files you can download onto your computer

Online Chats Self-Help Schedule
The same list of self-help groups that appeared in the Better Health & Medical Forum

Equal Access Cafe Chat Room
Access to live meetings and chat groups

Go to Better Health and Medical Forum

If you click on "Message Center," you'll see the following list of main topics plus "Go to Better Health & Medical Forum."

```
Assistive Technology Board
Blindness Board
Cancer & Related Concerns
Cerebral Palsy/Related Concerns
Deafness & Hard of Hearing Board
Diabetes & Related Concerns
General Discussions
Learning Disabilities Board
Mental Health Issues & Concerns
Multiple Sclerosis
Physically Disabled Board
```

If you click on "Equal Access Cafe Chat Room," you'll enter the public meeting room of the disABILITIES Forum. If a meeting is in process, feel free to listen in. If not, check to see if anyone is present. If so, strike up a conversation. If not, just wait a few moments and see if someone drops in to chat.

From the Equal Access Cafe (or any virtual room on AOL) you can click on "Rooms" and will be taken to the People Connection, where you'll see a list of all currently occupied rooms on AOL, along with a notation of how many people are in each room. If you don't find the group you're looking for, follow the on-screen directions at People Connection to open your own virtual chat room on any topic.

Points of Special Interest

- The "Assistive Technology Forum" has a database of Apple Computer's disability resources, an Assistive Technology Message Board, an Assistive Technology Software Library, and an Assistive Technology Reading Room, with files covering physical, visual, learning, and speech disabilities. Another folder offers a consumer's guide to disability software starting points, and yet another is titled "Macintosh Electronic Curbcuts."

- The "General Disabilities" message folder includes special-interest sections on introducing yourself, hemophilia, lupus, wheelchairs (best and worse), the Americans with Disabilities Act, and epilepsy.

- The "Software Library" contains an extensive collection of disability-related files and databases. An especially notable resource in the library is an extensive collection of logs of recent self-help mutual support group meetings.

- Clicking on the icon for the "Health Conference Room" takes you to the online room where many of the support group meetings are held. During the off-hours you may or may not find anyone here. (You'll see the screen name of anyone present in the room.) If you do find people in a meeting room between regularly scheduled meetings, feel free to say hello and ask them about themselves and their interests. You can also click on "Member Profile" (in the pull-down menu) for additional background information on any member you meet.

The Health Channel (Keyword: "Health")

AOL recently launched the Health Channel, a convenient and innovative directory of selected health-related chat groups, forums, databases, search services, magazines, news, etc. (See the sidebar on p. 68 for a list of topics.)

The Health Channel menu includes Reference, Magazines, News, MEDLINE, AIDS Daily Summary, Top Internet Sites, What's Hot in Health, Online Events Schedule, and Suggestion Box. There are also a small but important button labeled "Index"and the Community Forums scroll box.

Reference (Keyword: "Health Reference")

Reference offers the Knowledge Center and Reference Q&A (both described below) as well as providing MEDLINE searches and access to the AIDS Daily Summary.

The Knowledge Center The Knowledge Center icon takes you to the Better Health & Medical Forum's health database (see p. 61).

Reference Q&A Reference Q&A is a live chat room in which AOL staffers answer your questions and offer online advice on a wide variety of health concerns. While they can't give medical advice, they will point you in the right direction and help you get your questions answered. This service is available every evening (except holidays) from 8:00 to 12:00 Eastern time.

Magazines

Clicking on the Magazines icon lets you browse through a selection of articles from the following publications: *Backpacker Online*, *Bicycling Online*, *Consumer Reports* (food and health), *Elle* (fitness and health), *Longevity Online*, *Scientific American*, and *Woman's Day* (your body, mind & fitness).

News

The News icon takes you to a menu with a list of current health-related news headlines. You can click on any headline to see the complete article. The *New York Times*—Science Times and *San Jose Mercury News*—Science & Medicine icons let you read health-related stories in these two respected newspapers. You can browse through back issues by topic or search for your subject of choice. In the New York Times—Science Times, for instance, you can catch up on recent pieces from Jane Brody's weekly "Personal Health" column.

America Online's Health Channel Topic List

AIDS, HIV Info	Fitness
Allergies, Immunity	Heart & Circulatory
Arthritis	Hormone & Endocrine
Attention Deficit Disorder	Infant & Children's Health
Blood & Lymph	Infectious & Contagious Diseases
Brain or Spinal Cord Problems	Kidney, Urinary Tract
Cancer	Lung & Respiratory
Cerebral Palsy	Men's Health
Daily Living	Mental Health
Deaf & Hard of Hearing	Multiple Sclerosis
Dependency & Recovery Issues	Muscles, Bones & Joints
Development & Learning Disabilities	Parenting & Caregiving
Diabetes	Relationships
Digestive, Abdomen Disorders	Reproduction & Infertility
Disabilities	Skin, Hair & Nails
Divorce & Separation	Teeth, Gum & Mouth
Ear, Nose & Throat	Teens Issues & Concerns
Eyes & Vision	Women's Health

Personal Empowerment Network (Keyword: "PEN")

This new forum provides another topic-specific list of health resources. Click "Empower Me" to suggest a new message folder, start a new support group, or send a comment or suggestion to the forum hosts.

HOT TIP

In most AOL forums, the maximum capacity of the online rooms is twenty-three members. So if the directory tells you that there are currently twenty-three people in the room, that means it's full and you probably won't be able to get in until someone else leaves. Choose another group or come back later to see if a spot in the room has opened up.

"Join In, Tell Us About Yourself"

In the two AOL forums we've described—and in many other self-help forums—you'll find a special section devoted to self-introductions by new forum participants. On AOL this section is usually entitled "Join In, Tell Us about Yourself." It's a good place to post your first message to a new forum.

But before you do, be sure to browse through a representative sample of the self-introductions by other forum members. You'll learn a great deal about the forum and its participants, you may meet potential new friends, and you'll get ideas for doing your own posting.

A self-introduction is your chance to tell other forum members about yourself, to share your concerns, and to tell people what you are looking for. Also be sure to list areas that you know something about and the experiences you've had—in a way that indicates the kinds of information or support you might be able to provide for others.

In many support forums you'll also find a folder called "Looking for Information" or "In search of. . . " These are special sections for members looking for the answers to specific questions. Recent questions in one such folder in the disABILITIES Forum included inquiries on hair transplants, surgery to repair a torn rotator cuff, whiplash auto injury, brittle bone disease, hepatitis B shots, and sperm banks. There also was a note from someone who has just had an illeostomy (intestinal surgery) and wanted to talk to others who have been through the experience. Another series of postings provided information on a program that offers cancer patients free transportation to or from cancer treatment centers on corporate jets.

A wide variety of other special-interest categories can be found in the disABILITIES Forum's various Message Center folders. When I selected two dozen folders at random I came up with the following:

> Advice for Runners, AIDS/HIV, Back Pain, Cancer Tests and Treatments, Carpal Tunnel Syndrome, Chronic Headaches, Fibromyalgia, Foot Woes, Hair Loss, Head Lice at School, Health News Discussion, Heart Problems, Heart Surgery, Chronic Pain, Human Sexuality, Lyme Disease, Prozac, Scoliosis, Menopause, Seasonal Affective Disorder, TMJ, Twitching, Ulcers, Vocal Chord Abuse

Each of these folders (and many more) contains postings from people concerned with the listed topic. For instance, in "Cancer Tests and Treatments" you'll find postings from a wide variety of people who are in the process of being diagnosed with various types of cancer. There are questions and comments about different treatment centers, discussions about particular types of cancer, input from researchers, and exchanges with experienced self-helpers who have had the same kind of cancer and know the ropes.

Links Between "Live" Support Groups and Support Forums

In the special-interest folder "Depression Self-Help Group" in the disABILITIES Forum, you'll find a series of postings by people who are also participating in a scheduled support group called the Depression Support Network. This is something you'll frequently find in the online world—a scheduled support group (live interaction) that is connected formally or informally with a support forum (posted messages or e-mail) on the same topic. You'll find many other ongoing discussions associated with other scheduled self-help group meetings; e.g., many of the same people who attend the Menopause Support meetings are among those most active in the Menopause Support Forum.

When reading forum postings, it frequently works best to select the "Most Recent" postings, then read backward. Or you can select postings written after a specified date. If you don't choose one of these options, you may get a very long list of messages, beginning with some that are many months or even several years old.

Other Health Forums

Issues in Mental Health (Keyword: "IMH")

The introductory announcement for the Issues in Mental Health (IMH) forum provides a good overview of its contents:

```
THE PARENTING BOARD
Parenting is often taken for granted as a skill we all pos-
sess. Today, there are problems never before faced by par-
ents. Join other members in discussing issues of this
challenging task on this message board. Share YOUR insights
into Parenting on this message board.

THE DAILY LIVING BOARD
Day-to-day living can be exciting, and quite stressful. New jobs,
problems with your boss, moving to a new place, making the most
of a vacation, all aspects of making it in our world today can
be found here. Join members as they post questions, anecdotes
and stories about coping in today's hustle-and-bustle world.
```

THE RELATIONSHIP BOARD
Relationships can be puzzling. They start and end, hit rocky
ground and survive trying times in our lives. Recent statistics show that nearly 1 in 2 marriages will end in divorce.
Join other members in discussing how they coped with divorce
and separation, that first date, the upcoming wedding, or any
relationship issue on this message board.

THE DIVORCE AND SEPARATION BOARD
Discuss these trying times in your life with others who have
survived the breakup of a major relationship in their life.
Forums in the IMH Conference Room also address relationship
issues for you. Feel free to join in the discussions.

THE TEEN FORUM BOARD
Teens... this is a place just for you. Talk about problems
you're having with school, parents, friends, etc. Our caring
staff listens and will answer any question you have. You're
invited to share special moments with other teen friends
online, share ideas about your life, and chat with teens
online.
...

THE IMH LIBRARY
The IMH library contains transcripts of forums, prior special
feature articles, and general information files pertaining to
the mental health area.

CONFERENCE ROOM
The Issues in Mental Health Conference Room bustles with
activity every day and night. Our caring staff is here for
you with a schedule jam-packed with events of all kinds. Drop
by for an interesting evening conversing with other AOL members on a wide range of topics. You'll always be welcome!...

The forum host is Laura Packer (screen name Arrianne). Laura is a mental health professional with an M.A. in counseling and psychology. She has extensive experience in crisis intervention, parenting, relationships, and other family concerns. She is highly thought of in the AOL self-help community. Laura offers the following advice to new IMH forum participants:

Once you've located the IMH Forum (Keyword: IMH), I'd advise new users to check out the current schedule of self-help/support group meetings on the IMH Forum, along with times and screen name of the staff member who hosts that event. You should also scan the Daily Living folder for any postings from me (Screen name: Arrianne). These will contain recent news and updates on the support groups.

Next, you might want to browse through the special-interest message boards and library files for items on your special interests. You may wish to copy or download interesting files for later off-line reading to save on access charges.

As you read the postings and the files, try to zero in on the members and staff who coordinate the meetings and/or post most frequently on your top-priority topics. You may then wish to send them e-mail. Introduce yourself and ask for more information about forums, people, and groups concerned with your concerns.

We currently have more than 50 self-help groups meeting weekly in the IMH Conference Room. Look them over and check in with the group leaders of the groups that interest you most. Introduce yourself, ask any questions you may have, and ask if there is a mailing list for your topic. If so, ask to have your name added. This will help you keep up to date on what's going on with the group. You are cordially invited to drop in to the IMH Conference Room during any group meeting.

Finally, I recommend that new users contact me (Screen name: Arrianne) with any additional questions. I would also welcome your suggestions for new discussion topics or chat groups you'd like to see added to the forum.

Best regards,

Laura Packer (Screen name: Arrianne)

Issues in Mental Health Forum Leader

Here's a list of representative topics at the forum:

Parenting Board

Spanking, Attention Deficit Disorder Kids, The "Strong-Willed" Child, Infertility, Single Parent Problems, Parents of the Emotionally Disturbed, Oppositional Defiant Disorder, Dealing with Parental Anger, Problems of Gifted Children, Stress in Children, Helping Kids Handle the Death of a Parent, Twins

Daily Living

Widows and Widowers, Bipolar Disorders, Mental Health Professionals, Depression, Anxiety and Panic Disorders, Eating

Disorders, Multiple Personality Disorder, Repressed Memories, Shy People's Support Group [they're presumably too shy to have an actual live chat group], Survivors & Recovery, Adult ADD, Chronic Low-Grade Depression, All about Feelings, Suicide, Panic Disorders, Alcoholism, Adult Survivors of Sex Abuse.

Divorce and Separation

Widowhood, Custody, Loneliness, Letting Go and Moving On, Surviving an Affair, When to Break Up?, Not in Love but Have Kids, When You Don't Want It to End, Spouse Abuse, The Courage to Leave.

Relationships

Women Dating Married Men, Corporal Punishment, Changing Men, Borderline Personality Disorder, Psychotherapy, Dating Again, Incest Survivors & Their Partners, Dominance and Submission, Younger Men with Older Women.

Note: As we go to press, AOL has just announced that it is closing down the Issues in Mental Health Forum. IMH members and groups will be invited to become part of the new Personal Empowerment Network (see p. 68).

HealthZone (Keyword: "HealthZone")

HealthZone is a fitness, nutrition, and wellness center in cyberspace. This is a playfully guilt-free service where members can find and share information on weight management, nutrition, exercise, sports medicine, and spiritual and mental well-being. HealthZone's features range from a Craving Chocolate support group to a Sports Medicine board (complete with doctors to answer your questions), to a selection of low-fat recipes, to a Fitness Professionals network, to a Buddy Board where you can meet online or in-the-flesh support pals for your planned lifestyle upgrade.

The Positive Living Forum (Keywords: "AIDS," "HIV")

This is a forum devoted to AIDS and HIV support and information. Support group meetings take place in the Positive Living Conference Room. There are extensive lists of message boards, online support groups, publications organizations, and AIDS and HIV sites on the Internet. There is also a database of AIDS and HIV treatment information. You can send e-mail to the area coordinator at GLCFJeff.

SeniorNet Online (Keyword: "Senior")

SeniorNet Online describes itself as "the international community of computer-using seniors." It is an independent nonprofit organization that contracted an especially favorable member rate from America Online. All interested AOL members over 55 are invited to join. (It's not necessary to join to participate in the forum, but SeniorNet members can receive a special deal: an unlimited number of free hours on SeniorNet for a basic monthly fee of $9.95!) This is a terrific bargain for those who think they might spend a lot of time on SeniorNet.

The icon choices on the main menu are for SeniorNet Forums, Community Center, Computer Learning Center, and Showcase & Exchange. Scroll box choices on the main menu include:

```
Welcome to SeniorNet Online

Announcements

What's New & Events

SeniorNet Membership Application

SeniorNet Sourcebook

Senior Resources

SeniorNet Headquarters
```

SeniorNet's host of the day can be reached by sending e-mail to the screen name "SeniorNet."

Two popular message boards are Health & Wellness and Getting Into Computers.

The Health & Wellness board contains fifty special-interest sections. Topics include:

> WINK'S Club Laughter=Medicine, Sexuality & Seniors, Grief Discussion & Support, Fibromyalgia, Eyes/Vision, Exercise & Fitness, Diet Club & Support Group, Depression, Cooking for Health, Panic Attacks and Anxiety, Alzheimer's/Dementia, Alcoholics Anonymous, Announcements/Requests, Living with Cancer, Caregiving Support

The Communities Message Area board is a place to link up with other seniors who share your special interests. It has a Newcomers & Introductions section. This section is a good place to introduce yourself and read the self- introductions of other forum participants. Other sections of this board include:

> 1995 Get-Togethers & Events, Health Sharing with All, Discussion about Forum/Chat, Families of Gays & Lesbians, Senior Gay & Lesbian Issues, Widows & Widowers Talk, Women's Issues, Women/Men Communicating, Women Sharing

It may be partly due to this uniquely affordable fee structure, but there seems to be an especially strong sense of community here. You'll meet lots of regulars who spend a great deal of time on the forum.

One typical SeniorNet regular is "Yota," a 63-year-old retired computer salesman named Bill Mason, who lives in Eyota, Minnesota. He has health problems, a bad leg, and poor hearing and admits that he sometimes feels pretty lonely. He relies on SeniorNet as a regular part of his social connection. He talks to seniors all over the country. He says it's like "a group of people sitting around a big table, having coffee and kidding each other."

Another grateful SeniorNet member is R. B. LeClaire, a 58-year-old Palm Beach County woman. She is hard of hearing and has been homebound for the last seven years. Recently her online friends helped her get through the illness and then death of her mother. After she posted some of her experiences on a SeniorNet bulletin board devoted to grief, one cyberbuddy recommended a change in her mother's medication. It made her mother's last months much more comfortable.

A knowledgeable self-helper responding to Mrs. LeClaire's description of her hearing problems got in touch with a state agency and arranged for her to have a special telephone installed. Still others read about her postcard collection and began sending her additional cards from all over. "I don't know how I would have emotionally stood up under the weight of being homebound," she says, and of her online network of friends, "I feel like I'm wearing out the word 'wonderful'."

So far SeniorNet can brag of four marriages resulting from friendships initially formed online. And Charlie "Chuck" Brown had what turned out to be an X-rated online eighty-first birthday party. (It went on for 7,770 lines.) One of the guests typed in a picture of a birthday cake topped by a naked lady with the words "Hi, big boy." Everyone, including the women at the party, cheered.

This forum is so good and so affordable that even those of us who are younger than 55 may be tempted to add a few years to our age and join in the fun.

**Health Online Distinguished
Achievement Award**

To: SeniorNet and America Online

For: Best Support Forum for Seniors

The Five National Nonprofit Specialty Forums

There are five specialty health forums on AOL run by national nonprofit groups:

- The National Alliance for the Mentally Ill (keyword: "NAMI")
- The National Multiple Sclerosis Society (keyword: "NMSS")

- United Cerebral Palsy Associations, Inc. (keyword: "UCPA")
- The American Cancer Society (keyword: "ACS")
- The Diabetes Forum (keyword: "American Diabetes")

At the time this book went to press, these forums offered primarily searchable text files on their designated subjects, but many had plans for extending their offerings.

Health-Related Forums

Baby Boomers (Keyword: "Baby Boomers")

Baby Boomers, a forum especially for those born between 1946 and 1964, has a section called Baby Boomer Issues that includes these discussion groups:

> Parents of Twins & Triplets, Parents of Preemies, Single Again/In Midlife, Losing a Parent, Empty Nesters, The Sandwich Generation, Stay-at-Home Fathers, New Age Thoughts, Prozac/Zoloft, Widows and Widowers, Fitness for Boomers, Friends of Bill W. [a boomer AA group], Dating, Marriage & Divorce, Midlife Flirtations, Endometriosis, Over-35 Abortions, Juggling Job and Family, Infertility, Nursing Homes for Aging Parents, Blended Families.

On the Boomer Roll Call board you'll find groups devoted to sex for boomers weight loss, and a number of forums in which you can schmooze with others who share a particular year of birth.

The forum hosts are Laura Heinzel (screen name Shakina) and Alice (screen name Dearest). (Alice also hosts two other support groups, Forty-Somethings and Power Surge [Menopause].)

The Bicycle Network (Keywords: "BikeNet" or "bicycle")

In the Bicycle Network (BikeNet) there's a message board in the Message Center, Bicyclist Training & Fitness, which is a forum for sharing "information about training, fitness, nutrition, exercise, or anything else pertaining to the human body." Topics include:

> Heart Rate Monitors, Numb Hands, Returning to Biking at Midlife, Personal Coaches, Cycle Racing, Stationary Trainers Road Rash and Bicycle-Related Medical Problems.

The forum leader is Tim Oey (screen name TheCyclist.)

The Deaf Community Forum (Keyword: "Deaf")

The Deaf Community forum has its own message board. Topics on the board include:

> Cochlear Implants, Deaf Parents' Network, Deaf Senior Citizens, Deaf and Hard-of-Hearing Gays, Employment Issues and Experiences, Hearing Aids, Hearing Parents of Deaf Kids, Hearing Spouses & Significant Others, Humor & Comedy, Interested Audiologists, Learning American Sign Language, PC Pals' Teen Network, and Singles' Network

The Gay & Lesbian Community Forum (Keywords: "Gay" or "Lesbian")

The Gay & Lesbian Community Forum hosted by "QUIRK" includes the invaluable HIV/AIDS Forum, several HIV/AIDS online support groups, a listing of other AIDS resources on the Net, and a forum for support and recovery from addictions.

Longevity Online (Keyword: "Longevity")

Longevity Online carries present and past issues of *Longevity* magazine, which contains articles on anti-aging medicine, alternative health, and a variety of other wellness topics. The Forum also includes Health Exchange, a person-to-person message board where you can discuss the topics covered in the magazine's articles with other *Longevity* readers.

Parents' Information Network (Keyword: "PIN")

The Parents' Information Network contains a variety of useful resources, including the Adoption Forum, the Child Abuse Forum, and Family Health Issues. It sponsors scheduled support groups for parents who have lost a child and other topics. Support group meetings include:

> **Adoption Forum** (host: MRowland)
>
> **Pregnancy/Newborn Chat** (host: LINDARNC)
>
> **You Are Not Alone—for parents of children who have died** (host: LoisG2)
>
> **Breast Feeding Chat** (host: NeenH)
>
> **Child Abuse Forum** (host: TomHanna)
>
> **Couple's Relationship Forum** (host: MINATURE)

The Personal Empowerment Network (Keyword: "PEN")

The newest forum by Health ResponseAbility Systems, the Personality Empowerment Network offers menus for a variety of health topics, with a wide variety of online resources for each—mostly the same ones provided by the Health Channel. In addition, the Empower Me icon provides an easy way to request a new self-help group or forum if you don't find what you're looking for. If you click on "Meet the Empowerment Team," you can view photos and bios of Health Responsibility Systems staffers.

Health Online Distinguished Achievement Award

To: Health ResponseAbility Systems and America Online

For: Innovations in Online Health Forums

Exploring the AOL Forums

Now that you've had an overview of the health and health-related forums on AOL, the question naturally arises: How might you use them to help you find the resources you need right now?

Most people log on to a health or health-related support forum because of a specific need or concern—their own or that of a family member. Let's say you're currently dealing with the pain of a recent death in the family. You log on, follow the procedures described above, and open the Better Health & Medical Forum's "Death & Dying" folder. Among the messages you find there are the following:

```
Subj: My Dad
From: JoanneQ2
My Dad died of brain cancer in October. People who haven't
lost a parent don't seem to understand that time is not the
quick healer they all seem to think it is. It's been almost a
year, but I still feel that my life will never be the same.
I no longer have a dad. I can't celebrate Fathers Day. Or his
birthday. Or sing for him. Or hear his corny jokes. Or hug
him. Or feel his cheek on mine. I feel so alienated from the
great mass of mankind who still have two parents.
```

Subj: Having A Hard Time
From: Anita1437
My boyfriend died this week. It was quick, but unfortunately
not painless. He was 29 years old. Is there still a support
group for those of us dealing with Death and Dying? Please
let me know. I'd like to be able to hold onto the sweet memory of Raymond, but without the pain.

Subj: Life, death, & meaning
From: GeorgeDeV
My father is dying of heart failure. He's quite ill and
debilitated, and I'm watching him waste away a day at a time.
It's one of the hardest things I've ever had to do.
    The lesson? Live life. Love life. ALL of it. Love the
people with whom you share your days. You really never know
what can happen. It is such a fragile presence we share. The
real lesson is: Open your eyes. Pay attention. Relish your
loved ones. Look around. Take it all in. While you're here,
really try to really BE here.

Subj: Death & Dying Support Group
From: Dan Ash
Yes, there's a death & dying support group. It meets on AOL
every Saturday evening. Here are the details:
Death and Dying Support Group
8 p.m. ET in a private PEOPLE CONNECTION room. Keyword: TALK.
"A place to discover common threads in our existence of dying
as we honor the uniqueness of our own process, and to explore
what our dying means to our lives." Contact "MarilynUSA".

Subj: Finding Meaning
From: UtahGal
My husband recently died of melanoma at age 38. We both
learned many lessons. He truly learned to appreciate all he
had. At his sickest, he would tell me that he was the lucki-
est person in the world because he now knew how many people
truly loved him.
    He pardoned his enemies and forgave the friends and fam-
ily members who had upset him. He wanted to live more than
anything, yet he was not afraid of dying. Living through the
experience showed me how strong I could be.
    I now view life as a road strewn with obstacles, some
greater than others. But as long as we move forward, with
love and caring for others, we will deal with and overcome
each obstacle in turn, and have no fear or regret when we
reach our final destination.

Subj: Celebrating Your Dad
From: Larry49
Oh, Joanne, I feel your tears.

I wonder if you could think of this another way. Perhaps on Father's Day you could have a quiet moment thinking of how your Dad loved you. Or writing him a letter. On his birthday you could light a candle... You get the idea.

His relationship to you has of course changed. The person, the warm cheek, the hug are not physically there. But don't for a minute believe that our ability to "relate to" departed loved ones ends with their physical existence. We can carry them forever in a shrine inside our hearts.

This is not to say that they are necessarily "alive" on some spiritual plane, but that our minds and hearts can pre-serve them in our memories, and thoughts, and the feeling of connection can continue as long as we live.

Subj: my dad
From: JoanneQ2
Thanks to all for your kind words of wisdom. While I still can't find much meaning in my father dying, I'm so glad that I could be there for him. I gave him his medicine. I bathed him when he was too weak to take a shower. I rocked him like a baby when he wept from pain. I held him in my arms as he took his last breath.

Never in a million years could you have convinced me that I would be capable of doing such things. But when the time came, I did them.

But then again he was my father and I would have gladly given my life for his. The love was that deep.

Subj: To all who grieve
From: PerryCat
We found a lovely little poem among my mother's papers after her death. It was clear she'd left it for us, but we don't know if she wrote it or found it somewhere. She'd spent a year in a vegetative state after a massive stroke, and there was much unfinished business, but this little poem seemed to help wrap things up for us.

It advised us not to be gloomy or grim, but to think of her as a benign guardian spirit that would always be present in our lives, simply withdrawn into the darkness, waiting for us as we finish our own paths that will lead us to the same place.
It made me feel that we should all perhaps write a message of blessing and good-by to those we leave behind...

After reading these messages, you might decide to take a deep breath, wipe a tear from your eye, and post a message in which you share your responses to the earlier messages and begin to share your own experiences and feelings with your fellow forum participants.

Digging Beneath the Surface

It's important to keep in mind that on AOL as on all the computer networks, in addition to the resources listed for your special-interest topic (e.g., the support forums and scheduled support groups), there may be additional semiformal and informal networks, unofficial chat groups, informal e-mail lists, off-the-record gatherings of friends, and a variety of other informal resources. The best way to find them is to ask the active members of your self-help group or forum about other available resources.

To illustrate this point, I've asked AOL Recovery group coordinator "MarshHawk" to help me put together an in-depth listing of additional recovery resources on AOL. (Like many self-helpers, MarshHawk prefers to maintain his anonymity. He asked that I identify him by his screen name only.)

Here, then, is MarshHawk's listing of groups and people that might be useful to AOL members dealing with alcohol or drug-related concerns. In addition to serving as an example of the kinds of additional "underground" resources that exist in most virtual self-help communities, we hope that this will provide useful guidelines for AOL members looking for help with alcohol or drug-related problems:

```
The recovery community on AOL is a very friendly one.
Newcomers are always welcome. Just reach out and say "Hi."
And please feel free to ask plenty of questions of any mem-
ber. If you have a recovery-related concern and you're inter-
ested in learning more about our community, I'd suggest that
you first visit the RecoveryLink Chat Room, the Friends of
Bill W. Chat Room, or both. These informal get-togethers are
a great place to start meeting people and learning your way
around. Here are some good places to start:
```

RecoveryLink Brunch
Saturday and Sunday, 11 a.m. ET in the Public Rooms area of
People Connection. Keyword: TALK. Contact "MarshHawk" or
"LilyBet". (RecoveryLink is also open and hosted each evening
from 8 PM until midnight Eastern Time on Thursday through
Monday. You may find it open at other times on these days
without a host. Contact "HOST Tess", "HOST Maize", or "HOST
Serene".)

Friends of Bill W.
Saturday, 11 p.m. ET in the Member Rooms area of People
Connection. Keyword: TALK. Room name: Friends of Bill W.
Contact "MetalXXXXX" or "ZCardman" or "DanZen12". (Note:
Friends of Bill W. frequently meets outside its scheduled
time and can be attended almost every night of the week in
the above location.)

Alternatives to 12-Step Programs
There is a private meeting for those interested in learning
about newer alternative recovery programs that are not based
upon the traditional 12-step model. Please contact GabeCT or
PamCT for more information on this meeting.

    Recovery Chat Rooms like RecoveryLink and Friends of Bill
W. tend to be very relaxed and informal. RecoveryLink is not
affiliated with any particular recovery program, while
Friends of Bill W. maintains a loose identification with the
12-Step programs. These rooms are more like (sober) picnics
than regular recovery meetings. This is a time for members of
the recovery community to laugh and relax and have fun. If
you need a 'real' meeting (not listed here as it is a 12-Step
tradition to be invited to meetings by a sponsor) you can use
these gatherings to ask other members to recommend the best
ones to attend.
    As a second step, I'd suggest you look into joining an
issue based Recovery E-mail List. This is the least expensive
way to stay up-to-date on recent community news as little
online time is required. Once your name is entered on one of
the recovery mailing lists, you'll automatically receive all
bulletins listing upcoming events and the latest news in your
area of interest. As their name implies, e-mail Meetings are
conducted via e-mail rather than in live chat rooms. There is
usually one topic for the week to which people respond. The
contact people listed below can help you find your way to an
e-mail list of interest to you.

For Information On:	Send e-mail to:
Adult Children Issues	RuthanneB
Men's E-mail list	ALOrlando

```
Attention Deficit         AngieDixon

Bills House               Gerundo

Codependents Group        KathyNor

Women's E-mail Group      Tamyers, Camillav, DiannaN

Friends of Bill W.        MetalXXXXX, ZCardman, Danzen12

Friends of Jimmy K        Zenhog

Friends of Lois W.        KMcF, Mamadread

Food Disorders Issues     BusbyDad

RecoveryLink              Host Tess, Host Serene, Host Maize

Alternatives to           GabeCT, PamCT
  12 Steps

Sober & Clean Brunches  LilyBet, MarshHawk
```

```
Master E-mail Recovery List
You can also ask to have your name added to the unofficial
AOL recovery mailing list and receive copies of periodic
updates about the AOL recovery community. To do so, please
send an e-mail message to "MarshHawk." The message should
include the screenname you'd like to have listed. You need
not send your real name.

A Final Note:
You can also create your own Member Room in the People
Connection (Keyword: Talk) for a recovery-related topic any
time of day or night. For example, If you can't find Friends
of Bill W. just go to People Connection and use the "Create
Room" button to open a "Friends of Bill W." or "Recovery"
room yourself. You'll usually be joined within a few minutes
by others from the recovery community. Warm wishes to all who
are interested in our online community. Please send me e-mail
if I can help. I hope to see you online.
--MarshHawk
```

Health Databases on AOL

A medical database can be found in the scroll box in the main menu of the Better Health & Medical Forum (keyword: "Better Health"). The main headings are:

Multimedia Self-Care Showcase	Men/Women/Children's Health
Lifestyles & Wellness	Senior's Health and Caregiving
Mental Health and Addictions	Alternative Medicine
Human Sexuality	Home Medical Guide
Informed Decisions	

One of the choices in the main menu's scroll box is "Search Health Forum." You can use this entry to search all sections of the database for your topic of interest.

Under "Lifestyle & Fitness" you'll find selections on the following topics:

Lifestyles and Wellness

Employment and Empowerment

Exercise

Environment

Safety, Accident Prevention

Stress Management

Smoking, Chemical Dependencies

There's an extensive list of interesting suggestions on the Weight Loss and Management support group.

Much of the medical material can be found under the selection "Home Medical Guide." The main subtopics are:

Diseases & Disorders	Tests
Symptoms	Surgeries
Medications	Rehabilitation/Assistive Devices

Database Listings Under the Heading "Diseases & Disorders"

About Diseases & Disorders	Heart & Circulatory Disorders
Abdomen & Digestive Disorders	Hormone & Endocrine Disorders
AIDS	Infectious & Contagious Diseases
Allergies & Immune Disorders	Kidney & Urinary Tract Disorders
Arthritis	Learning & Communication Disorders
Blood & Lymph Disorders	Lung & Respiratory Disorders
Brain & Nervous System Disorders	Mental Health Disorders
Cancer	Multiple Sclerosis
Diabetes	Muscle, Bone, & Joint Disorders
Ear, Nose, and Throat Disorders	Skin, Hair, & Nail Disorders
Eyes & Vision Disorders	Teeth, Gum, & Mouth Disorders

MEDLINE (Keyword: Medline)

MEDLINE, the National Library of Medicine's database of references to the medical literature, is the world's largest biomedical database. AOL's version has the easiest interface to use for this distinguished medical database that I've ever seen. It offers three levels of searching: Standard, Advanced, and InfoStar. The Standard search is child's play—just type in the keywords you'd like to search for, and in a few seconds you'll see a list of articles. The Advanced search is also highly intuitive. Even the InfoStar search (expert level) is easier than most other MEDLINE systems, although you'll probably want to click on the Help icon on the main MEDLINE screen for directions and guidelines. There are user forums devoted to discussions of all three levels of searching. Other message forums provide an opportunity to compare experiences with other users and to exchange messages with AOL MEDLINE honcho Allen Douma (AlDouma).

Please note that MEDLINE doesn't provide the full text of the articles. Some listings give the title, authors, and journal only. Others include article summaries. So if you're not planning a trip to the medical library, you may wish to limit your search to those with summaries. AOL hopes to offer full text printouts of articles by mail—for an additional fee—at a later date.

The AIDS Daily Summary (Keyword: "AIDS Daily")

The AIDS Daily Summary offers news reports on a variety of social, political, and scientific news stories relating to AIDS and HIV.

Top Internet Sites

Top Internet Sites lists the Health Channel staff's picks of the best health-related Web sites. It also gives you an opportunity to do a Web Crawler search for Web pages on your topic of choice.

The Health Index

The Health Index is a directory of many of selected health resources on AOL. As we go to press, the listings are:

AIDS Daily Summary	*Bicycling Magazine*
AIDS, HIV Forum	*Consumer Reports Complete*
AIDS Positive Living Forum	*Drug Reference*
American Cancer Society	*Consumer Reports Food*
American Diabetes Association	*and Health*
Backpacker Online	disABILITIES Forum
Better Health & Medical Forum	*Elle* Fitness/Health

Health News (CNN)	National Multiple Sclerosis Society
Health Reference	*New York Times* Science Times
Home Medical Guide	Reference Q&A
Knowledge Center	Personal Empowerment Network
Longevity	*San Jose Mercury News* Science
MEDLINE	*Scientific American*
National Alliance for the	United Cerebal Palsy Association
Mentally Ill	*Woman's Day* Body & Mind

Community Forums

The Community Forums scroll box on the Health Channel directory (keyword "Health") lists a variety of health-related topics, for example:

> AIDS/HIV, Cancer, Diabetes, Fitness, Heart & Circulatory, Men's Health, Mental Health, Reproduction & Infertility, Women's Health

Clicking on a topic takes you to a master screen that lists a wide variety of online resources for that topic: topic-specific databases, related forums and chat groups, and links to relevant publications and Web pages. This is an extremely helpful resource for those looking for information on a specific condition.

Here are seven more searchable databases or forums that include a database:

- The American Cancer Society (keyword: "ACS")
- The American Diabetes Forum (keyword: "American Diabetes")
- The National Alliance for the Mentally Ill (keyword: "NAMI")
- The National Multiple Sclerosis Society (keyword: "NMSS")
- The Parents' Information Network (keyword: "PIN")
- Scientific American (keyword: "Scientific American")
- United Cerebral Palsy Associations Inc. (keyword: "UCPA")

HOT

TIP

On many AOL health forums' main menus, you'll find an icon labeled "Software Library." It will lead you to a listing of longer health-related articles you can read on screen, print out, or download onto your hard disk. On the disABILITIES Forum, for example, you can download files on anti-depressants, anti–side-effect medicines, mood stabilizing medicines, anti-anxiety and sleeping medications, electro-convulsive therapy, and Bill W.'s greatest hope and inspirations.

Self-Help Support Group Meetings on AOL

The following schedule of live chat meetings on AOL was compiled by online self-help community organizer Todd Woodward (SHIC@aol.com). (For more on Todd, see the Author's Notes.) All times are Eastern. The list represents only some of the meetings currently being held. Many others are private, have unlisted hosts, or are publicized only on the forums. Others are spontaneous member-initiated group meetings. Note that the list changes frequently. For updated information, check the list for the following forums or contact the individual group leaders:

- Issues in Mental Health (keyword: "IMH"; host: Arrianne)
- The Better Health & Medical Forum (keyword: "Health"; host: ESilveous)
- The Gay & Lesbian Community Forum (keyword: "GLCF"; host: QUIRK)
- The Parents' Information Network (keyword: "PIN"; host: GenK)

```
SATURDAY
Gamblers Anonymous (12 Step) 10 a.m. (Contact "Pwerles")
RecoverLink Brunch 11 a.m. (Contact "MarshHawk")
SeniorNet Diet Club 11 a.m. (Contact "JessieA2")
Serenity (AA) Noon (Contact "AlBucko" or "PamSew")
Dissociation Support 1 p.m. (Contact "Metwelve")
Young ADDults 1 p.m. (Contact "EricNJB")
Herpes Support 3 p.m. (Contact "EarthStar")
Depression Support 6 p.m. (Contact "RoseTatTwo" or "StInAspen")
Haven (General Mental Health) 7 p.m. (Contact "StInAspen")
Friends/family of those with ADD  8 p.m. (Contact "MaryDeee")
Death and Dying Support Group 8 p.m. (Contact "MarilynUSA")
disABILITIES FunTime Meeting 9 p.m. (Contact "DacLilly")
Gay, Lesbian & Bi Disabilities  9 p.m. (Contact "GLCFZinc")
Mood Disorders Support 9 p.m. (Contact "DanAsh" or "JanaBike")
RecoveryLink 9 p.m. (Contact "Host Tess" or "HostCraig")
Dissociation/Women Only  9:30 p.m. (Contact "Windpuppy" or "EllenAll")
Multiple's (MPD)/Women Only 9:30 p.m. (Contact "DONNA ULTD")
Friends of Bill W. 11 p.m. (Contact "MetalXXXXX")
Panic Disorders Support Group 11 p.m. (Contact "Shalynnn")
```

(continued on next page)

SUNDAY
Overeaters Anonymous 10 a.m. (Contact "Bearynice")
RecoveryLink Brunch 11 a.m. (Contact "LilyBet")
Dissociation Support Group 1 p.m. (Contact "Metwelve")
Kids with ADD 2 p.m. (Contact "SusanS29")
People of Color Conference 4 p.m. (Contact "GLCFBabe" or "GLCFTasha")
Welcome to ADD 4 p.m. (Contact "Wetmores")
Teen Conference 5 p.m. (Contact "GLCFErin")
Chronic Illnesses & Conditions 6 p.m. (Contact "DACxSajx")
Bisexual Conference 7 p.m. (Contact "GLCFFuzz" or "GLCFSpyce")
PC Pals Deaf Teen Chat 7 p.m. (Contact "Chrisx24")
Life's Gentle Journey 7 p.m. (Contact "YshiDaremo")
LIVING with Cancer 7 p.m. (Contact "Lil Mousey")
Fibromyalgia Self-Help Group 8 p.m. (Contact "Begete" or "LuvBirdJan")
Deaf Community Networking 8 p.m. (Contact "GERALD1192" or "Carlanne")
Male Point of View 8 p.m. (Contact "HostSteel")
RecoveryLink 8 p.m. (Contact "HostTess" or "HostCraig")
Nurses' Station 8:30 p.m. (Contact "MsLadyKatz")
Chiropractors' Networking 9 p.m. (Contact "DrDubin" or "DBrady")
Co-Dependents Anonymous 9 p.m. (Contact "LindadYneX")
Down Syndrome Babies Support 9 p.m. (Contact "RClementi" or "MDMFamily")
Gender Conference 9 p.m. (Contact "GLCFGraci" or "GLCF Wendy")
HIV/AIDS Support Group 9 p.m. (Contact "MartyHwrd" or "Magg2")
Power Surge (Menopause) 9 p.m. (Contact "Dearest")
Childcare Professionals 9:30 p.m. (Contact "ChildAtHrt")
Al-Anon 10 p.m. (Contact "MamaDread")
Alternatives in Recovery 10 p.m. (Contact "PamCT" or "GabeCT")
Battered Partners 10 p.m. (Contact "GLCF Cat" or "GLCF Spur")
Jewish Parenting 10 p.m. (Contact "Scharff")
Narcotics Anonymous 10 p.m. (Contact "TerryJFT")
Rheumatoid Arthritis Self-help 10 p.m. (Contact "CASD")
Issues in Mental Health Open Forum 10:30 p.m. (Contact "JessieIMH")
Weekend Blues 12:30 a.m. (Contact "Samatha88")

MONDAY
Stay-at-Home Moms 3 p.m. (Contact "CherieLG")
Infertility Support 6 p.m. (Contact "FrancescaQ")
Seniors Who Are Alone 7 p.m. (Contact "EWGRED")
Anxieties and Phobias 8 p.m. (Contact "PennyAP")
Dissociation Support Group 8 p.m. (Contact "Metwelve")
Endometriosis Self-Help Group 8 p.m. (Contact "Luv2Spike")
Infertility Support Group 8 p.m. (Contact "Bellegonia")
RecoveryLink 8 p.m. (Contact "Host Tess" or "Host Craig")
Chronic Fatigue Syndrome 8:30 p.m. (Contact "MDHarris")

Adoption Issues Conference 9 p.m. (Contact "Mrowland")
Arthrogryposis Multiplex Congenita 9 p.m. (Contact "GabyH")
Multiple Sclerosis Self-Help Group 9 p.m. (Contact "DACRoger")
Occupational Therapists 9 p.m. (Contact "Organic1" or "Tigertvii")
Parents & Friends of Lesbians & Gays 9 p.m. (Contact "GLCFSteve" or
  "GLCFSam")
SugarShack (Unstress with humor) 9 p.m. (Contact "CupCake")
Widows/Widowers Support Group 9 p.m. (Contact "MrMom SK" or "Jayemay")
Cancer Survivors 10 p.m. (Contact "KittyBa" or "JPLyons602")
Partners & Friends—HIV/AIDS 10 p.m. (Contact "GLCFKent" or "GLCFPat")
StressBusters 10 p.m. (Contact "LadyMJB")
Attention Deficit Disorder (12 Step) 11 p.m. (Contact "AngieDixon")
Dating, Mating and Relating 11 p.m. (Contact "LovingUniv")
Down Syndrome Midnight (Contact "SherrySch" or "JoanieM5")

TUESDAY
Getting It Done 11:30 a.m. (Contact "Debette")
Sober Today 1 p.m. (Contact "Byuself")
Over 50 5 p.m. (Contact "DolFlorida" or "JenG3")
ADD Support 7 p.m. (Contact "Debette")
Loved Ones of Cancer Survivors 7 p.m. (Contact "Lil Mousey")
Widowed World 8 p.m. (Contact "Carol94901")
Juvenile Rheumatoid Arthritis 8:30 p.m. (Contact "AlKal" or "UPCAST")
Couples Conference 9 p.m. (Contact "GLCFDara" or "GLCFJoe")
Down Syndrome 9 p.m. (Contact "C1NDYSUE" or "Kalismom")
Epilepsy Support Group 9 p.m. (Contact "RICTER")
Starting Over 9 p.m. (Contact "Diadem")
You Are Not Alone (Death of a Child) 9 p.m. (Contact "LoisG2")
Multiples (MPD) Support Group 9:30 p.m. (Contact "DonnaUltd")
Post Polio Survivors 9:30 p.m. (Contact "DAC JPL" or "TominCal")
Adult Children of Alcoholics (ACoA) 10 p.m. (Contact "ACoATed1")
Bills House (AA-Speaker Meeting-Protocol) 10 p.m. (Contact "Gerundo")
Down Syndrome 10 p.m. (Contact "C1NDYSUE" or "Kalismom")
Herpes Self-help Group 10 p.m. (Contact "EarthStar")
Post-Traumatic Stress Disorder Support 10 p.m. (Contact: "GiselaR41")
ADDults Only Midnight (Contact "Annie12345")

WEDNESDAY
Breastfeeding 1 p.m. (Contact "NeenH")
ADD Support 2 p.m (Contact "Debette")
Fibromyalgia Self-Help Group 4 p.m. (Contact "DKellyU" or "JaneFC")
Late Deafened Chat 7 p.m. (Contact "BobDeafie")
Parenting 7 p.m. (Contact "HomeParent")
Cerebral Palsy Self-Help Group 8 p.m. (Contact "DACJon")
Dissociation Support Group 8 p.m. (Contact "Metwelve")

Parents of ADD Kids 8 p.m. (Contact "JimAMS")
HUGS 9 p.m. (Contact "StarGypsy")
Adoption Forum Chat (CUB Online) 9 p.m. (Contact "MargyMc")
Codependency Issues 9 p.m. (Contact "KathyNor")
Mensa/Gifted Children 9 p.m. (Contact "TabithaB")
Obsessive-Compulsive Disorder 9 p.m. (Contact "Slobert" or "Ethomp")
Power Surge (Menopause) 9 p.m. (Contact "Dearest")
Repetitive Strain Injury 9 p.m. (Contact "AlKorn" or "Merryl")
Vegetarians Online 9 p.m. (Contact "NurseBobbi")
Bills House (AA 12-Step) 10 p.m. (Contact "NoBooz")
Challenging Children 10 p.m. (Contact "CiaO" or "InsaneDad")
Gay & Lesbian 12-Step 10 p.m. (Contact "GLCFSissa" or "GLCFJoell")
Parents Conference 10 p.m. (Contact "GLCFBean" or "GLCFVixen")
Chronic Conditions Chathouse 11 p.m. (Contact "DACLilly")
Depression Support 1 a.m. (Contact "Loner33")

THURSDAY
Stay-at-Home Moms 10 a.m. (Contact "MyCamelot")
Parents of ADD Kids 2 p.m. (Contact "SallyF")
Getting it Done 3:30 p.m. (Contact "Debette")
Muscular Sclerosis Self-Help Group 6 p.m. (Contact "Oishda")
Seasons of the Heart 7 p.m. (Contact "RoseTatTwo" or "StInAspen")
Counselors Corner 8 p.m. (Contact "Ceres6")
RecoveryLink 8 p.m. (Contact "Host Tess" or "HostCraig")
Al-Anon 9 p.m. (Contact "MamaDread")
Autism Forum 9 p.m. (Contact "DACTravis" or "Robin124")
Child Abuse Discussion Group 9 p.m. (Contact "TomHanna")
Epilepsy Support Group 9 p.m. (Contact "RICTER")
HomeSchooling 9 p.m. (Contact "MyCamelot" or "RETROMOM")
Teen Forum 9 p.m. (Contact "Tangerine")
The Women's Room 9 p.m. (Contact "EvaS")
Widows/Widowers Support 9 p.m. (Contact "Donnaburke" or "Javgunner")
Multiple's (MPD) Support Group 9:30 p.m. (Contact "DONNA ULTD")
Serenity (AA) 9:30 p.m. (Contact "AlBucko" or "PamSew")
Abuse Recovery 10 p.m. (Contact "Arrianne")
Inclusion Chat 10 p.m. (Contact "KarenL2888" or "EG12")
Bisexual Conference 10 p.m. (Contact "GLCF Fuzz" or "GLCF Spyce")
Eating Recovery 11 p.m. (Contact "Comity")
One Day at a Time Midnight (Contact "Comity")

FRIDAY
Women with ADD 3 p.m. (Contact "Wetmores")
Café Expressions 7 p.m. (Contact "RoseTatTwo")
Divided Minds (Dissociation) 8 p.m. (Contact "Spektrum")
Coming Out Support 9 p.m. (Contact "GLCF McBee" or "GLCF Erin")
Muscular Dystrophy Support Group 9 p.m. (Contact "Chalant")
Mothers of Multiples 10 p.m. (Contact "MomOTwins")

Chapter 6

CompuServe

"These [online physicians and self-helpers] are wonderful to give so freely of their time. And the advice I've received online is more complete and more useful than what I get face-to-face from our attending physician."

Linda Kerwin
A CompuServe self-helper

———— ◆ ————

Signing Up

To sign up for CompuServe, call (800) 848-8199. In Ohio, call (614) 457-8650. For technical support, call (800) 609-1674. You'll receive your free software (specify for DOS, Windows, or Mac) in the mail in about seven to ten days. Your first month's membership is free. After that, there's a monthly membership charge of $9.95. Special rates are available for heavy users. Members get unlimited access to basic services. Extended services marked by "+" are billed at an additional $4.80 per hour. Premium services marked by "($)" cost $4.80 per hour plus an additional surcharge that varies from service to service. You'll see a listing of surcharge fees before you enter those areas. There are additional charges for higher access speeds and for sending or receiving more than about sixty pieces of e-mail per month.

WHEN IT COMES TO HEALTH RESOURCES, CompuServe has two special strengths: a much wider selection of health and medical *databases* than either America Online or Prodigy and a large number of *helpful online health professionals* willing to respond to your questions and provide information and advice. And, like AOL and Prodigy, CompuServe boasts a sizable number of active self-helpers with strong altruistic inclinations.

CompuServe has two noteworthy drawbacks as well: The system interface can be a bit intimidating to new users, and because of its three-layer pricing and additional fees for e-mail, CompuServe can be very expensive, especially if you send or receive lots of e-mail or spend a lot of time using the high-priced premium services.

But it is the databases and the wealth of helpful and knowledgeable health professionals that make it worthwhile. Indeed, I found more physicians, nurses, chiropractors, dentists, and other health professionals (both alternative and traditional) on CompuServe than on the other two services combined.

This e-mail message from Kentucky-based CompuServe self-helper Raymond Green (ID 75340,1354) illustrates how important access to health professionals can be:

> I can hardly put into words how helpful CompuServe has been to us. My wife Pamela was recently hospitalized and near death from an accidental overdose of acetaminophen (Tylenol). I was so overwhelmed with what she was going through and how easily it happened that I felt the need to warn others, so I posted a message on CompuServe's Health & Fitness Forum warning people about the potential dangers of OTC medicine and its improper use. I got a number of responses, one of them from a wonderful nurse named Marianne Burns (75120,3220).
>
> Marianne posted a good letter about acetaminophen to the Forum, and we communicated daily throughout Pamela's hospital stay. Marianne literally kept me fully informed of all the technical aspects of what was happening.
>
> The team of doctors tending to Pam knew their stuff but seemed unwilling or unable to keep me up to date on what was happening. Late one night (11:00) one of them was making rounds and told me "I don't know what's keeping her going but if she's not giving up we're not either." I later learned that by the third or fourth week they couldn't understand why she was still alive and really didn't know what to tell me.
>
> I overheard the things her doctors said. I read her chart. I made notes of the medications she received. Then at night I'd rush home and send all this information to Marianne. And she would explain everything and would tell me straight out what she thought.
>
> Our life is a lot more peaceful now. Pam is much improved and I've recently started running to lose some of the weight I gained during our hospital ordeal. In fact, I'm now training to run a marathon—thanks to the advice and motivation I've been receiving from the Running & Racing section of the Health & Fitness Forum on CompuServe. I started out just wanting to lose a few pounds, but after hanging around with this online bunch, I'm ready to tackle a major race.

Meredith's Story

Another online self-helper who benefited from the databases and the health professionals she found on CompuServe is Meredith Gould Ruch (71223,3716), who described her experiences in a recent article in the magazine *Natural Health*.

Meredith was doing some heavy lifting when she felt a pop in her back—followed by an excruciating pain that burned from hip to ankle. She tried chiropractic, body work, visualization, and movement therapy without relief. A magnetic resonance imaging (MRI) test revealed a ruptured disc pressing on the nerve to her affected leg. Meredith's neurologists advised immediate back surgery.

Faced with a pressing need to decide whether to have the recommended surgery, Meredith posted several messages on CompuServe. When she logged back on a few hours later, she found a number of helpful responses. One came from Sandra Pinkerton of the Texas Back Institute Foundation in Dallas (pinks10@aol.com). Sandra suggested that Meredith consider a consultation with a physiatrist, (physiatry is a relatively new physician specialty combining physical medicine, physical therapy, and rehabilitation). Sandra's message continued:

```
Most likely, a physiatrist will have you get a CT and/or MRI
scan from a reputable radiologist. Then after giving you some
anti-inflammatory medication and/or acupuncture treatments to
get past any acute pain you may be experiencing, he or she
will put you through a program of 'Back School.' You will go
through a graduated exercise program with the physical thera-
pist that will help strengthen your lower abdominal and leg
muscles. These will help hold your back in a 'neutral' posi-
tion, thus helping your herniated disc to heal and increasing
your ability to continue your daily activities during the
healing process, which may take some time....
```

Meredith was amazed, startled, and very grateful. "I didn't even know this person," she wrote, "but here she was extending considerable help, and offering more if I needed it." Other databases and self-helpers offered new information and perspectives. The accumulating evidence suggested immediate surgery, so she then went back to CompuServe to seek advice on preparing herself, encouragement, and comfort. The surgery went well. Finally when Meredith was able to log on to CompuServe again, she found a long list of e-mail get-well messages.

The "Look and Feel" of CompuServe

The CompuServe interface is straightforward, powerful, and attractive, but it is not always as intuitive, as uniform, or as easy to use as that of AOL. Part of the reason is that different databases and forums sometimes operate in very different ways. It was my distinct impression that the typical CompuServe user is older, more likely to be a professional, more likely to be male, and more technically experienced than the average user of either AOL or Prodigy.

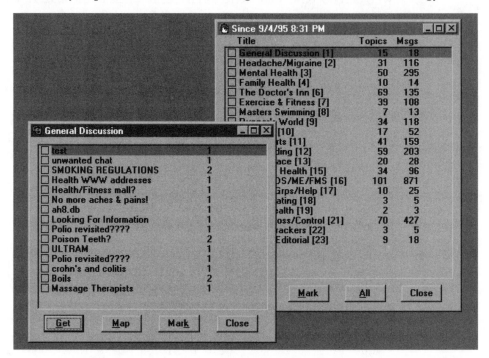

CompuServe is more text-based than other services. This is how a forum's message center looks when accessed with WinCIM. Click on a message to designate it for retrieval. (Design © CompuServe)

HOT

TIP

Here's another unique feature of CompuServe: With AOL and Prodigy you can use only one piece of software to access the service—the one they send you. With CompuServe, in addition to using the free software the service provides, you can use a number of generic telecommunications packages, including some that experienced onliners may already be using. There's also a program called Navigator, available from CompuServe for an additional fee, which automates the log-on process and allows you to do a great deal off-line to save on access fees. It's worth the extra initial investment if you plan to visit forums often. Because CompuServe can be accessed by so many different software packages, your onscreen results may sometimes look different from those described in the chapter.

Information Overload

Exploring CompuServe can be a bit like wandering around in the Library of Congress. To the online newbie, it may sometimes seem as if CompuServe has too much information, in too many formats, with too many different pricing structures. This is largely because many of the databases available here—especially those offering the full text of magazines and newspapers and academic citations—are run by other companies and have their own unique organization.

Yet like AOL and Prodigy, CompuServe has a wide variety of very special resources that are available nowhere else. So while it may be hard to learn, if you need what they have to offer, it's definitely worth it. Even though the system may be a bit intimidating in the beginning, once you learn your way around, you'll be able to focus on the resources themselves without being distracted by the interface.

CompuServe's Health and Health-Related Forums

Let's now take a look at some of the most popular health-related destinations on CompuServe—the health forums. We'll start out by walking through two general-topic and three specific-topic health forums. Then we'll consider more briefly other health and health-related forums. The first forums we'll explore will be:

- The Health and Fitness Forum
- The Holistic Health Forum
- The Cancer Forum
- The Attention Deficit Disorder (ADD) Forum
- The Human Sexuality Forum
- The Recovery Forum

HOT TIP

The primary command for navigating your way around CompuServe is "Go," e.g., "Go Goodhealth," "Go Cancer," or "Go HLTDB." It operates like the "Keyword" command on AOL, taking you where you want to go by simply entering "Go" and the word for the resource you want to visit.

Finding Support Group Meetings on Your Forum of Choice

Before we go further, I need to introduce you to a general characteristic of all CompuServe health forums. While there *are* growing numbers of scheduled support group meetings on CompuServe, they are listed separately within each forum. At the time I visited there was no systemwide central listing of chat groups.

The support group meetings are held in rooms located within the forums themselves. You may visit the rooms at any time, though unless there's a meeting scheduled, they may be empty. To learn more about the scheduled support group meetings for a given forum, log on to that forum and read the announcements. For example, if you're looking for information on support groups for diabetes, simply log on to the Diabetes Forum and read the announcements.

Unfortunately, the meeting announcements don't always give the name of the person facilitating the meeting. (CompuServe sysops take note: They should. It would be a big help to newcomers.) If you'd like to find out who's leading the group and make contact with him or her before attending, send an e-mail request to the forum sysop requesting the name and CompuServe ID of the meeting coordinator, or check the sysop roster under announcements. Or you may be able to figure out who the meeting coordinator is by reading recent postings in the appropriate special-interest section.

The Health and Fitness Forum ("Go Goodhealth")

The Health and Fitness Forum is the place you'll find the most in-depth discussions of conventional health care approaches, although there is a section on alternative health as well. You'll find lots of health professionals here, especially in the section called The Doctor's Inn.

Please note, though, that while "The Health and Fitness Forum" is the official title, you'll find most online self-helpers referring to it as "The Goodhealth Forum."

When you log on, you'll find hundreds of wide-ranging health and medical discussions in process. The forum administrator, Alan Stevens (76702,562), and the assistant administrator, Chuck Etienne (76711,100), will be glad to direct you to the people or resources you want to find or to help you with any other problems or questions you may have.

The first thing you'll see when you log on to this or any CompuServe forum is a small box that announces the arrivals and departures of other CompuServe members as they log on or off the forum. You can also click on the Who's Here icon to read a complete list of everyone logged on. If you see somebody you know, you can use the "Talk" command on the menu bar to send them an instant message. Or you can invite several people to join you in a group conversation.

You can also view several announcements from the forum sysops. Pay close attention to these announcements, as they serve as a key source of information on most CompuServe forums. (You may find additional announcements when you select a section within a forum.) Reading them regularly is a good way to keep up to date on what's going on in your forums of choice. Other files from the Forum Library will provide additional forum information.

On a recent visit, the welcome announcements for the Health and Fitness Forum included special bulletins for swimmers, for runners, for those participating in the NordicTrack Fitness Challenge, and for several other categories of self-helpers.

In this, as in other CompuServe forums, after you've read the welcome announcements, you'll have a chance to read a number of *standard information files* about the forum. Topics include:

> General, Conference, Library, Membership, Sysop Roster, New Members, Messages

Once you've read through the announcements, you can click on the Read Messages icon to view recent postings. Postings are organized under the subject headings listed below. You can also review titles and abstracts for a list of downloadable files in the forum library. Another icon will take you to the meeting rooms within the forum.

The special-interest sections in the Health and Fitness Forum are:

General/Help	Headache/Migraine
Mental Health	Family Health
The Doctor's Inn	Exercise and Fitness
Runner's World	Nutrition
Martial Arts	Women's Health
Chronic Fatigue Syndrome	Support Groups/Help
Inline Skating	Weight Loss/Control
Nordic Trackers	Opinion/Editorial

Note that a number of vital health topics are *not* included on the list above. That's no accident. A number of specific medical conditions are discussed in separate forums, as described in the listings below.

Exploring the Health and Fitness Forum Libraries

For each of the special-interest sections listed above, you can access either a message board containing recent messages or a substantial forum library, containing a wide variety of files, databases, and even some software. A few quick examples of files in the library:

- "M.D. Pearls" in The Doctor's Inn section library is a lookup utility for a database of more than 10,500 acronyms and abbreviations found in the medical literature and in clinical practice.
- "BackMan," another downloadable file, is a Windows-based animated screen saver showing you how to sit and move during the workday to avoid backache. When your computer is idle, the program appears onscreen, showing you a series of back care guidelines and exercises that can help you relax your back and neck.

- "Spouse's Depression," another in the Mental Health section library, is a fascinating file. It contains the transcript of a long series of forum messages in which a wife reaches out for help and advice in dealing with her husband's gradually worsening gloomy moods.

You'll find a separate list of library files in each section. The best way to see what's there is to browse through the list for the sections you're interested in. The files are listed by date of upload, with the most recently uploaded files listed first.

The Sysop Roster

In each CompuServe forum, under the "Announcement" listings, you'll find the Sysop Roster. The roster is a good way to track down the sysop who deals with your topic of interest. Here's an excerpt from the Sysop Roster for the Health and Fitness Forum:

```
Forum Administrators
Chief Sysop               Allan Stevens (76702,562)
Associate Sysop           Chuck Etienne (76711,100)
General/Help              Chuck Etienne (76711,100)
Headache/Migraine         Harry Kaplan (71023,371)
                          Carvel Gipson, M.D. (72520,3172)
Mental Health             TomL! (72510,636)
                          Brian Crabtree (72303,1003)
Family Health             Tom Koch (71600,1123)
Doctor's Inn              Michael Mayer, M.D. (76437,1156)
Exercise and Fitness      Allan Stevens (76702,562)
Runner's World            Benji Durden (70304,1752)
Nutrition                 Susan Robbins (70303,1152)
Martial Arts              Mike Janay (70762,2066)
Women's Health            Marianne Burns, R.N. (75120,3220)
Chronic Fatigue           Ellen Atwood (71740,1212)
Support Grps/Help         Ed Madara (70275,1003)
Inline Skating            Bill Lorenz (73572,3141)
Weight Loss/Control       John McNerney (74536,2011)
Nordic Trackers           Denyse Stevens (73700,1070)
You can also contact us by phone or snail-mail:
Allan Stevens (513) 445-6441
GO GOODHEALTH
P.O. Box 292496
Kettering, OH 45429
```

Sample Postings from the Health and Fitness Forum

From the Women's Health section, here are excerpts from an ongoing discussion on colposcopy:

Subj: Colposcopy
I recently had a colposcopy (a scoping procedure used to view the vagina and cervix) and cervical biopsy. It was painful, probably because my doctor gave me no warning. He just did it. I'd been complaining of pain during intercourse, and that was his solution. No explanation, nothing. He found nothing and the pain is still there-except worse.
   After the colposcopy, I went to work. Big mistake I could hardly walk from the pain.
   I hope you have a kinder doctor.
Diane

Subj: Colposcopy
I'm an ob/gyn physician and do 30-50 colposcopies a month... They are usually NOT painful... obnoxious like a pap... yes... mildly painful... but usually not more than menstrual cramps and then only for a few minutes... so don't let someone scare you.
   The colposcopic exam is done like a pap smear except we look in at the cervix with a microscope. It takes 5 to 10 minutes with the speculum in place so it's a bit obnoxious. By looking at the surface contour, color, vessels patterns and the like we can see common findings consistent with normal tissue, viral infections, or precancerous changes from mild to moderate to severe, and cancerous changes with or without invasion. There are common finding identifiable with each of these progressions from normal to mildly precancerous to moderately precancerous and so on.
   When we see areas that may be consistent with precancerous changes we back that up with SMALL biopsies. Since there aren't many nerves on the cervix it's usually a matter of bad luck to land on top of one and get pain with a biopsy. If there is pain at all it will be like a quick pinch or menstrual cramp and just lasts a few minutes at the most...
   Your pap results are mild in nature. Mild precancerous changes will revert to normal on their own about 70 to 80 percent of the time. Since a given pap can miss a greater abnormality up to 20 to 40 percent of the time you need a colposcopy to find out several things... Is it mild/moderate or <unlikely> farther up the line? Is it a big spot or a small spot? Is there a viral infection <called HPV> associated with the finding? Most of the time it'll be no more than what your pap states.

```
      It would be UNLIKELY for you to have anything serious that
  can't be either watched with serial paps every 3-4 months or
  so or can't be COMPLETELY removed EASILY AND COMFORTABLY in
  the office with a "LEEP" procedure <a larger but still easy
  biopsy about as uncomfortable as getting a filling>. <3
  ladies out of over 200 have told me the LEEP biopsy hurt. The
  rest tolerated it very easily>. Most of the time all you will
  need is a small biopsy with the colposcopy you're having.
      BTW [By the way].. if your doc finds mild precancer and
  says to follow it with paps alone, he/she will be right.
  That's the way to follow mild dysplasia. Most go away on their
  own. Even cancer that hasn't invaded yet goes away on its own
  25% of the time.... Though we don't sit on it obviously....
      This doesn't cover everything and it should not be con-
  sidered medical advice but I hope it helps... Don't lose any
  sleep over this... It's normal to have a mild abnormality and
  it will be easy to deal with.

Mark D. OB/GYN
```

The Holistic Health Forum ("Go Holistic")

The Holistic Health Forum may be of interest to those looking for alternative or complimentary medical approaches. It "is based on a vision of the health consumer as a whole person, not just as a collection of organ systems" and takes a complimentary view, working in conjunction with, not in opposition to, traditional medicine. There are sections in the libraries devoted to vitamins and minerals, herbs and plants, homeopathy, Chinese and ayurvedic medicine, massage and body work, diet and exercise, the mind-body link, and much more.

The forum sysop is Skye Lininger (76702,1101), a chiropractic physician in Portland, Oregon. Dr. Lininger says, "When people have a choice, they often make a choice for variety. I see holistic medicine as the middle ground, and this is the progress area. Holistic medicines, in most cases, are as good or better than mainstream medicine." He will be happy to help you find what you're looking for or answer your questions.

Special-interest sections in the Holistic Health Forum include:

Corner Juice Bar	Holistic Medicine
Dietary Supplements	Herbs & Plants
Homeopathy & Bach Flower Remedies	Chinese/Ayurvedic
Chiropractic	Massage & Bodywork
Foods, Diet & Water	Health Politics

Healing & the Mind

Birth & Child Care

Exercise & Yoga

Holistic Pet Care

Natural Products

Rethinking AIDS

Women's Health

Weight Control

Holistic Dentistry

Health Education

Folk Remedies

Sysop Roster for the Holistic Health Forum

Skye Lininger, DC (76702,1101) [Wizard Sysop]
   Skye Lininger is a chiropractic physician with more than a decade of clinical experience. He teaches Practical Nutrition at Western States Chiropractic College in Portland, Oregon.

Edward Brown, DC (71154,674) [Wizard Sysop]
   Edward Brown has been in practice as a chiropractic physician since 1981, and has taken post graduate training in nutrition and acupuncture.

Donald Goldberg, RPh (70206,76)
   Don Goldberg is a pharmacist with over 25 years of experience with nutritional supplements. He is part owner of a pharmacy that specializes in nutritional supplements, homeopathic products, and herbal remedies.

Michael Janson, M.D. (72702,3653)
   Michael Janson is a physician with 17 years experience in holistic medicine. He uses nutrition and vitamin therapy, orthomolecular medicine, chelation therapy, allergy/clinical ecology, stress management and exercise as his primary approaches to health care.

Kris Keller, D.C. (76260,703)
   Kris Keller is a chiropractic physician with a BS in agriculture and experience in organic farming dating back to 1970. As president of his local chiropractic association he oversaw the granting of hospital privileges to DC's this summer.

Jeff Gordon (71154,1431)
   Jeff Gordon is a developer of nutritional diagnostics software for health professionals.

Charles Dort, MD (73117,2174)
   Charles is a Psychiatrist and Medical Director of a drug and alcohol treatment center.

David R Schryer (71601,375)
    David Schryer is a research chemist at a major government research
laboratory. He is interested in the role of nutrition and nutritional
supplements in the attainment and maintenance of good health, and the
prevention and cure of diseases.

Tony Martinez (73110,2754)
    Tony is a graduate of Brooklyn Law School. In 1991, he co-founded
NPHPAC, the National Progressive Health Political Action Committee,
formed to bring nutrition, wellness, and alternative health care issues
into the national political arena.

Susan Robbins (73447,1410)
    Susan is a doctoral candidate in genetics, with a long-standing
interest in health, nutrition, and medical research. Her area of special
interest is dietary carcinogens and anticarcinogens.

Sarah Fisher, M.D. (75430,775)
    Sarah is a board-certified obstetric anesthesiologist and a former
assistant professor of anesthesiology at Temple University. She consults
in pain management and natural healing.

The file listings in the Holistic Health Forum contain a huge collection of
"threads"—transcripts of forum discussions on a wide range of health topics—
from acupuncture to Zoloft, from tai chi and toddler's diarrhea to sunscreens
and sperm allergies. Other files offer information on amalgam fillings, brain
tumors, hot peppers and cancer, humor and healing, meditation, recumbent
bikes, and weaning while pregnant.

- The forum traditionally holds an "Informal, No-Host, Come as You Are,
  Don't Forget the Snacks Conference on Holistic Health" on Sunday
  evenings, at 9:00 Eastern time. A parenting discussion is held on Saturday
  nights, also at 9:00 Eastern time. Kids are welcome.
- You'll also find lots of interesting holistic health information in the
  Diet/Herbs/Health section of the New Age Forum (see p. 117).

The Cancer Forum ("Go Cancer")

The Cancer Forum is a support forum for people with cancer, their families,
and interested health professionals. It is an active forum where thousands of
people who are fighting cancer (and their friends and families) get support and

encouragement on a regular basis. Here's a testimonial I received from a self-helper who found the Cancer Forum especially useful:

Dear Tom,
My husband has advanced colon cancer. So I joined the Cancer Forum on CompuServe right away. I didn't know quite what to expect, but the response was incredible. I found emotional support that I hadn't been able to find anywhere else. For someone like me who expresses thoughts and feelings better in writing, it's been a wonderful experience.

My husband's condition recently took a turn for the worse, and we didn't feel we were getting the right attitude from our oncologist, so I mentioned it on the Cancer Forum. Within two days, we had an appointment scheduled at our local University Medical Center. Our experience there has been wonderful.

While we might have eventually found our way to the University anyway, these people made getting there a much easier and more pleasant process. They have been considerably more helpful than the American Cancer Society. There's always someone ready to listen and answer questions. I really don't know what we would do without this service.

Thanks for the chance to share my experiences on this matter.
--Valerie Brown (75537,1767)

The forum's message sections include:

General/Newcomers	Support Group
Breast Cancer	Gynecologic Cancer
Prostate/Testes	Head/Neck/Lung
Bladder/Kidney	Brain/Spinal Cord
Skin/Melanoma	Sarcomas/Bone & Soft Tissue
Gastrointestinal	Hematologic
Pediatric cancer	Misc. cancers
Insurance Issues	Health Care Politics
Grand Rounds	Hospice
Nutrition Issues	New Research
Ranting & Raging	Hot Topic!
The Coffee Shop	

Diagnosing His Own Cancer

Another CompuServe self-helper who recently benefited from the Cancer Forum is Paul Hansen (76702,475), sysop of a CompuServe computer forum (Practical Peripherals Forum). Paul was having back pain and a routine physical exam revealed a large mass in his abdomen, so Paul did some research in the CompuServe health databases, then quickly signed on to the Cancer Forum.

The docs he contacted there were able to help him understand the medical lingo, and he was able to tentatively diagnose himself based on the information he found online: He had retroperitoneal sarcoma, a rare type of cancer. The diagnosis was later confirmed by his physicians.

Paul soon learned that he needed more high-tech resources than he could find in his hometown of Westlake Village, California. The Cancer Forum self-helpers referred him to the UCLA surgical oncology group and to a sarcoma specialist in L.A. Armed with his online research, Hansen began appearing at his doctor's visits with a printed list of questions and a tape recorder.

Sysop Roster for the Cancer Forum

Primary Sysop: John Ross (76703,551)
   John has no medical background, but is deeply interested in the field of Cancer, and in providing a forum for those interested as well. John also manages the CP/M forum on CompuServe.

Assistant Sysop: Gene Feaster (76704,56)
   Gene has a Ph.D. in Physics and has worked in Medical Physics at three hospitals. He retired in 1987. Gene holds 12 U.S. Patents, and is the inventor of SuperFlab, which is used in most of the radiation therapy treatment clinics in the U.S.

Assistant Sysop: Roger Honkanen (76704,55)
   Roger is a free-lance writer in the Detroit, Michigan area. He has fought off seminoma, a form of testicular cancer, twice and has been in remission since January, 1989.

The Cancer Forum is an official distribution site for the National Cancer Institute's PDQ (Physician's Data Query) files (see Chapter 9). These in-depth files review the current state of the art of medical knowledge for just about every known kind of cancer. The forum maintains an up-to-date database of all PDQ files in Library 22, the Protocol Library. Caution: Be sure to check the size of the file before downloading. Many of them are extremely large and may take many minutes to download. Be sure they don't exceed your available disk space.

Here's another particularly useful downloadable file: "Cancer FAQ from the Internet," in the Support Library, Section 2.

The Attention Deficit Disorder (ADD) Forum ("Go ADD")

The ADD Forum is a very active support group with over twenty-six thousand members from the United States and around the world. This friendly community of people includes parents of children with ADD, adults with ADD, employers, friends, and spouses of people with ADD, and professionals (e.g., physicians or therapists) who work with people with ADD. The forum also includes a section for discussion of other neurobehavioral disorders such as Tourette's syndrome, a genetic disease that produces involuntary motor movements and verbal ticks such as explosive language (heated words and profanity). You'll encounter many active members of national organizations for ADD on the forum.

Message sections include:

Forum News & Chat	Newcomers: Hi & Help
Family/Social Life	Preschool Parenting
Elementary/Preteen Parenting	Schools & Learning
Parenting Teens	Student Union
Adult ADD	Work/Career Issues
Relationship Issues	Success/What Works
Is it ADD?/Diagnosis	Therapy/Medication
SOS - Need Help NOW	Ask the Doctors
Alternate Therapies	Books/Media/Meetings
TS/Aut/PDD/NBDs	Legal & Advocacy
Debate & Argument	Computer Chat/Query

Sysop Roster for the ADD Forum

Thom Hartmann (76702,765)

   The Primary Sysop for the ADD Forum, Thom is the founder (with his wife, Louise) and former Executive Director of the New England Salem Children's Village in Rumney, New Hampshire, a residential treatment facility for children. He is the author of "Attention Deficit Disorder: A Different Perception," and the parent of an ADD teenager.

Dave deBronkart (76702,1140)

   Dave is a successful ADD adult who didn't discover the trait until he was 42. He is writing "Hyperthink: The Edison Trait," which argues that Thomas Alva Edison's "kaleidoscopic mind" was almost certainly ADD.

Dale Hammerschmidt, M.D. (72662,76)

   Dale is an Associate Professor of Medicine at the University of Minnesota, and is Senior Editor of the Journal of Laboratory and Clinical Medicine. He and his wife run a support group for families with neurobehavioral disorders (ADD, OCD, Pervasive Developmental Disorder and Tourette's), and are the parents of two children with TS.

Elisa Davis (74431,117)

   A former financial analyst and strategic planner, Elisa is now an amateur expert on neurobehavioral disorders because of her children. Her older son has a variety of behavior difficulties, and her younger son has been diagnosed with high-functioning autism.

Ann Linden (71333,2236)

   Ann, a freelance writer and publisher, lives with her daughter in Marietta, GA. She's editor of The ADDed Line, a newsletter for people interested in ADD.

Hal Meyer (71333,2770)

   Hal is on the Board of Directors of Children and Adults with Attention Deficit Disorders and, with his wife Susan founded Ch.A.D.D. of New York City which they now coordinate. Hal and Susan lecture on helping teach and reach students with Attention Deficit Disorders.

Cj Bowman (72614,1003)

   Cj, a homeschooled ADDer and advocate for people with ADD, was born in 1979. In the summer of 1993, at age 13, he became one of the youngest Sysops on CompuServe.

Janie Bowman (72662,3716)

   Janie is a volunteer for the Olympia Chapter, L.D.A. of Washington (state), and editor of their Attention Deficit Newsletter.

```
Carla Nelson (73020,1421)
   Carla, the mother of two ADD children, is a communications consul-
tant and a self-styled "computer addict and cyberspace cruiser."

Wendy Hoechstetter (76300,363)
   Wendy first discovered ADHD in adulthood while a sales rep for Abbott
Labs. After her diagnosis, she was unable to find any support services, and
so started the ADD support group on CompuServe's Education Forum in 1992.

Glenda Serpa (72262,214)
   Glenda manages the forum's burgeoning libraries. She is the mother
of a 10 year old ADHD son.

Morgan Adcock (72357,1100)
   (Beth Ann) Morgan Adcock is a RN working with people with multiple
disabilities, including ADD. She is the mother of a teenager with ADD,
who is doing well in a school district which incorporates many special
ed techniques in "normal" classrooms.
```

I recommended these files from the ADD Forum Library:

In Library 1:

ADDMST.LST	A complete list of available files in the ADD Library.

In Library 4:

DIAGNOS.TXT	Thread with medical folks about diagnosing ADD
DSM.TXT	Diagnostic criteria used by psychiatrists
ISTHIS.TXT	Thread about "Is this ADD or something else?"
BAADS.TXT	Some interesting ideas on ADD

In Library 6:

PHARM.TXT	Drug therapy for ADD in Adults

In Library 7:

DIAG.TXT	An unofficial diagnostic questionnaire for Adults
RATEY.TXT	Lecture about Adult ADD (comprehensive)
LIKE.TXT	What is it like to have ADD?
50TIPS.TXT	Non-medical treatments for ADD

In Library 12:

TELS.TXT	Telephone numbers for local ADD support groups
MEDS.TXT	About kids taking medicine for ADD
KIDMED.TXT	Doctor's hints on administering meds to ADD kids
50CLAS.TXT	50 tips for teachers (and parents) dealing with ADD kids

Additional information and discussion about ADD can be found in the Education Forum ("Go Edforum"), the Disabilities Forum ("Go Disabilities"), the MedSig Forum ("Go MedSig"), the Student Forum ("Go Stufo"), and the Holistic Health Forum ("Go Holistic").

The Human Sexuality Forum ("Go HSX," "Go HSX100," "Go HSX200")

The Human Sexuality (HSX) Forum is a support forum for the discussion of "human sexuality, relationships, emotions, and life in general." In the 1980s, it was a leader in developing online services for the AIDS community. This very interesting resource now comprises three parts—a searchable database ("Go HSX") and two separate forums, the Human Sexuality Open Forum ("Go HSX100") and the Human Sexuality Adult Forum ("Go HSX200").

An extremely active forum, it offers live chat conferences on a wide variety on topics throughout the day. Topics include communication, relationships, single life, shyness, recovery, and other special interests—ranging from the therapeutic to the frankly erotic. Forum chat groups listed on a recent schedule included:

> Adult Babies, Erotic Tickling, Foot Fun, For Women Only, Fun and Fantasy, Global Village Hot Tub, Late Nite in Cyberspace, Long-Distance Love, Men Talk, Online Addicts, Overcoming Inhibitions, Sexual Enrichment, Shyness Workshop, Single Parents, Spiritual and Gay, Successful Dating

Members see the Human Sexuality Forum as something much more sophisticated than an e-mail version of a 900-number hot chat line. Regulars tell of forming lasting online friendships and many have met in person, developing lasting "real-world" relationships. During the month I was writing this chapter, there were four reported weddings between members who had met on HSX.

The chief sysops for the forum are Howard and Martha Lewis (76703,303). Howard and Martha have a long history of providing useful information drawn from medical sources. Their books include *Sex Education Begins at Home, The Parent's Guide to Teenage Sex,* and *Sex and Health: A Practical Guide to Sexual Medicine.* The Lewises have been editors of the *Journal of Sex Education and Therapy* and *Medical Aspects of Human Sexuality.* Their articles on health and sexuality have appeared in *Reader's Digest, Good Housekeeping,* and *Consumer Reports.*

While hot sexual chatting can be found in a few discreetly hidden closed sections of this forum, there is a well-defined etiquette involved in meeting potential hot chat partners. New members must subscribe to the HSX Membership Agreement (available in the Help library), in which they pledge not to subject other forum members to uninvited or persistent requests for chat. Instead, members are encouraged to participate in scheduled online groups. As one sysop explained, "Once people get to know you, they'll be more open to chatting privately." The purpose of this policy is to help create "a compassionate community in which all members feel safe in sharing their feelings and experiences." For more on recommended online etiquette, see the file MANNERS.TXT in the Help library, which contains guidelines and commentary written by the women of HSX.

HSX Sysops

The HSX forum managers are Cathy (70007,2270), Victor (70007,3673), Mike M. (76703,4051), Gail S. (70007,2300), Maggie (70007,5153), Linda W. (76711,1142), and Paula (76703,2040). Special-interest section leaders include:

```
Paula  (76703,2040)      HSX Helpline
Joanne (76570,1051)      "Dear Joanne"
Sam    (72070,3605)      Family Crisis
Eileen (71163,1505)      Singles Club
Polly  (70254,3564)      Shyness Workshop
Caren  (71652,2110)      Pen Pals
Roy R. (76060,1012)      Living With AIDS
Tony J (73564,3301)      Tony's Teen Talk
```

The HSX Open Forum

Here is a representative list of the open forum's special-interest sections:

HSX Helpline	Dear Joanne
Family Crisis	Counselor's Corner
Gay Alliance	Singles Club
Matters of Morals	Software Exchange
Shyness Workshop	Pen Pals
HSX Contest	More than Skin Deep
Naturist Lifestyles	Living with AIDS
Sex and the Law	Global Village
Jens' Kuschelecke	Breaking Up
Financial Affair$	Tony's Teen Talk

Participants in the sections are expected to observe a "PG" level of discourse and language appropriate to a publicly accessible group.

The HSX Adult Forum

As noted, all the special-interest sections in the adult forum require advance contact with the group coordinator. Here's a selected list:

Patti's Pub

General adult discussions

"I Was Abused"

Restricted to survivors of sexual, physical, or emotional abuse

For Women Only

Restricted to females

Personal Physician

Expertise in emotional and sexual aspects of health-related issues from a board-certified family practitioner

Biways

Restricted to bisexuals and to people interested in exploring their possible bisexuality

Fantasyland

Fantasies, dreams, and other aspects of the unconscious

Gays and Lesbians

Discussions of emotional issues, restricted to gays and lesbians 18 and over

Intimate Partners

Exploring and improving intimate relationships

Men Talk

A warm, supportive place where men can discuss their feelings in an all-male setting (State that you are male)

Over 50

Restricted to members who've reached the half-century mark

"Yes I Can!"

Personal challenges of people with disabilities. Supporters are welcome

In Recovery

Restricted to those seeking freedom from all forms of addiction and co-dependency and to their supporters

Loving a Survivor

Restricted to those who are in a relationship with a survivor of emotional, physical, or sexual abuse

Triumph over Trauma

Helps survivors and loved ones get on with life after being emotionally stricken by extreme stress (e.g., violence, illness, bereavement)

Gay Young Adults

Restricted to people age 18 through 21 with a sympathetic interest in gay and bisexual concerns

There are a number of other sections devoted to sexual concerns that some readers might find offensive, and many of the groups have very frank and open sexual discussions. Admission to these groups is subject to the approval of the group leaders. Those who wish to join a closed section must first contact the group facilitator. For more on the closed sections, go to the HelpFiles and look for the HSX Closed Section Agreement file, CLOSED.TXT. It contains a list of rooms and groups and instructions for gaining access.

The MedSig Forum ("Go MedSig")

MedSig is a health-related forum run by the American Medical Informatics Association. It was established as a professional forum for physicians and other health professionals and researchers. There is much discussion of the technical aspects of medical computing as done in hospitals, medical centers, and research, but there is also much talk of everyday medical problems. You'll find lots of physicians here and layfolk are welcome.

Sysop Roster for the MedSig Forum

Frank W. Meissner, M.D. (71333,3377) Primary sysop. Frank is a cardiologist and emergency medicine specialist with the Air Force in San Antonio.

Sue Frisch (76702,1724) Assistant Sysop. Editor, Medical Software Reviews President and Editorial Director; Healthcare Computing Publications.

John Farrer, M.D. (76702,1725) Assistant Sysop. General practitioner in a small coastal town in BC, Canada. Australian by Birth, British by Training, Canadian by Choice.

Marvin Gozum, M.D. (72307,2362) Co-Sysop. Chief, Medical Informatics, Division of Internal Medicine, Jefferson Medical College. Chief, Medical Consults, Wills Eye Hospital.

Keith Davis, M.D. (72256,3155) Section Leader, Family Pactice/ Pediatrics/Ob/Gyn section. Keith is a Family Practitioner in Shoshone, Idaho.

Sylvia Steiger, RN (71511,2253) Section Leader, Nursing. She has worked in oncology and home IV therapy and has reviewed insurance claims. She lives in Dallas with a husband and 2 preschool children.

Nancy Tice, M.D. (71370,2740) Section Leader, The Lounge/Students/Employment. Forum House Cleaner. Nancy is a Psychiatry Resident at the Albert Einstein School of Medicine.

Susan Robbins (73447,1410) Section Leader, Research and Bioethics. Susan is a graduate student in genetics at West Virginia University. Her research interests include genetic toxicology. She is a self-admitted CompuServe junkie.

Sam Feinstein, DMD (76046,257) Section Leader, Dentistry. Author of "100 Things You Didn't Learn in Dental School" and "Common Sense About TMJ & Occlusion."

Tom Anderson (70732,3020) Section Leader, Total Quality Management & the Computerized Medical Record. Director of the Research and Management Initiative at the Massachusetts Rate Setting Commission.

Bertram Warren, M.D. (73307,3023) Section Leader, Mental Health, Clinical Director, Union County Psychiatric Clinic, Past President, New Jersey Psychiatric Association, Member of Committee on Information Systems, American Psychiatric Association.

Steven Zweibel, M.D. (71543,1345) Section Leader, Palmtops/Laptops, Internal Medicine Resident at Columbia Presbyterian Hospital, New York City. "I've never gotten so much pleasure from holding something in the palm of my hand!"

The Recovery Forum ("Go Recovery")

The Recovery Forum is an active support group for those dealing with alcohol, drugs, smoking, eating disorders, and other aspects of recovery. You can read or post messages, attend a live Alcoholics Anonymous or other Twelve Step meeting, schedule a special conference on a topic of your choice, or drop into a recovery chat room twenty-four hours a day.

Here are some representative message sections on the recovery forum:

Soberspace Cafe	Adult Children
Friends & Families	Alcoholism/12 Steps
Drugs/12 Steps	Eating/12 Steps

Nicotine Addiction   Compulsive Debt

Rational Recovery   Dual Diagnosis

AIDS and Recovery   Relationships

Recovery Resources

Here's a current listing of live online Twelve Step meetings and other recovery-oriented support groups on the Recovery Forum. One Byte at a Time is the online version of One Day at a Time—these are Alcoholics Anonymous groups. All times are Eastern.

Sunday, 1:00 P.M.	International One Byte at a Time
Sunday, 8:00 P.M.	Narcotics Anonymous
Sunday, 9:30 P.M.	One Byte at a Time
Monday, 9:30 P.M.	Overeaters Anonymous
Tuesday, 8:00 P.M.	Narcotics Anonymous
Tuesday, 9:30 P.M.	Al-Anon
Wednesday, 4:30 P.M.	International One Byte at a Time
Wednesday, 9:30 P.M.	One Byte at a Time
Thursday, 9:30 P.M.	Rational Recovery
Thursday, 9:30 P.M.	Adult Children of Alcoholics
Friday, 4:00 P.M.	One Byte at a Time
Friday, 9:30 P.M.	One Byte at a Time
Saturday, 9:00 A.M.	International One Byte at a Time

If you'd like to set up a new conference, send an e-mail message to conference coordinator Angel H. (75601,1242) listing the topic you'd like to discuss and the day and time that would be most convenient. For further information, help, or questions, contact the sysops listed below.

Sysops for the Recovery Forum

```
Wendell F. (76702,3501) Forum Administrator
Debbie M. (75450,2501) Assistant Forum Administrator
Angel H. (75601,1242) Conference Coordinator
```

Other Health and Health-Related Forums

The Diabetes Forum ("Go Diabetes")

The Diabetes Forum is a self-help and support forum for discussions not only of diabetes but also of hypoglycemia and related chronic metabolic conditions. It was founded by diabetics who believed that there was a need for an open forum in which diabetics and their friends, families, and health care professionals could discuss the lifestyle issues, physical facts, and emotional dimensions of this condition.

General Discussion meetings are held on Thursday nights at 9:00 Eastern time, and there are informal chats on Wednesday and Sunday evenings, at 9:00 Eastern time. As the sysop's welcome message says, "This is the place to ask questions, learn conferencing, make new friends, and generally enjoy yourself. Please do drop in!" The forum sysops are Dave Groves (76703,4223), Jim Beyer (73060,1544), and Corky Courtright (76326,1673). They all welcome your questions.

The Disabilities Forum ("Go Disabilities")

A self-help and support forum, the Disabilities Forum, is open to anyone who is concerned with disabilities: people with physical or emotional handicaps, their friends and families, their health care professionals, those who employ the disabled, and others. The forum sysop is Dr. David Manning (76703,237), director of the Mainstream Center at the Clarke School for the Deaf in Northampton, Massachusetts.

Special-interest sections include Developmental Disabilities, Emotional Disturbances, Deaf/Hard of Hearing, Learning Disabilities, Vision Impairments, Mobility Impaired, Multiple Sclerosis, Rights/Legislation, Education/Employment, Family Life/Leisure, and General Interest.

The Seniors Forum ("Go Seniors")

The Seniors Forum is devoted to a wide variety of issues relating to the second half of life. Elder care, health and medicine, loss, and grieving all are discussed in the special-interest sections. The For Our Boomers section is for forty and fifty-somethings who want to share ideas about their coming elderhood.

The forum is a place where seniors can congregate and get answers, support others with their experiences, and enjoy swapping amusing stories. It can serve as a source of new friendships, conversation, chatting, and advice from people around the world. Typical discussions involve losing a loved one, managing health problems, and caring for a family member. The forum is also open to younger visitors who like to benefit from the members' accumulated wisdom. Other special-interest sections are Caregiving, Health/Medicare, Relationships & Sex, Retiring, and Social Security.

The primary sysop for the forum is Victoria Chronister (71154,1266). The leader for the Caregiving section is Barbara J. Holt (71022,3244). Other sysops are Betty Clay (76702,337), Carmen Flak (74163,2637), and Jeff Finn (71154,750).

Library 4 features files on health and medicine for seniors.

The Family Services Forum ("Go MYFAMILY")

This is a support forum for everyone who has, or hopes to have, a close personal relationship with other family members. Forum members assist each other with a wide range of family-related concerns: day-to-day relationship maintenance, dealing with traumas, healing old wounds, and managing chronic conditions. No pseudonyms are allowed. Forum participants must use their real names.

Here are some representative message sections on the Family Services Forum:

Just Us Two	Pregnancy/Birth
Newborns/Infants	Toddlers/Kinders
Grade Schoolers	Adolescents/Teens
Adoption/Foster Care	Grown Children
The Extended Family	Single Parenthood
Family Abuse	Divorce/Widowhood
Illness and Death	For Moms Only
For Dads Only	For Kids Only
For Teens Only	

The Education Forum ("Go Education")

Sysop Hal Meyer (76446,613) helps lead the discussion of attention deficit disorders in the special-interest section on ADD and hyperactivity of the Education Forum. Dale Hammerschmidt, a psychiatrist and an associate professor at the University of Minnesota, helps parents with a variety of children's neurological diseases, ranging from ADD and hyperactivity to the autismlike pervasive developmental disorder (PDD).

Besides contributing his professional experience and wisdom, Hammerschmidt brings a personal perspective. He and his wife have two children with Tourette's syndrome. Hammerschmidt is frequently able to help people whose kids have not been appropriately diagnosed or treated. He can also help parents avoid problems relating to punishing children for behavior that is beyond their control. "Physicians often don't know enough to diagnose it, school officials can't recognize when a student should be evaluated, and few teachers know appropriate classroom strategies," he says "My wife and I recognize that there are a lot of non-professionals out there with problem kids who don't have our background or resources, and could use some help. We like to give it." To connect with him, go to the ADD/Hyperactivity section and leave a message.

The Cooks Online Forum ("Go Cooks")

The Cooks Online Forum offers support, advice, and conversation for anyone with an interest in food, cooking, and nutrition. The message section "Nutrition/Fat Free Club" is an excellent source of low-fat and non-fat recipes. I learned to make Fettucine Alfredo with nonfat sour cream and evaporated skim milk. Additional recipes can be found in the forum library.

Sysops and Section Leaders for the Cooks Online Forum

Larry Wood (76703,704)	Forum Administrator
Jenee Burns (70007,3367)	Sysop
Judy Gruhn (76702,3141)	Salads & Dressing/Pizza & Pasta
Lon Hall (76702,3147)	Breads/Soups and Sauces
Nicole Novak (71750,3061)	Ethnic Foods
Hansje Kalff (100135,1326)	Nutrition
Kevin Souza (76702,3144)	Conferences
Nanette Blanchard (76702,3406)	Desserts and Sweets
Gary Jenanyan (70733,3614)	Culinary Professionals/Schools
Randall Carlson (76702,3135)	Meat, Poultry & Fish/General
Overton Anderson (72701,667)	Outdoor Cooking/General
Judi Johnson (72137,3045)	Herbs & Spices/Microwave

The Issues Forum ("Go Issues")

The Issues Forum features discussions of current news issues. Handicapped issues and human rights are frequent topics of conversation. Other special-interest sections include Minority Issues, The Parent Connection, Middle-Age Boomers, Men's Issues, Village Elders, Ethics/Human Rights, Women's Issues, Lesbian/Gay Issues, and Generation X. There's also a Parenting Issues support and discussion group.

The New Age Forum ("Go NewAge")

The Body/Mind/Health special-interest section of the New Age Forum offers discussions of a variety of alternative health approaches. Other health-related sections include Dreaming/Mind/ESP, Western Paths, Eastern Paths, Native American Paths, Men's Group, Women's Circle, and Sciences & Technology. For the latest word about what's new in the New Age community, check out the forum newsletter, *The Village News Kiosk*, in message section 2, or the monthly *Town Scryer* in Library 1, About the New Age Forum.

The forum administrator and wizop is Neil Shapiro (76703,401) and the sysops are Rilla Moulden (76702,1766) and Brad Hill (71333,2165). The forum librarian is Suzanne Carter (72233,1273), the conference manager is Ariadne (71700,3044), and the forum's public relations contact is Devika Meredith Ruch (71223,3716).

The Muscular Dystrophy Association Forum ("Go MDAForum")

The Muscular Dystrophy Association Forum offers discussions and support for those with Muscular Dystrophy, their friends and families, and interested health professionals.

The AARP Forum ("Go AARP Forum")

This forum, coordinated by the American Association of Retired People, includes message areas for "Health/Daily Living" and "Support Center." AARP members who register in the AARP Forum Club will receive an extra free online hour per month in this forum. This is a comfortable place for new online elders to make friends and get more comfortable with CompuServe. The Support Center message area, formerly titled Alzheimer's Support, contains a great deal of information about this and related topics.

Health and Medical Databases on CompuServe

Among the Big Three, CompuServe is the king of the health and medical databases. No other service can hold a candle to the millions of bytes of health information that can be searched and browsed through on CompuServe. So it should be no surprise that CompuServe is the hands-down winner of our Health Online Award for the best health and medical databases.

**Health Online Distinguished
Achievement Award**

To: CompuServe

For: Best Health and Medical Databases

Now we'll take a look at four representative CompuServe health databases. They are arranged in order of complexity, with the easiest to use listed first.

- **HealthNet**—an electronic health encyclopedia
- **Consumer Reports Complete Drug Reference**—an easily searched simple database of drug information
- **Health Database Plus**—a powerful yet fairly easy-to-use mid-level database of both popular and professional sources
- **PaperChase (MEDLINE)**—a more difficult and expensive but extremely powerful way to search the professional medical literature

HealthNet Reference Library ("Go HNT")

You can think of the HealthNet Reference Library as a giant medical encyclopedia. This easy-to-use database provides a wealth of consumer information on a wide variety of health topics. It is comprehensive enough to provide at least a preliminary overview for most questions on a specific disease, a specific symptom, a particular type of surgery, a medical test, or a specific drug, making it a good first stop in your quest for health and medical information.

The HealthNet Reference Library is divided into several basic categories:

> Disorders and Diseases
>
> Symptoms
>
> Surgeries/Tests/Procedures
>
> Obstetrics
>
> Ophthalmology
>
> First Aid
>
> Home Care
>
> Drugs

Each of these broad categories contains a long list of more specific topics. Under "Surgeries," for instance, the list is broken down into the specific areas of the body (gastrointestinal, abdominal, etc.). Further divisions take you to even more specific topics, like laparotomy or cholecystectomy. For each type of surgery, there is a list of reasons you might want to have the operation, a description of the surgery itself, descriptions of potential complications, instructions for post-surgical care in the hospital, and guidelines for recovery at home.

If you search for information on a specific symptom, say, abdominal pain or numbness and tingling radiating down one leg, HealthNet will display a list of possible causes. There is further information on how each symptom is typically evaluated and diagnosed and the potential treatments for each diagnosis.

Here's an excerpt from a typical HealthNet listing:

```
Breast Cancer
   Over one out of twenty women in the United States will
develop breast cancer, and this makes it the commonest cancer
in women. It is one of the commonest fatal diseases of women,
yet it has been estimated that over one half of all cases are
curable. Men can also develop this disease, but with only a
hundredth of the frequency of that in women.
   Spontaneous occurrences of breast cancer are very common,
but certain factors are associated with an increased risk.
These include a mother or sister with the disease, absence of
pregnancy in the past, first pregnancy after age thirty, and
either early onset of menstruation or late onset of
menopause. Almost all patients discover their cancer them-
selves, and around one half of these have already spread
(metastasized) at that time. Thus efforts have been aimed at
screening for the purpose of detecting tumors at an earlier
stage, when cure rates are highest. Screening implies that no
obvious abnormalities are present--it refers to the appar-
ently healthy woman.

Screening
   Mammography is one aspect of screening; this is actually
a specialized form of x-ray which in recent years is accom-
plished with doses of irradiation which are quite low.
Research has shown that in women over age 50, periodic mam-
mography combined with a breast exams by a physician can
decrease mortality from breast cancer. Current recommenda-
tions are for a baseline mammogram between ages 35 to 40,
every two years or so thereafter. Some physicians think this
is excessive, others feel it is insufficient. Only one's per-
sonal physician can make this judgment on an individual
basis.
   A breast exam by each adult woman every month at a con-
sistent time of the menstrual cycle improves the prognosis of
cancers that are detected. A physician exam periodically will
add to this benefit. Many masses which are detected turn out
to be benign cysts or other noncancerous problems, but only
through biopsy or other techniques can this be determined.
```

```
Diagnosis
Once a lump or abnormal mammogram is detected, some sort of
biopsy is necessary to make the diagnosis. Some cystic lumps
can be drained through a simple needle and syringe, but this
decision requires careful judgment and follow-up. Consensus
of opinion currently is to do an initial biopsy of the lump
under local or general anesthesia, with definitive therapy
decided upon after the final biopsy results are analyzed.
Definitive therapy depends upon the stage of the disease, as
discussed below....
```

Consumer Reports Complete Drug Reference ("Go Drugs")

A very easy-to-use database of consumer drug information, the Consumer Reports Complete Drug Reference is compiled by the U.S. Pharmacopeia. It provides general guidelines on the use of medicines, as well as in-depth listings on most commonly used prescription and over-the-counter drugs. Information on medical tests is also available.

To find information on a particular drug or medical test, go to the database's main menu and select "Search for a Drug or Medical Test." You'll be presented with a blank line and asked to enter the term you wish to search for. If you were to enter "Cytoxan" (a brand name), you'd be presented with the following choices (cyclophosphamide is the generic name for Cytoxan):

```
Overview: CYCLOPHOSPHAMIDE (Systemic)
Brand and Common Names
Description
Before Using This Medicine
Proper Use of This Medicine
Precautions While Using This Medicine
Side Effects of This Medicine
Additional Information
```

You'd then click on the selections you wished to read.

The database contains general information about the correct use of all medicines, as well as specific entries for more than seven hundred individual medicines or drug families. It's a good idea to read both the general information under "General Information on Medicine Use" in the main menu and the information specific to the medicine you are concerned with.

In some searches—especially when you enter a brand name—there may be more than one index term that matches your search term. For example, there are many variations of the brand name "Anacin"—Anacin, Anacin-3, Anacin-3 Children's Tablets, etc. In those cases, the database displays a menu of all the drug names in the index that begin with the name you entered. You must choose the name from this menu that exactly matches the medicine you are taking.

Also, please note that the entry for a single generic drug (e.g., aspirin) may cover many different brand-name medicines.

Health Database Plus ("Go HLTDB")

Created by Information Access Company, Health Database Plus provides an easy way to search through a huge selection of more than two-hundred thousand articles excerpted from more than one hundred consumer and professional health magazines. Articles cover a wide variety of health topics, from nutrition to health care politics. Selections are updated weekly, keeping Health Database Plus nicely current.

At the heart of the database is a collection of publications with health, medical, nutrition, and fitness coverage oriented to nonprofessional readers. Most popular articles include the full text, and coverage begins with January 1989. Core publications range from such newsstand titles as *American Health, Parents' Magazine, Nutrition Today,* and *Shape* to more specialized reports and journals like *AIDS Weekly* from the Centers for Disease Control, *Morbidity and Mortality Weekly Report, Patient Care,* and *RN.* The collection also includes a number of pamphlets issued by such organizations as the American Lung Association.

The database also encompasses an extensive library of technical and professional journals, such as the *Journal of the American Medical Association, The Lancet,* and *The New England Journal of Medicine,* as well as a large number of more specialized medical titles. Research and professionally oriented journal articles usually don't include the full text, but they do include an abstract specially written for nonprofessional readers. The author's original abstract is sometimes included as well.

There are also a large number of health-related articles from nonhealth publications. These articles have been carefully selected to provide you with an even greater range of information than would be possible with specialty publications alone. They generally contain the full text. In addition, an online help forum is available if you have questions.

To use Health Database Plus you'll have to work with a rather old-fashioned command-line interface—in which you type the number of your chosen command from a menu instead of simply clicking on a selection. But it's a simple interface to master and the database is very easy to search.

A friend asked me about sleep apnea, so in my most recent session in Health Database Plus, I entered the condition as my search term. It took Health Database Plus less than a second to tell me that it had 238 articles that matched my query. I reduced the list a bit by specifying that I wanted to see only those articles for which the full text was available. That brought the number down to 177.

I then flipped quickly through the list of articles, chose three that sounded appropriate to my needs, and printed them out. The whole search took less than ten minutes, and my friend found the information quite satisfactory.

As a result of the diverse publications available, the information is extremely wide ranging and nicely varied. You'll typically find several different perspectives on your chosen topic, but layfolk may need a medical dictionary to decipher some of the professional journal articles. There's a $1.50 surcharge for each article read or printed. Abstracts are $1.00 each.

The bottom line: Health Database Plus is extremely useful and moderately priced. I use it frequently.

PaperChase ("Go PaperChase")

A full-fledged professional medical database, PaperChase is not for the faint of heart. However, it does provide at-home access to MEDLINE, the National Library of Medicine's database of references to the medical literature, which is the world's largest biomedical database. At the time I last searched it, it contained 8,633,005 references to articles in more than 4,000 journals. Approximately twenty-five thousand additional references are added each month.

Additional resources available include AIDSLine, the National Library of Medicine's database of AIDS information, and CancerLit, the National Cancer Institute's database of cancer information. PaperChase automatically searches all of its linked databases in a single search.

One of the more expensive databases on CompuServe, PaperChase costs $18 per hour from 7 P.M. to 8 A.M. weekdays and all day on weekends and $24 per hour 8 A.M. to 7 P.M. weekdays.

Unfortunately, there isn't enough storage in the host computer for the complete text of eight million articles. However, as you display or scan references online, you may press F, for "Fotocopy," to request that a photocopy of the full text of the article be mailed to you. Each photocopy costs $10 by first class mail or $25 by fax or express delivery within North America.

In addition, abstracts are available online. You may display the abstract online or print or download it with the list of references at the end of your search.

New users should use PaperChase's "Feedback" query at the end of the session to request the free online user's guide. It's a great introduction to the online search process.

Search Tips for PaperChase

- Be brief. It often works best to enter less rather than more in your search term. Usually the root of the word suffices. For phrases, type only the root of the most significant word. The less you type, the broader the selection of terms from which you can choose, and the less the chance of making a spelling or typing error. If you enter the search term "Lupus," PaperChase gives you the following choices:

```
Medical Subject Headings                 Number of References
and Title Words
1 Lupus                                   11,020
2 Lupus Erythematosus, Panniculitis       13
3 Lupus Erythematosus, Cutaneous          170
4 Lupus Erythematosus, Discoid            1,368
5 Lupus Erythematosus, Systemic           16,692
6 Lupus Nephritis                         439
```

- Be specific. Since over a quarter of a million words are in the database, almost any term you search for is probably there. Don't search for "Eye Disease" if you mean "Cataracts."
- Use standard medical subject headings. These are highly specific index terms assigned to each article on the basis of content. For example, if you want articles on the disease AIDS and you choose the term "AIDS" rather than the medical subject heading "*AIDS (ACQUIRED IMMUNO-DEFICIENCY SYNDROME)," your list will include references about hearing aids and audiovisual aids, but will miss references in which the author didn't use the word "AIDS" in the title.
- Use the subheading "MAJOR TOPIC" (abbreviated "MX") with your search term. This subheading restricts the search to articles in which that medical subject heading is the major topic. For example, to find references in which "aspirin" is the major topic of the article, search for "Aspirin/MX."

Search Options Menu

You can get a bit of a feeling for what using PaperChase might be like by taking a look at the search options menu:

```
1 Exit PaperChase
2 Display List
3 Look for Topic
4 Find References Common to Two or More Lists
5 Include References from 2 or More Lists
6 Put All References from a List on Print Queue
7 Restore/Remove Lists in Display
8 Change/View Choices for Printing
```

Is PaperChase for You?

Compared with the popularly oriented databases described earlier, PaperChase isn't a simple database to search. When you're dealing with eight million items, reducing your list of options to a manageable size can be quite a task. But by the standards of professional medical databases, PaperChase is relatively easy. However, you should be ready to spend considerable time during your first few searches learning your way around the system.

You can get off to a good start—and save a substantial amount in online fees—by *reading all the instruction files in the PaperChase Welcome menu before beginning your search*. And don't be afraid to call the 800 number below for help if you get stuck.

PaperChase was created and is supported by Boston's Beth Israel Hospital, a teaching hospital of Harvard Medical School. Questions or requests for further information should be directed to the PaperChase Customer Support Line, (800) 722-2075; in Massachusetts, call (617) 278-3900.

One final thought: Another option might be to hire a professional medical researcher to do a search for you. For more on this approach, see the section "Using a Health Information Broker" in Chapter 12.

Other CompuServe Health and Health-Related Databases

AIDS News Clips ("Go AIDSNews")

AIDS News Clips lists daily news updates on AIDS furnished by the Associated Press, Reuters, United Press International, and the *Washington Post.*

CCML AIDS Articles ("Go CCMLAIDS")

CCML AIDS Articles provides full-text articles on AIDS from leading medical journals, textbooks, and reference books, all found in the Comprehensive Core Medical Library.

The Handicapped Users Database ("Go HUD")

The Handicapped Users Database supplies information on resources for the handicapped. The sysop for the Handicapped User's Forum is Georgia Griffith (76703,266).

The welcome menu for the database offers the following choices:

Welcome	Reference Library
Software & Hardware	Rehabilitation
Organizations	Research/Development
News Notes	IBM/Special Needs Exchange
Recent Additions	Index

The database covers a wide range of topics, from "Preschools for the Blind" to "Hearing-Ear Dogs," from "Empowering the Disabled" to "Wheelchair Basics."

An index of all the items in the database can be accessed directly ("Go HUD-7500"). Individual files can be accessed by using the "Go" command plus the page number: To read an article on page 2,345 of the database, use the command "Go HUD-2345."

The Human Sexuality Databank ("Go HSX")

The Human Sexuality Forum (see p. 108) offers a searchable database on sex-related information. Topics covered include urology, gynecology, psychiatry, and other areas of sexual medicine and therapy.

Information USA/Health ("Go InfoUSA")

Information USA/Health allows users to access free, up-to-date health information resources from the U.S. government. From the main menu, select option 13, "Free Health Information and Care."

The IQuest Medical InfoCenter ("Go IQMEDICINE")

The IQuest Medical InfoCenter links several important medical, pharmaceutical, and related health databases, such as Alternative Medicine, MEDLINE, Cancer Research Weekly, and AIDS Weekly. Users can search for their topics using a single database or Multi-Database SmartSCANS, which scans a group of databases to find the best sources of information on a given topic. There is a substantial surcharge.

The Knowledge Index ("Go KI")

The Knowledge Index links a number of major medical and pharmaceutical databases, such as CancerLit and PsycINFO, at reduced rates. It costs $24 per hour or 40¢ per minute and is available only in the evenings and on weekends. Beginners should search using the Menu option, which gives instructions for each step in the process. Advanced users can search using the Command option.

Magazine Database Plus ("Go MAGDB")

Magazine Database Plus contains full-text articles on many subjects, health included, from more than 130 general-interest magazines, journals, and reports, dating back to January 1986. There is a surcharge of $1.50 for each article viewed or downloaded.

The NORD Rare Disease Database ("Go RDB")

The NORD Rare Disease Database, maintained by the National Organization for Rare Disorders (NORD), is designed for use both by the public and by health professionals. Keyword searches can provide information on specific illnesses regarding any or all of the following: synonyms, general discussion, symptoms, causes, affected population, related disorders, standard therapies, investigational therapies, resources and organizations, and references. When searching, you should use the singular form of the name of the disease. If you have difficulties, check the index for correct spellings.

Although there are no message board sections, there are newsletters, updates, immediate sign-up for the database's networking program, and a Feedback to NORD section. For more information, write NORD, PO Box 8923, New Fairfield, CT 06812, or call (203) 746-6518.

Physicians Data Query ("Go PDQ")

Physicians Data Query consists of four separate databases dedicated to cancer: Directory File, Protocol File, Consumer Cancer Information File, and Professional Cancer Information File. You can use specific or generic names to search. The Consumer Cancer Information File has basic information on more than eighty types of cancer, including alternative treatments, stages of each type of cancer, and general prognoses. This information is also available as downloadable files on the Cancer Forum (see p. 102).

PsycINFO (Psychological Abstracts) ("Go Psycin")

A huge scholarly database of abstracts, produced by the American Psychological Association, PsycINFO covers psychology and the behavioral sciences. Among the topics are:

> Applied Psychology, Developmental Psychology, General Psychology, Experimental Psychology, Communication Systems, Education, Personnel and Professional Issues, Psychometrics, Treatment and Prevention, Social Processes

You can search by author, subject, publication date, or language. There is a surcharge of $5 for the first ten titles found, another $5 for each subsequent ten titles, plus $5 for each full abstract selected.

Odds and Ends on CompuServe

- *Very Important Note on the Comma and the Dot*—Please note that when you are on CompuServe and are sending e-mail to another CompuServe member, you use the member's regular CompuServe ID with a comma, e.g., 76702,562 for Allan Stevens. But if you're on another system and are sending e-mail to Allan, you need to send it to his Internet e-mail address, which is 76702.562@compuserve.com (with a dot in the ID). As this is a key point, let me go over it again: Each CompuServe member's on-system CompuServe ID contains a *comma*, whereas his or her Internet e-mail address is made up of the same series of numbers, but with a *period*, followed by "@compuserve.com".

- One of the problematic features of the CompuServe message system is that older forum messages are automatically deleted, so you'll ordinarily see only recent postings. You may be able to retrieve older messages by setting the search date parameters to an earlier time. But some older messages on some forums may be lost forever—unless some kind soul has preserved them and uploaded them into the forum library.

- Many of CompuServe's medical databases impose a hefty surcharge, so it's easy to run up a big bill finding the information you're looking for. Be sure to keep track of the access charges you're incurring. I was shocked when I got my bill for researching this chapter.

- If you ever lose your way while looking for health resources, you can always choose "GO HEALTH" and you'll be presented with the CompuServe Master Health Menu, which lists many of the more popular health resources covered in this chapter.

- I *always* got a busy signal at the CompuServe customer service line. I would need to dial the number repeatedly, usually ten or twelve times, before my call went through. After several frustrating attempts, I learned an important shortcut: If you need technical support, call the support personnel directly at (800) 609-1674.

Chapter 7

Prodigy

. . . all that sharing, all that caring, all that wealth of information, it's all there daily, even hourly, whenever I need it. It's made such a huge difference in my life.

Barbara Lea
Prodigy self-helper

————————◆————————

Signing Up

To sign up for Prodigy, call (800) PRODIGY or (800) 776-3449. You'll receive your free software (specify for DOS, Windows, or Mac) in the mail in about seven to ten days. Your first ten hours of online time are free. After that, the base rate is $9.98 per month, which includes up to five hours per month of connection time. Premium services are extra. Additional hours are billed at $2.95 per hour. Special rates are available for heavy users.

PRODIGY'S BRIGHT, COLORFUL INTERFACE is simple to use and offers some unique features, but it lacks the sophistication and polish of its competitors. It is unintimidating for the new user and may be especially attractive to children, but for the sophisticated user accustomed to word processing or e-mail on AOL or CompuServe, sending e-mail on Prodigy seems clunky and awkward. Revising text while online can be so cumbersome that it sometimes seems hardly worth the bother.

Prodigy system administrators promise that much of what currently irritates—the old-fashioned look, the clunky feel, the primitive text editor—will soon be improved by software upgrades. They're also moving to tone down the relentless parade of unsolicited advertisements that flash on and off at the bottom of your screen, making the whole Prodigy experience like trying to watch TV with a commercial running in a lower corner.

But while there are admittedly many things about Prodigy (often abbreviated onscreen as "*P") that may frustrate or infuriate the sophisticated user, you shouldn't necessarily let that stop you, particularly if you're a new user or have children who'll be using your online service. Prodigy contains some valuable self-help resources that are currently unmatched by any other commercial service.

Fortunately, those pesky ads don't follow you into the health and medical bulletin boards and the chat areas. And once you get there, you'll be glad you stuck it out, because things start looking considerably better.

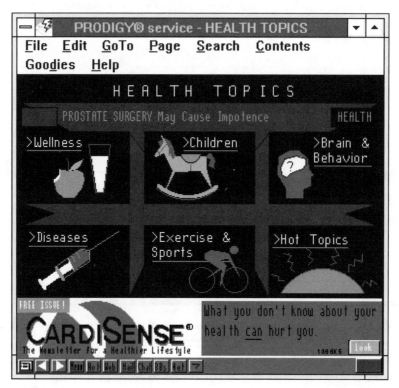

Prodigy has a simple interface that is especially appealing to children. Note the advertisement at the bottom of the screen. (Design © Prodigy)

Chat on Prodigy

Prodigy's chat rooms—on all topics—are all located on a single forum, called, appropriately enough, the Chat Forum (Jump: "Chat"). You must enroll in this forum and choose a nickname before you can enter the chat rooms.

To see a list of current chat rooms, go to the Chat Forum, click on "About Chat," then select "Chat Areas and Chat Rooms." To see a list of scheduled meetings, click on "Chat Calendar." To read scripts of past chat groups, click on "Chat Transcripts."

Many of the health-related support groups can be found in the following chat areas:

Family Issues

Medical/Health

Self Help/Insight

Social Issues

Women Online

You'll find two kinds of chat rooms—Prodigy rooms (public rooms created by Prodigy on topics picked by the network administrators) and member rooms created by members. To create a member room, select the jumpword "Chat" and then click on the Create a Room button.

Chat hosts are available for all online chat groups on Prodigy. Although they may not be present while you're there, you can summon them by clicking on the Alert button. So if you notice online bad behavior, you can call for help. Chat hosts may enter chat rooms without their presence being announced.

The "Pseudo Chat" area is devoted to role-playing, fantasy, and adult conversations. Parental controls are available, so you can keep your children out of certain chat rooms if you wish. Chat on Prodigy is a premium service for which surcharges apply.

HOT TIP

Use "jumpwords" to move directly to your desired destination.

Jumpword	Takes you to
medical support bb	Medical Support Bulletin Board
health bb	Health Bulletin Board
Crohn's & colitis	Crohn's & Colitis Bulletin Board
multiple sclerosis	Multiple Sclerosis Bulletin Board
consumer reports	Consumer Reports
health news	Health News
chat	Chat group listings
member list	List of Prodigy Members
health topics	Prodigy Health Menu
women's health	Women's Health

The Prodigy self-help forums do have a considerable following and can boast a devoted and generous network of self-helpers. Self-helper Annie Little (WHCW66A@prodigy.com), who is active in the self-help forums on both Prodigy and America Online, describes one reason Prodigy users like it:

> One nice feature of Prodigy is the "path" option. Once you choose your selected sequence of "places" you usually like to go, the system will automatically take you there. For me it's Medical Support Bulletin Board, Games Bulletin Board, Travel Bulletin Board, and Weather.
>
> And once you arrive at your chosen bulletin board area, you have several options: reading all messages posted there, reading only new messages since your last visit, or choosing messages by date, sender, or recipient. No other system allows you to do this. This makes it especially easy to read all the notes from a particular correspondent.
>
> Prodigy's bulletin boards are very convenient to use. Whereas messages on AOL are sorted by date, on Prodigy postings are arranged by thread. This makes it easy to read the original message and all the responses to it. On AOL this can be quite a hassle.
>
> If I wrote a note on the Diabetes board asking: "Where can I get information on food exchanges?" then went back to check, I'd find all the responses in one place. On AOL, I might have to read through dozens of messages to find the ones I wanted.

Ed Madara is also a big fan of Prodigy as a self-help resource:

> Another great thing about the support boards on Prodigy is that it's much easier to develop new user-initiated subject headings there than on any other service. So when you go to the Medical Support BB on Prodigy you'll see a wider variety of topics than you will on AOL or CompuServe. Check the "Other Medical" section and you'll find a variety of unique new groups, like "Gall Bladder Club," which as far as I know don't yet exist anywhere else--either online or in the face-to-face self-help community.

Confessions of a Prodigy "Doc of the Day"

Another interesting custom on some Prodigy health boards is to invite a series of "Docs of the Day" to "appear" on certain forums to answer members' questions. In fact, there appears to be more of an emphasis on "Ask the Expert" resources on some of Prodigy's health boards than on those of the other two services. Indeed, I was recently invited to be the Doc of the Day on the Health Bulletin Board on Prodigy (see page 142 for some examples of the questions I received and my answers). On the whole, it was a very positive experience, but I do have a few mixed feelings about the practice.

On the one hand, it is without doubt a tremendously valuable service to Prodigy members to give them easy access to knowledgeable medical experts. I would think that the many Prodigy members who are able to receive prompt and accurate answers to their questions would rate this feature highly. But I must say that it does change the chemistry of the interactions on the forum considerably. Certainly the quality of the interactions were quite different than those on some of the other self-help forums I've visited, especially those that had developed a strong lay leadership. I couldn't help wondering whether these visiting "experts" might get in the way of developing a core group of responsible self-helpers who can provide members with good answers to the same kind of technical questions—and in addition can provide positive personal models, shared experiences, and continuing support.

While definitive answers to such concerns are beyond the scope of this book, I suspect that we'll find that at least in some situations, unless it is done with the utmost sensitivity for self-help principles, having outside experts as visiting authorities on self-help forums is not an altogether good thing. (For more on this question, see the Epilogue.)

Prodigy's Bulletin Boards

The Medical Support Bulletin Board (Jump: "Medical")

The Prodigy support bulletin board most frequently mentioned by Prodigy self-helpers—often with a reverence bordering on awe—is the Medical Support Bulletin Board (frequently abbreviated online as "MSBB"), one of the largest and most active health forums on any of the commercial services. This is clearly one place where Prodigy has done everything right. The Medical Support Bulletin Board was recently chosen as one of the best computer bulletin boards in the nation in a recent contest sponsored by *Boardwatch* magazine.

"I've frequently needed to post the same query on the health boards of AOL, CompuServe, and Prodigy," Ed Madara explains. "I get good answers from all the systems. But I usually get the most responses on Prodigy. It does appear that the MSBB has more active members than the health boards on either America Online or CompuServe."

"Daily, Even Hourly, Whenever You Need It"

Prodigy self-helper Barbara Lea describes her experience with the Medical Support Bulletin Board as follows:

> I joined Prodigy two years ago, after my older son had been diagnosed with attention deficit disorder (ADD). I'd read several books on the subject and we had a fine pediatrician and a good psychologist, but I still felt very much alone. I was stunned to discover such a supportive and knowledge-able group of people on the Prodigy ADD board. Everyone knew just what I was going through, and could listen and care without judging.
>
> They helped me realize that I had ADD myself, and so did my younger son. They recommended books, organizations, maga-zines and tapes that helped me educate myself, my family, and our professionals. My Prodigy friends and I laugh and cry together. We send electronic hugs to those who are ready to give up. Knowing there are others who understand and care and accept us without judgment or blame means so much to us. We've all been pretty hard on ourselves.
>
> Now that I have some feel for this condition, I tried to give back what I was given. I hope I've helped others as they pass through the stages of discovery, grief, and acceptance. What's especially wonderful about online help, is that all that sharing, all that caring, all that wealth of informa-tion, it's all there daily, even hourly, whenever I need it. It's made such a huge difference in my life. If you're having a crisis, just post a note and you'll almost instantly receive helpful suggestions, or just words of kindness. I'd be happy to hear from any of your readers who might have questions or need advice.
> --Barbara Lea (PJEYO5B@prodigy.com)

The Number One Self-Help Bargain

One of the best features of the Medical Support Bulletin Board is financial: The MSBB has a separate sign-up procedure, and once you enroll, you get five addi-tional free online hours on the MSBB each month. And after your monthly five free hours are up, each additional hour is priced at the very moderate rate of $1.20. This progressive "self-help discount" makes the MSBB the number one self-help bargain on the Big Three commercial services. Prodigy manage-ment deserves a special commendation for offering this special discount rate to active self-helpers.

**Health Online Distinguished
Achievement Award**

To: Medical Support Bulletin Board
and Prodigy

For: Best Special Rate for Those with Chronic
Health Problems

Getting Around on the Medical Support Bulletin Board

The MSBB's board leader is Beth Nye (BBAP15B@prodigy.com). You're invited to e-mail Beth with any questions or concerns about the board. She'll either get back to you directly or ask the appropriate MSBB staffer or volunteer to respond. You can also send e-mail questions to MSBB staffer Nancy Eggleston (AFVE44B@prodigy.com).

On MSBB, as on the other Prodigy bulletin boards, the main categories are known as "topics" and subtopics are called "subjects." Prodigy establishes the topics, but any user can create a new subject.

Here's a list of the main topics you'll find on MSBB:

AIDS	Eating Disorders
Alcohol Abuse	Grief/Death
Alzheimer's	Heart Disease
Arthritis	Infertility
Attention Deficit	Lupus
Cancer	Multiple Sclerosis
Caregivers	Neurological
Chronic Fatigue Syndrome	Rare Diseases
Crohn's/Colitis	Respiratory Problems
Deaf/Hearing Loss	Sexual Abuse
Depression/Anxiety/OCD	Smoking
(obsessive-compulsive disorder)	Transplants
Diabetes	Vision Loss
Disabilities	Weight Loss
Drug Abuse	Other Medical

Select your topic, click on the option "Read Comments," and you'll be presented with a list of subjects to choose from. For instance, for "Cancer," you'll see a subject list that includes:

BC (breast cancer)

BMT (bone marrow transplant)

Drug Effects/Hair Loss

Euthanasia

Hair Loss after Chemo

Hodgkin's

Home from Houston

Interferon

Liver Cancer

For each subject there may be as few as one or two to as many as dozens of comments. Once you've read the postings on a subject, you can add a posting of your own, send private e-mail to the poster, or move on to another subject or topic.

The "Other Medical" topic serves as a catch-all for a wide variety of health concerns. Checking this list is a good way to get a quick overview of new or unusual topics. Representative subjects—just a few of many—that I saw on a recent visit included:

acne	hepatitis C
aging parent	kidney disease
breastfeeding	Lyme disease
celiac disease	menopause
chronic pain	osteoporosis
cleft palate	Reye's syndrome
fibromyalgia	scoliosis
genital warts	stroke group
headaches	thyroid disorders

Here are some representative messages from the Medical Support Bulletin Board's thread on infertility:

```
To: All
From: Charlotte E.
Hello all. Well the time has come--I'm about to have my first
visit with this new fertility expert. I was just wondering,
what can I expect from this first visit? Will tests be done?
An internal exam? My appointment is with Dr. Andrew Pickford
of [name of city and hospital]. Has anyone had any experi-
ences with him?
Thanks,     --Charlotte
```

```
To: Charlotte E.
From: Debbie H.
They'll take a complete medical history of both you and your
husband. Your doctor will go over the necessary tests. Then
they do an internal exam. They'll probably do blood tests,
hormone tests, and a prolactin test. Some of the tests will
depend on where you are in your menstrual cycle. Make sure
you let the doctor know about all your concerns, any limita-
tions, and how aggressive you want to be. Do you have any
time limits? Make sure your doctor is aware of anything else
that may affect your treatment.


To: Charlotte E.
From: Carol W.
Hi, Charlotte. I used to work at the hospital where Dr.
Pickford practices and I must tell you it is an excellent
facility. Their OB/GYN services are world-renowned. I do not
personally know your doctor, but my friend Martina, who is a
nurse there, is very pleased with the team. She herself is
suffering from infertility.
Best wishes.   --Carol
```

The Health Bulletin Board (Jump: "Health bb")

Another major health resource on Prodigy is the Health Bulletin Board. The board leader, once again, is Beth Nye. While the MSBB is organized by categories of illness, the Health Bulletin Board is oriented more toward preventive and holistic medicine and general wellness concerns. The goal of the forum is "to provide an online destination where members can exchange information and experiences concerning a wide variety of positive health practices."

There are currently four member-doctors on the board who have been granted special contributor status. They visit the board regularly to answer medical questions. Currently the four are a holistic doctor, a dentist, an endocrinologist and a podiatrist. Other special guests appear from time to time to lend their added expertise. (I recently had the opportunity to be the Doc of the Day on this bulletin board.)

Once a week, a medical forum takes place on the chat BB where members discuss various health issues in real time. You can send e-mail to Beth Nye (BBAP15B@prodigy.com) for the time and date of the next meeting. She will be happy to answer any questions about Prodigy and will be glad to help you find your way around the Health board.

The main topics for the Health Bulletin Board are:

Bodybuilding	Injuries/Healing
Chiropractic	Internal Medicine
Consumer Issues	Men's Health
Cosmetic Enhancement	Mind/Body Connection
Dental Care	Pregnancy
Diet & Nutrition	Prescription Drugs
Emotional Issues	Skin Care
Exercise	Sleep/Dreams
Eye Care	Sports Medicine
Family Medicine	Vitamins
Foot Care	Weight Control
Herbal Medicine	Women's Health
Home Remedies	Other
Homeopathy	

Here are some sample postings. This thread was under "Emotional Issues—Anxiety and Depression":

```
To: All
From: Maria K.
Subject: Anxiety and Depression
I've been having panic attacks, usually in the morning when I
wake up with rushes of adrenaline and a pounding heartbeat.
(I suffer from allergies, am 29, and have a toddler.) In the
midst of one recent episode, I was also experiencing an upset
stomach and some weakness, so I went to my doctor. He did
blood tests and checked for pregnancy. The results came back
fine. He informed me that my white blood cell count was per-
fect and advised me not to worry.
    I was fine until yesterday (three days after my doctor's
visit) when I threw up twice, had heart palpitations, and
felt the adrenaline rushing through my body, pounding heart,
etc., so I called the doctor again. He recommended that I
take a sedative:  Xanax three times a day or as needed.
    As you can imagine, I'm feeling very depressed because I
think something else may be wrong, even though the blood
tests were normal. I must also add that my husband had open
heart surgery three months ago, so I suppose this could be
coming back to haunt me. All I feel like doing is crying and
I can't spend my day lying around because I have an active
young child to care for. Has anyone else ever experienced
anything like this?
```

Maria received a number of reassuring replies. Most advised her to find a doctor who would take her anxiety attacks seriously and help her work through her emotional upsets. Here is one example:

> To: Maria K.
> From: Lori W.
> Dear Maria--I've had a similar problem--severe anxiety attacks--since an accident at work and now have a chronic pain disorder and am at home by myself a lot with no one to talk to. I've been taking Ativan 2 mg., four times daily. This works pretty well to keep the attacks away while I work on what is causing them. I won't go into details, but I am seeing a therapist and have a lot to work on in my own life right now.
>
> I hope you can find someone to help you find the peace of mind you seek. And I hope you can find a medicine that will really help you get through this difficult time. It has helped me to remember that our pain and fear is often a signal that there is something we need to change or some way in which we need to grow. Hang in there and Good Luck!

Sometimes when you're reading the messages in a self-help forum, you may notice that certain messages that other self-helpers refer to are "missing" from the forum. What is happening is that other self-helpers are responding to the original poster by private e-mail rather than by posting so that you are seeing only one side of the conversation. As one such example, self-helper Elaine N. posted the following message on the thread "Heart Trouble":

> From: Elaine N.
> I really need some help. I recently had mitral valve replacement surgery and am now home and doing okay--except in two areas. The major area is sleep. I can only tolerate sleeping on my bed on my left side with a pillow behind me for about four hours. After that I seem to get short of breath and it just becomes agony and I wake up. Tonight I tried sleeping in a recliner--but sleep was difficult and only lasted for about two hours. I'm getting desperate. (It sounds like when I had my baby--definite sleep deprivation, but I didn't have to deal with as much pain then.) Secondly (and this is much less important) this little valve is so noisy. Anyone know of techniques to quiet it down? I'm going buggy. I have a Saint Jude's valve.

Helen then apparently received a private e-mail message from a self-helper named Tim—so it didn't appear in the thread. She responded:

```
From: Elaine N.
Thank you so much, Tim, for your excellent explanation about
needing to elevate my head more than I'd been doing. I fol-
lowed your advice--I'm using two fat pillows, and I'm sleep-
ing so much better now! The last two nights I've been able to
sleep eight hours straight, without waking up once. What a
difference it makes to my frame of mind! I'm a little stiff
when I first get up, but that's a small price to pay. (And
the noise of the valve doesn't even bother me. I'm getting
used to it.)
Sincerely, Helen.
```

Here's an exchange from the thread "Eye Care—Radial Keratotomy":

```
From: Ken E.
I've been seriously thinking of taking the big step, having
Radial Keratotomy, and throwing my glasses away. Has anyone
had it done? If so, can you report on any good or bad
results? Did it hurt? And where there any unpleasant side
effects of the procedure?
```

Ken received many responses. Here are two:

```
To: Ken E.
From: Henry M.
I had RK a number of years ago, and the results were not
what was promised. I suggest doing lots of research before
you "take the big step." My vision was pretty poor in the
beginning (20/300), but after surgery in one eye, I couldn't
go through with having the other worked on. The incisions
were so deep that I now have a very bad glare when driving
at night. Furthermore, after surgery, the one corrected eye
regressed somewhat. Now I have one eye that is very near-
sighted, with the other being farsighted. I wouldn't rule it
out completely. You may be different from me and they may
have advanced the art somewhat, but by all means do look
before you leap.
```

```
To: Ken E.
From: Linda Grant
Carl, I had RK done on my left eye on Aug. 12, and my right
eye on Sept. 9. I am very pleased with the left eye. I saw
immediate improvement, but so far I'm disappointed with the
right eye. I went for my first check-up three days after
surgery. The doctor says it's too soon to be upset. He says
there's some corneal irregularities. I was hesitant to have
the right eye worked on because of a scar from a childhood
injury. I'm hoping it will improve. I will still need reading
glasses because I wore bifocals before the surgery, but I knew
that going into it. I'm still not sorry I had it done because
the improvement in the left eye still makes it possible for me
to go without glasses in a social situation, which is what I
was aiming for. Let me know if you have any more questions.
```

In the Family Medicine section of the Health Bulletin Board, you can post medical questions and receive answers from volunteer medical specialists. One Prodigy member recently posted the following question:

```
From: Kathy P.
Subject: Questions for Urology Doctor
Our 8 mo. old son was born with an undescended testicle. The
testicle was lodged in the cavity next to the scrotum. What
are the chances that this testicle will naturally descend
into the scrotum by age 2? Would surgery be necessary, and if
so would it be recommended?
```

His question was answered by Barry Bodie, M.D., an associate professor of urology at Southern Illinois University:

```
From: Dr. Bodie
Subject: Undescended Testicle
Dear Kathy,
   Earlier surgical therapy is becoming well accepted as
treatment for undescended testicles (cryptorchidism). I sug-
gest you get your son to a urologist as soon as possible. The
risks from surgery and anesthesia are minimal, particularly
in an 8 month old child. The benefit of waiting to see if
the testicle will descend is minimal and medical therapy is
more often unsuccessful than not. If you have any further
questions, please feel free to contact me by e-mail.
```

I too recently had an opportunity to be the Doc of the Day on this bulletin board. Former Health Bulletin Board sysop Jim Callan announced that I would be responding to members' inquiries about specific self-care resources. Here were some of the questions I received and my answers:

```
Subject: Alternative Approaches for Cancer
From: Denise F.
I'm a clinical social worker helping a patient with advanced
melanoma. She is currently going through all known medical
therapies and so far none have done much good. She has asked
me for information on alternative therapies for cancer, but
aside from a local acupuncturist I have no info on this
topic. Can you suggest a good resource in this area?

Subject: Alternative Approaches for Cancer
To: Denise F.
The best source I know for information on alternative
approaches to cancer is the Commonweal Cancer Help Program in
Marin County, California. Call program director Waz Thomas at
(415) 868-0970. They can send you an information packet on
their one-week residential programs. Your client should also
order their book, *Choices in Healing*, by Commonweal's head
honcho, Michael Lerner (It's available from the same number).
Best of luck to you and your client,
Tom Ferguson

Subject: Managing My Blood Pressure Without Drugs
From: Jill D.
I'm 27 years old and am currently on Isoptin for high blood
pressure. I'd like to get off medication because I plan to
have a baby soon and I know that this is a major risk factor
for problem pregnancies. Also, I am a nervous person by
nature, so any tips on how to calm down and relax would be
appreciated. I do not want any more medication!

Subject: Managing My Blood Pressure Without Drugs
To: Jill D.
Dear Jill,
   There is a great deal most people can do to reduce or per-
haps even eliminate your need to take anti-high-blood-pressure
medications. The best book I know on this subject is called
*The HART Program: Lower Your Blood Pressure Without Drugs* by
Dr. Ariel Kerman. You can reach her institute (in Chicago)
directly at (312) 493-HART for further information and to order
the book. (It's also available through local bookstores.)
```

```
    Everyone with high blood pressure who'd like to know what
they might do to take more control of this problem should read
this book.
Best wishes,
Tom Ferguson

Subject: Support Group for Weight Watchers?
From: Ginnie Q.
I've heard that there's a Weight Watcher's support group on
Prodigy but haven't been able to find it. Can you help direct me?

Subject: Support Group for Weight Watchers?
To:  Ginnie Q.
The Weight Watchers support group on Prodigy can be found on
the Medical Support Bulletin Board under "WW-Buddies Lose
Here." Contact: Toby Hecht (EGMP88A@prodigy.com).
Best of luck,
Tom Ferguson
```

The Crohn's & Colitis Bulletin Board (Jump: "Crohn's & Colitis")

The Crohn's & Colitis board is a freestanding information resource operated by the Crohn's & Colitis Foundation of America. When you arrive at the Crohn's & Colitis BB, you will be offered six choices:

> Library
> Research
> More News
> Specialist BB
> Send E-mail to CCFA
> About CCFA

"Library" offers an extensive library of frequently asked questions on inflammatory bowel disease. Choices include:

> Basic Facts, Complications, Diagnosis, Medications, Surgery, Coping, Insurance/Legal, Glossaries

Choices under "Research" include:

> Overview, Genetics, Immunology, Epidimiology, Clinical, Other

"More News" lists current headlines of news articles related to inflammatory bowel disease.

When you click on "Specialist BB" you see the names and e-mail addresses of the month's special guest (when I checked in it was Peter Nielsen, "body-builder, author and Crohn's Disease sufferer"), as well as the month's online medical specialists (Dr. Mark Miller of Baylor and Dr. Philip Grossman of Cedars Medical Center in Miami). The e-mail addresses of the special guest and the medical specialists are given so that you can send them private e-mail. Click on "Select Topic" to review previous postings on the BB or add your comments.

"About CCFA" provides further information about the Crohn's & Colitis Foundation of America, "Send E-mail to CCFA" lets you do exactly that.

There is no patient-to-patient forum on this board. However, you will find an active Crohn's/Colitis section on the Medical Support Bulletin Board.

Here's a sample of one typical series of exchanges from the Expert BB section on the Crohn's & Colitis Bulletin Board. It is on the topic "Medications."

```
From: Malcolm M.
I'm interested in finding more information on the use of
antibiotics for treating Crohn's or Colitis, and would wel-
come any response from anyone who has been prescribed either
Metronidazole or Ciprofloxacin for treatment. What have been
your success, failures, or side effects during treatment?
Would you have any specific advice to give others based on
your experience of having taken these drugs.

To: Malcolm M.
From: Brett Gemlo, M.D.
Metronidazole remains the Gold Standard in the treatment of
infectious perianal Crohn's disease, but more information
about other antibiotics is growing. None are clearly superior
to Flagyl at this point, but that may change in the future.
```

The next thread is titled "Question to Doctor."

```
From: Eleanor W.
I've been reading some of the letters explaining symptoms of
Crohn's disease and would like to know exactly why it is that
the eyes and joints are affected. Does eye involvement mean
problems with vision or something similar to allergic symp-
toms, such as redness, itching, or swelling? Is joint pain
similar to arthritic pain and can it occur in any joint or
just in certain areas of the body? Thanks for your help.
```

```
To: Eleanor W.
From: Philip Grossman, M.D.
Eye and joint problems are a well-known part of the compli-
cations of Crohn's. The joint symptoms are similar to many
other forms of arthritis. However, there is a particular
pattern somewhat specific for IVD, called sacroileitis, or
arthritis of the sacroiliac joints in the lower back. The
eye problems can manifest as redness, swelling, and vision
changes. It is important to have regular eye check-ups.
Also, steroids frequently used as therapy may cause tempo-
rary (and if long-term, permanent) changes in vision. Thanks
for the question.
```

The Multiple Sclerosis Bulletin Board (Jump: "Multiple Sclerosis")

Like the Crohn's & Colitis BB, the Multiple Sclerosis Bulletin Board is a free-standing, separate board run by an illness-specific nonprofit organization, in this case, the Multiple Sclerosis Society. The goal of the board is to provide a wide range of information about multiple sclerosis (MS).

When you jump to the Multiple Sclerosis board, you're offered four choices:

> Compendium
>
> MS News Update
>
> Fact Sheets
>
> Pamphlets Online

The Compendium is essentially a FAQ (set of frequently asked questions) about MS. It is an exhaustive and authoritative source of information on MS. The MS News Update is a brief listing of recent news stories that involve MS, and Fact Sheets and Pamphlets Online each provide a listing of articles about a variety of common problems or concerns related to multiple sclerosis.

HOT

TIP

There's no message section for MS on this board, but there is a very active one on the Medical Support Bulletin Board (Jump: "Medical Support BB").

Jumpword: "Health"

There are many other health resources on Prodigy. You can see the whole list of them by selecting "Health" as the jumpword. This calls up the Prodigy Health & Fitness master list, which includes these options:

Classifieds	Health BB
Community Services	Health News
CR [Consumer Reports]	Health Topics
Diet & Nutrition	Keeping Fit
CR [Consumer Reports] Exercise	Medical Support BB
CR [Consumer Reports] Health	Multiple Sclerosis
Crohn's & Colitis	Sports
Exercise Equipment	Women's Health

You can go to your section of choice either by clicking on the topic listing or by using the "Jump" command and entering your selected topic as a jumpword. Here's what you'll find under each of the listings above.

- *Classifieds.* Classified ads for health-related products and services. Prodigy is the only one of the Big Three that carries classified health ads.
- *Community Services.* A mixed bag of ads and public service announcements.
- *CR Diet and Nutrition, CR Exercise, and CR Health.* (See "Consumer Reports Health Resources on Prodigy," below.)
- *Crohn's & Colitis.* (See "The Crohn's & Colitis Bulletin Board," p. 143.)
- *Exercise Equipment.* Consists mostly of ads for golf club manufacturers and other retailers of sports or exercise-related merchandise.
- *Health BB.* (See "The Health Bulletin Board," p. 137.)
- *Health News.* Lists latest news bulletins and stories on health-related trends and biomedical breakthroughs.

Classified Health Ads on Prodigy

You can place your ad on Prodigy for 30 days for $20 for the first page (screen) and $1.00 for each additional page. Here are two classified ads from the Health section:

```
Diabetic Supplies by Mail
  Preferred Rx, a mail-order pharmacy in
  Cleveland, Ohio, has since 1988 saved
  families all over the country hundreds
  of dollars a year on costly prescription
  drugs and diabetic supplies. Maybe
  you've seen our ads in Diabetes Forecast
  or Diabetes Self-Management.
  -Preferred Rx ships prescriptions to
  your home without advance payment.
  -Preferred Rx bills your insurance
  company.
  -Preferred Rx, in most cases, accepts
  insurance reimbursements as
  payment-in-full.
  For more information, contact us by
  e-mail or call 1-800-843-7038, 8:30-5:30.
  Sorry, no Medicare or Medicaid accepted.
Free Health Newsletter!
  Looking for support motivation for
  your fitness program?  THE LIFE
  PRESERVER, a newsletter for people
  seeking healthy lifestyles, contains
  news & info about research, nutrition,
  recipes, & exercise. For a FREE SAMPLE
  COPY, hit the reply button & give your
  name & address. Or send name & address to:
          ORCHARDS PUBLICATIONS
          11500 NE 76TH ST. A-3  Suite 234
          VANCOUVER, WA  98662-3939
          E-MAIL:  PVGA74A
```

- *Health Topics*. A mixture of recent press releases and news stories on a variety of health topics. Main headings include Wellness, Children, Brain and Behavior, Diseases, Exercise & Fitness, and Hot Topics.
- *Medical Support BB*. (See "The Medical Support Bulletin Board," p. 133.)
- *Multiple Sclerosis*. (See "The Multiple Sclerosis Bulletin Board," p. 145.)
- *Sports*. Sports news and updates from ESPN and a list of available sports chat groups and forums.
- *Women's Health*. Includes news articles on women's health, a list of women's health groups, and cross-references to other Prodigy health services.

Consumer Reports Health Resources on Prodigy

We'll wind up this whirlwind tour of Prodigy by describing the most extensive database of health and health-related information to be found on the system—the complete collection of recent *Consumer Reports* articles on health and medical topics. These can be found under three separate headings: "Consumer Reports Health" (jumpword: "CR Health"), Consumer Reports Exercise (jumpword: "CR Exercise"), and Consumer Reports Diet and Nutrition (jumpword: "CR Diet"). You may also select the jumpword "CR Library," then choose the "Consumer Reports Index." This index provides an extensive listing of articles, both health and nonhealth, listed from A to Z.

It's not possible to do an automated topic search of the Consumer Reports database. You must review the lists of titles and select the articles you wish to read.

Under "CR Health," you'll find the following master topic list:

Body Systems	Injury/Emergency
Drugs & Medicine	Insurance/Care
Environment	Lifestyles
Food Safety	Medical Records
Genetics	Medical Treatments
Health Products	Pesticides
Infection/Disease	Question of Health

Simply click on the topic you're interested in to see a more detailed list of available articles. For instance, here are three article lists you'll find:

Drugs & Medicine

Another Pill for Aches and Pains	How to Buy Drugs for Less
Antacids, Aspirin/Half Dosage	Miracle or Media Drugs
Buying Vitamins	New Pain Relievers
Can You Live Longer?	Psychiatric Drugs to Fight Anxiety
"Cholesterol-Reducing" Pills	Pushing Drugs to Doctors
Costly Medicine for Triaminic Drugs	Taking Vitamins
Estrogen Therapy	The High Price of Prescriptions
Generic Drugs	

Medical Treatments

Acupuncture	Hysterectomy Decisions
Are Ovaries Dispensable?	Hysterectomy: What To Expect
Can Surgery Free You from Glasses?	Laser Surgery
Can You Live Longer?	Maker of Viralizer to Temper Ad
Cesarean	Claims
Chiropractors	Miracle Drugs or Media Drugs?
"Cholesterol-Reducing" Pills	Not-So-Hot Cold Remedies
Costly Little Aspirins against Heart Attacks	Psychiatric Drugs to Fight Anxiety
Eye Surgery Follow-Up	Pushing Drugs to Doctors
Generic Drugs	The Estrogen Question
Homeopathy: Much Ado about Nothing?	The Facts about Alternative Medicine
How to Lower Blood Pressure	The Prostate Puzzle

Diet/Nutrition

A Costly Way to Cut Down on Salt

Advocating the Prudent Diet

Are You Eating Right?

Blood Pressure, How to Lower

Butters, Margarines and Spreads

Calcium Supplements

Can You Live Longer?

Cheese, American: Nutrition

Cholesterol

"Cholesterol-Reducing" Pills

Cholesterol Test, Take-Home

Coffee and Cholesterol

Coffee and Health

Eating Right at Holiday Time

Eating Right: It's Easier
   than You Think

Eggs and Egg Substitutes

Fast Food

Fast Food for Fat-Watchers

Fats in the Diet

Food Labels, Better

Food Labels: New and Improved?

Food-Label Hype

Food Pyramid, FDA's
   "New, Improved"

Frookies: Sour Grapes over
   Fruit Sweeteners

Frozen Desserts, Low-Fat

Frozen Light Entrees

Losing Weight: What Works?
   What Doesn't?

Margarine, The Trouble with

Meals-In-A-Can Should Stay There

Milk: Why 2% Is Really 35%

New Data on How We Eat

No-Fat Foods

Nutrition IQ

Olive Oil

Olive Oil and the Heart

Olive Oil: Follow-Up

Salt/Sodium

Sports Drinks

Vitamins, Buying

Vitamins, Taking

Yogurt: Diet Food or Dessert?

Other Self-Help and Health-Related Resources on Prodigy

Cultures Bulletin Board (Jump: "Cultures BB")
Deaf Culture

Education Bulletin Board (Jump: "Education BB")
Special Education Issues

Lifestyle Bulletin Board (Jump: "Lifestyle BB")
Gay/Lesbian Issues

Science & Environment Bulletin Board (Jump: "Science BB")
Social Sciences (health care)

Seniors Bulletin Board (Jump: "Seniors BB")
Retirement Issues

Veterans Bulletin Board (Jump: "Veteran")
Disabled Vets
Desert Storm (Persian Gulf War Syndrome)

Odds and Ends on Prodigy

- A wide range of Internet newsgroups are available on Prodigy. Use the Jumpword "Internet" to select the newsgroups you wish to read. (See Chapter 13 for suggestions.) The World Wide Web is also currently available from the Internet Menu.
- Watch out for the plus services. Use any of them just once and Prodigy'll tag on a charge of $7 per month. Plus services include the Health Bulletin Board, and the *Consumer Reports* database.
- You can use the Bulletin Board Note Manager (choose the jumpword "BBNM" for more information) to download just the notes you want so that you can read and reply off-line without incurring additional fees.

Chapter 8

The Best of the Other Commercial Services

◆

HERE ARE BRIEF NOTES on several other computer networks with interesting or unique resources for online self-help. These services were the most frequently mentioned and recommended in my explorations in self-help cyberspace. (But watch for three very interesting new online health resources from Microsoft, AT&T, and IBM.) I welcome your suggestions of additions and updates for the next edition. (See "How to Help Us Update This Book," p. 281.)

eWorld

After America Online, CompuServe, and Prodigy, which are described in the preceding chapters, and the Microsoft Network (MSN), which was launched too late to be covered fully in this edition, eWorld is the largest computer network. It is currently accessible only to those with a Macintosh computer, although a Windows interface is promised soon.

One forum on eWorld that will be of special interest to self-helpers is Transformations—A Self-Help and Support Group Community. It is run by sysop Becky Boone, Ph.D., a psychologist and psychotherapist (BeckTF@eworld.com) who cut her teeth as an active staffer on the self-help boards of America Online.

Scheduled Support Groups in eWorld's Transformations Forum

AA Open Discussion	Gamblers Anonymous
AA Step Meetings	Gay and Lesbian Support
Abuse Survivors	Gay Teen Support
Adoption Search	Grief and Loss
Adult Children of Alcoholics	Health Care in the '90s
Alanon	Lesbian Support
Attention Deficit Disorder	Life Management Support Group
Bisexual Support	Living through Depression
Cancer Survivors	Narcotics Anonymous
Chronic Fatigue Syndrome	Overeaters Anonymous
Chronic Pain	Parenting Support
Codependents Anonymous	Post-traumatic Stress Disorder
Emotions Anonymous	Stop Smoking Support
Fibromyalgia	Teen Support

Becky fears that AOL, at five million–plus members, may have grown too big too fast to support the kind of forum she yearns for. She likes the laid-back atmosphere of the eWorld self-help community. Becky says that what distinguishes eWorld's support community from AOL's (in addition to being less crowded) is a strong commitment from the host to provide support for grassroots initiatives from online self-helpers. This means extensive handholding for newcomers and active staff help and support for those who want to start new chat groups or establish new topics in the message center.

Becky writes: "From my personal experiences with the healing power of twelve step self-help groups, and my years of experience on CompuServe and America Online, I have come to be a staunch believer in self-help groups. I would love to hear from anyone who would like to contribute to our store of information, or who needs information from us."

The Transformations Forum is located in the Arts & Leisure Pavilion, under "Home, Health & Environment." It's divided into three subforums: Medical Health, Mental Health, and 12-Step Programs.

The forum's Health Information database comes in two parts. The first, "Beginning the Journey," contains shorter files (less than 29K) that can be read online. The second, "Download Library," contains larger files and health applications that can be downloaded and read off-line.

The screen names of the key forum staffers are Moon TF, Earth TF, World TF, Angel TF, Perk TF, Light TF, and Star TF. Feel free to contact any of them for help or guidance.

Becky recently launched her second forum on eWorld—Women Online Worldwide (WOW). It contains additional files on women's health topics.

To subscribe to eWorld, call (800) 521-1212, ask for extension 969, and request free startup software.

Transformations Forum: Message Board Topics

Allergies	Heart Disease
Alternative Health Practices	Lupus
Back/Neck Pain	Menopause
Bell's Palsy	Panic Disorders
Bone Marrow Transplants	Pregnancy/Reproductive Health
Bruxism	Rehabilitation
Canavan's Disease	Salmonella
Carpal Tunnel Syndrome	Sinus
Chronic Epstein-Barr	Skin Issues
Deafness	Strokes
Death and Dying	TMJ
Dermatomyositis	Velo-Cardio Facial Syndrome
Finding the Right Provider	Wellness and Prevention
Gallbladder	

GEnie

GEnie is another medium-sized computer network. There are four "RoundTables" (GEnie's word for forums) of special interest to online self-helpers. Each offers a support forum, information in file libraries, and real-time conversation. Access to sections labeled "Private" requires prior contact with the group coordinator. You'll see instructions on how to reach them when you log on.

The disABILITIES RoundTable (Keyword: "ABLE")

The disABILITIES RoundTable covers such disability-related topics as rights, resources, laws, agency information employment, education, leisure, and technology. Message board topics include:

> Specific Disabilities, Computers and Software, Vision Impairment, Deaf/Hard-of-Hearing/Speech, Mobility Impairments, Learning Disabilities, Chronic Fatigue Syndrome, Americans with Disabilities Act Support Center, Internationally Able

The Family and Personal Growth RoundTable (Keyword: "FAMILY")

The Family and Personal Growth RoundTable covers all aspects of family life, interpersonal relationships, and personal growth. Special features include private bulletin boards for kids and for teens (no grown-ups allowed!) and several adults-only areas for frank discussions of sexuality. Other message board topics include:

> Singles; Getting and Staying Married; Divorce and Remarriage; Adoption and Foster Parenting; Illness; Dying, Death, and Bereavement; Personal Growth; Working the Twelve Steps; For the Recovering Alcoholic; For the Family and Friends of the Alcoholic; Overcoming Overeating; Survival and Recovery

The Medical RoundTable (Keyword: "MEDICAL")

The Medical RoundTable is a forum for the discussion of medical topics. Both health professionals and layfolk participate. Special features include person-to-person support for various illnesses and private forums for physicians, nurses, and allied health professionals. This roundtable is also home to PsyComNet, which has an extensive library of psychiatric and psychological files for all to share. Message board topics include:

> Clinical Consulting—General Questions and Answers on Medical Topics, Psychiatry—Biological/Medical/Major Disorders, Ask the Doctor—Specific Questions about Your Health Problems, Computers and Medicine, Drugs/Pharmaceuticals/etc., Alternative Health Care, Pregnancy/Childbirth and Gynecology, Heart Disease, Eyes/Ears/Noses and Throats, Orthopedics and Podiatry, AIDS

The Public Forum/NonProfit Connection RoundTable (Keyword: "PUBLIC")

The Public Forum/NonProfit Connection focuses on news and issues of interest to the public sector. It covers a wide range of subjects, from using computers on the job, to sexism and what can be done about it, to religion, ecology, addiction, nonprofit management and the role of technology in social change. Message board topics include:

> Technology for Nonprofits, Working for Social Change, Public Gay/Lesbian/Bisexual Issues, Twelve-Step Programs, Religion/Spirituality/Personal Growth, Biomedical Issues, "Anonymous" Twelve-Step Programs, Abuse Survivors and Friends

Self Help for Hard of Hearing People Online (Keyword: "SHHH")

Self Help for Hard of Hearing People (SHHH) is a network of face-to-face self-help groups with more then 275 local chapters. This new service offers three areas of interest to people with hearing loss: the Bulletin Board serves as a message forum for hard-of-hearing self-helpers, the software library contains articles from the SHHH Journal as well as a variety of other useful files, and the real-time-conference area offers a scheduled support group meeting each Tuesday evening at 9:30 P.M. Eastern time. There are also some private areas, accessible to SHHH members only. This forum can be found on page 1680 in the Medicine and Science area. Use the code SHHH123 when you sign up for GEnie to take advantage of a special $50 bonus offer. Deaf users can get GEnie information at (800) 238-9172 (TTY).

GEnie can sometimes provide private discussion categories and file libraries to nonprofit organizations. For more information on GEnie, or to order a startup kit, call (800) 638-9636 or (301) 340-4000.

Delphi

This medium-sized computer network was the first to offer a direct Internet connection. Health-related forums include Living Healthy, Child Health Forum, New Age Network, and Alternative Science. Delphi also provides a useful list of health-related Internet Gopher sites. For information or software, call (800) 695-4005.

The Well

The Well is a small but influential online network based in San Francisco. Most members live nearby, but membership is now available nationwide. One of the special benefits of Well membership to those who live near San Francisco is the legendary monthly Well parties, where online chums actually get a chance to meet each other face to face.

The Well's unofficial "house doctor" is Flash Gordon, M.D. (I'm not making this up). He's often called on to answer members' medical questions. You can reach him at flash@well.com.

Ongoing conferences on the Well include:

> Aging, AIDS, Couples, Disability, Dreams, Drugs, Eros, Gay, Health, Holistic, Kids Online, Life Stories, Men Only, Night-Owls (12 to 6 A.M. Pacific time), Optical Problems, Parenting, Psychology, Recovery, Sexuality, Therapy, True Confessions, Virtual Communities, Women Only

For further information about the Well, send e-mail to info@well.com or call (415) 332-9200.

Women's Wire

The percentages of women on the Big Three have been estimated as follows: CompuServe, 20 percent; America Online, 30 percent; and Prodigy, 40 percent. If you prefer a women-centered network, you might want to check out another small San Francisco Bay Area service called Women's Wire (Women's Worldwide Information Resource & Exchange).

Women's Wire was established to serve the "information and networking needs of women." Although men are allowed to join, only about 10 percent of the members are male, so this service is indeed provided primarily by and for women.

Many women's organizations, like the National Education Center for Women in Business and the National Association of Women Business Owners, have information available online. There are ongoing forums on health and fitness. Live chats are also popular. Its more than 270 ongoing conferences cover such issues as parenting, health, politics, and feminism. Downloadable files include health and other articles from *New Woman, Working Woman, Ms.,* and *Self.*

Women's Wire provides extensive handholding to new members and supplies good online training and continuing support. For more information, send e-mail to info@wwire.net or call (800) 210-9999 or (415) 615-8989.

The Microsoft Network

This new online service comes as a part of the system software for the Windows 95 operating system and is currently available only to those who are using that system. As we go to press, the Microsoft Network (MSN) is just a skeletal system in its early stages. By the time you read this, there should be a good selection of health resources.

If you are currently running Windows 95, you can sign up for the Microsoft Network by double-clicking on the MSN icon on your Windows 95 desktop. A piece of software called a "wizard" will guide you through the sign-up process. The Microsoft Network offers a standard plan with a monthly minimum and a discounted rate for heavy users.

Microsoft is currently working on software that will allow Macintosh users to access MSN. This network will not be available via earlier Windows systems.

For more information on the Microsoft Network, you can sign on to MSN, click Member Assistance, double-click Member Support, and double-click the MSN Help Desk. Or you can call (800) 840-9890.

Part III

The Internet and Beyond

The Internet (frequently called just the Net) is a sprawling collection of more than 20,000 interlinked computer networks, connecting governmental, military, research, academic, and commercial sites, plus millions of private citizens, to each other—and to a wide range of computer resources, services, and information.

The growth rate of the Internet is hard to verify, but even at the most conservative estimates, it is impressive. According to some recent news stories, certain parts of the Net are now growing at a rate of 20 percent *per month,* and research reports toss out numbers like thirty-seven million Internet users. Even Socks, the presidential cat, has a place on the Internet, sharing a World Wide Web home page (http://www.whitehouse.gov) with the nation's first family.

While these big numbers may suggest that just about everyone is on the Net, that's far from true. The thirty-seven million figure reflects the number of people with Internet e-mail addresses. As we go to press, only an estimated eighteen to twenty-four million actually browse around the network looking for files, newsgroups, or World Wide Web sites. Compare that number with the sixty million who typically watch the Super Bowl and you'll conclude that the Net, while impressive, still has a long way to go. But at its present rate of growth, it will get there pretty quickly.

Much of the recent rapid increase in Internet traffic has taken place on a section of the Net called the World Wide Web (the Web for short). The growth of the Web is due largely to a new type of online browser program (like Mosaic and Netscape Navigator) that makes it possible to navigate the Net by means of a point-and-click graphical interface. (You'll learn more about the World Wide Web in Chapter 11.)

The Internet was originally developed twenty-five years ago by the Defense Department to enable military organizations and research institutes to share computer resources and to pass information around. Like many technologies that came out of the military world, it was not designed for ease of use. As recently as a year or two ago, it was still fairly difficult to navigate.

The worst thing about the Internet today is that it can be a bit overwhelming. The best thing about it is that you can safely ignore ninety-nine percent of it. And you'll probably find most of the good stuff in one of the following categories, which we'll be covering in the subsequent chapters:

- Internet mailing lists
- Internet newsgroups
- World Wide Web home pages
- Other Internet resources

Q *Who uses the Internet?*

A All kinds of people: grandmothers sending e-mail to their grandkids, patients e-mailing their doctors, high school students playing elaborate computer games. Publicists sending out their latest electronic press release, sweethearts sending love notes, and ordinary business people keeping in touch with customers, suppliers, and co-workers.

While exact statistics are hard to find, most Internet users agree that on much of the Net, males exceed females, the young exceed the old, and the well-schooled outnumber those with less formal education. However, in the self-help communities of cyberspace, the male-female ratio is much closer to 50-50 and the average age is considerably older.

Q *Exactly what kinds of information can and can't be sent over the Net?*

A If it can be reduced to digital form (a string of ones and zeros), you can send it over the Net. Text is the most common content of Internet messages, but photographs, video and audio clips, music, computer programs, games, and fine-art reproductions are just a few of the other things that are frequently sent through the modem-and-phone-line pipe.

Q *Is there a Yellow Pages or phone book of things you can find on the Net?*

A No. Despite a number of ambitious attempts to construct a "card catalog" for the Internet, all have serious limits. The Net is probably too gigantic and fast changing to be completely covered in any single source. No one has ever done it. And since the Net is growing and changing so rapidly, it's extremely unlikely that anyone ever will.

There are a number of good guides to certain topics on the Net (like this book), and there are good directories to certain functions (like Yahoo for the World Wide Web—see p. 240). But it's unlikely that there will ever be a definitive Yellow Pages.

Q *Isn't there any way to look up a friend's e-mail address?*

A While there are some online search tools that in some cases can help you do this (e.g., finger and whois), in general the most convenient way to find friends' e-mail addresses is to call them up and ask.

Q *Who really owns and runs the Internet?*

A No one—and everyone. While corporations, governments, schools, small businesses, and individuals may own the hardware and the on-disk files at their particular sites, the big data conduits (backbones) that connect those sites are owned and maintained by several hundred different telecommunications companies, government agencies, and universities. Several organizations work to make sure the Net runs smoothly (the Internet Society sets certain standards and the Virginia-based Internet Network Information Center acts as a central registry and clearinghouse for Internet addresses), but there's no central governing body.

Q *Are America Online, CompuServe, and Prodigy the same as the Internet?*

A Not exactly, but they're all connected. The Big Three offer complete or near-complete, easy-to-understand access to nearly all Internet features. But if you have a direct Internet connection, you can't access America Online, Prodigy, or CompuServe unless you sign up for your own account.

Q *Am I likely to encounter criminals, pornographers, racists, drug dealers, pickup artists, hackers, dirty old men or women, or other unsavory characters on the Internet?*

A In my two years of explorations of the online world, I have experienced no such unpleasantness. But just as in real life, it mostly depends on where you go. Most cities have adult book stores and pickup bars. If you don't want to meet their customers, all you need do is simply stay away. Similarly, it's usually pretty easy to tell what kind of area you're in, in cyberspace. The self-help neighborhoods are usually quite benign.

One advantage of the commercial services is that they're constantly monitored for signs of bad behavior. You can exercise parental control, and it's always possible to call in a sysop to report an infraction. Participants who misbehave are warned. If they continue, they can be kicked off the system.

Traffic on the unregulated portions of the Internet is somewhat more unpredictable. Flaming and other forms of verbal abuse are common on certain newsgroups and mailing lists. But if you find you don't like a conversation, escape is always a mouse click away.

Q *Are my kids going to be safe on the Net?*

A Despite a recent rash of lurid TV headlines, your kids should do just fine in cyberspace. But while they'll certainly be a lot safer than they would be in almost any other public place, some parental supervision is advised, and kids should be taught the basics of online self-protection:

- Be aware that people you meet online may not be who they represent themselves to be.

- Don't give out personal or family information (such as phone numbers or addresses) to people you don't know.

- Never respond to abusive or suggestive messages. The solution to bad behavior is to break the connection.

- Report anything that seems offensive or strange to your parents—just as you would in real life.

America Online and Prodigy offer parental advisories and methods for restricting your kids' access to certain adult features of their systems.

A useful pamphlet, "Child Safety on the Information Highway," is available from the National Center for Missing and Exploited Children. To request a copy, call (800) 843-5678.

Chapter 9

Internet Mailing Lists

We're probably better people for having had the humbling experience of a debilitating illness. We've found our strengths. We've identified our true friends. And we welcome the sunrise a little differently than those who take life for granted.

> Rita Weeks
> *Parkinson's Disease Information Exchange Network*

———————◆———————

BOB BROEDEL ISN'T A GUY who spends a lot of time blowing his own horn. A mild-mannered computer specialist in the meteorology department at the University of Florida at Tallahassee, Bob is the host and list keeper for the ALS Interest Group-ALS Digest, an Internet mailing list for people with amyotrophic lateral sclerosis (ALS, or Lou Gehrig's disease) and their friends and families. Bob doesn't consider his work anything special or unusual.

Many of the other online members of the worldwide ALS self-help community (ALS patients, their families and friends, and health professionals and ALS researchers) would strongly disagree. They believe that by establishing a mailing list for ALS and sending his modest weekly electronic newsletter, *ALS Digest*, out to over one thousand subscribers, Bob may have done more to support people with ALS and their families than any other single person or even any agency in the United States.

Subscribing to an online mailing list feels much like participating in the self-help forums described in the previous chapters, but the underlying technology is altogether different. Let's take the ALS list as an example. Here's what Bob Broedel does:

1. He collects the e-mail addresses of people who send him e-mail asking to be added to the list. He adds each incoming name to his ALS master list.

2. He receives and reads each piece of incoming mail directed to the list.

3. He copies each piece of incoming list mail into a working file for the next issue of the newsletter. When it's time to send out the new issue, he adds a header and a table of contents to the file.

4. He mails the completed newsletter file out to the whole list once a week.

As a member of Bob's list, you receive the *ALS Digest*, containing messages Bob has received that week.

If you want to participate in a self-help forum on your commercial service, you'll need to log on and go to your forum of choice to read the new postings at regular intervals. But if you subscribe to a mailing list, its postings will automatically arrive in your mailbox. With some lists, you'll receive each message separately. With others, like Bob's, you'll receive a daily or weekly mailing, usually called a digest.

Running a self-help mailing list is one way that a single volunteer can use the power of the new information technologies to improve the lives of hundreds of people. As one subscriber to Bob's newsletter writes:

> I was diagnosed with ALS a little over two years ago and subscribed to Bob Broedel's wonderful ALS DIGEST shortly thereafter. I now have eight notebooks full of back issues (25 issues per notebook) and refer back to them frequently. Here are some of the ways the newsletter helps:
>
> - We can find out about new drug trials and research studies for ALS.
> - We can read about other patients' experiences with this disease and offer and receive support.
> - ALS Digest serves as a *Consumer Reports* for drugs, doctors, hospitals, and assistive technologies.
> - Researchers can "advertise" for volunteer subjects for their studies.
> - ALS patients who are no longer able to talk (a common occurrence in this condition) can still communicate electronically with their national network of ALS friends.
>
> Bob Broedel has certainly managed to produce a wonderfully helpful resource with the ALS Digest. For people like me, it's definitely the best source of online information and support I know.
> Warm wishes,   --Hardy Carroll (hardy.carroll@wmich.edu)

Bob got started in the electronic mailing list business after his wife, Carmen, was diagnosed with ALS. (ALS is an inherited disease of the nervous system that usually does not become manifest until midlife.) Carmen recently died of ALS, and many list members were worried that Bob might stop running the list and editing the newsletter. But fortunately for the ALS community, he decided to continue—in Carmen's memory.

Here's the first page of a recent issue:

```
Subj: ALSD#179 ALS-ON-LINE
From: broedel@geomag.gly.fsu.edu
X-From: broedel@geomag.gly.fsu.edu (Bob Broedel)
To: als@huey.met.fsu.edu
=======================================================
==        ------ ALS Interest Group ------        ==
==             ALS Digest                         ==
==                                                ==
== --- Amyotrophic Lateral Sclerosis (ALS)        ==
==    --- Motor Neurone Disease (MND)             ==
==       --- Lou Gehrig's disease                 ==
==          --- Charcot's Disease                 ==
==                                                ==
== This e-mail list has been set up to serve the  ==
== world-wide ALS community. That is, ALS patients, ==
== ALS researchers, ALS support/discussion groups, ==
== ALS clinics, etc. Others are welcome           ==
== (and invited) to join. The ALS Digest is       ==
== published (approximately) weekly. Currently    ==
== there are 1080+ subscribers.                   ==
==                                                ==
== To subscribe, to unsubscribe, to contribute    ==
== notes, etc. to ALS Digest, please send e-mail  ==
== to:bro@huey.met.fsu.edu (Bob Broedel)          ==
== Sorry, but this is *not* a LISTSERV setup.     ==
==                                                ==
== Bob Broedel; P.O. Box 20049; Tallahassee,      ==
== FL 32316 USA                                   ==
=======================================================

CONTENTS OF THIS ISSUE:
1. Announcements
2. ALS Digest on Floppy Disks
3. als@huey
4. Ask the Experts on April 30
5. re: stiffness
6. re: Managing Swallowing Problems
```

```
 7. some questions
 8. powerlessness/power/control
 9. Riluzole
10. CNTF & BDNF & Neurontin & more.
11. BDNF and GDNF
12. Patients suffer while FDA dithers
13. Battelle looks at the future
```

Each issue of the newsletter contains ten to fifteen short selections. Some are personal accounts or questions from people with ALS (or both). Some are responses to earlier questions, often with answers and suggested resources. Others are reports of recent research studies and messages from clinicians and researchers.

Unlike a printed newsletter, which is typically written by a single editor, the *ALS Digest* serves as a vehicle by which the wisdom of the entire group is made available to all group members. Topics range from recent scientific breakthroughs to experiences with various therapies to personal musings by ALS patients and their family members and friends.

Here's a representative posting from a recent issue, an essay a group member wrote in the form of a letter to express a common problem.

```
Dear Friend,

You haven't been by to see me in quite some time. I wondered
about what happened. Did I say something that offended you? I
started asking around.

Word finally got back that you were uncomfortable around me
because of my illness. That's why, instead of calling, I
thought I might write you a note. Maybe I can explain a lit-
tle better to you about the way I feel.

The last time you came over, I was having a lot of physical
problems. This illness is like that; good for two days, bad
for three. Before you come, call. I'll tell you honestly if
I'm up or down. That way you know what to expect.

But don't avoid me. Inside, I am still the same person I
always was. I can still beat you at chess, still out-talk you
over religion and politics. I can still laugh at all your
jokes, still feel sad when we talk about some of our lost
friends. I'm still me.
```

Don't be afraid to talk about the things you see. My hands shake, my walk is unsteady. I know that. It isn't a secret. I'll tell you about what I'm going through, about the medications and stuff. You need to know so you will feel comfortable when you see something happen.

Just because I've accepted my disease doesn't mean I've accepted defeat. I'm still fighting. But the fighting would be so much easier if you were around. Why? Because we used to talk about everything and I miss that. We used to laugh at stupid stuff and I miss that. We used to punch one another in the arm, work on our cars together, tell lies, talk about kids--and I miss all of that. We used to get sad together, remembering the things in the past. We made a vow never to talk about those things outside of our friendship and I need to talk about them with you.

I'm still the same. Nothing inside has changed, only the outside. That's why you don't need to feel uncomfortable around me. We've traveled too many miles together to let something like this come between us. So I'm asking you--call me. Come visit. Let's talk about today, tomorrow, ten years from now, because the future will be so much richer if you're around, and so much poorer without you.

Sure, I'm battling a chronic physical condition, but you snore. So I'd say we all have problems.

I've missed you. As always, I'll be here for you, waiting for you to call.

Sincerely, Your friend

Like hundreds of other Internet support-group list keepers, Bob Broedel has helped to create an important outpost on the new frontier of online self-help.

Health Online Distinguished Achievement Award

To: Bob Broedel

For: *ALS Digest*

The Brain Tumor Mailing List (BRAINTMR)

In describing this list, I can do no better than to quote the following (lightly edited) e-mail message from Samantha Scolamiero, the group's founder:

As a brain tumor survivor, I began BRAINTMR in 1993 with the simple hope of helping people concerned with brain tumors share information and experiences. In less than two years BRAINTMR has moved far beyond that initial vision.

Of our 650 members, roughly three-fourths are patients and family members. We layfolk share information and advice about the best medical centers, about little-known clinical trials, nutrition, rehabilitation, alternative therapies, doctor/patient relationships, and other resources on the Internet. Patients use printouts of list messages to get their doctors to help them sign up for the latest clinical trials.

The issues and problems we deal with on the list are more immediate and useful than information gathered from books, articles and other sources. The list helps to ease our isolation and depression and provides us with a coping strategy for difficult times. People who might be intimidated by face-to-face meetings can participate in a friendly, non-clinical, mutually-supportive exchange. BRAINTMR is a welcome haven for those with no local group. And with adaptive input/output equipment, even the disabled can participate.

About one-fourth of our members are neurosurgeons, nurses, psychologists, epidemiologists, pathologists, social workers and other clinicians and researchers. Our doctor members have told me that monitoring the list helps them understand the specific physical, emotional and spiritual needs of their patients. Such insights can be difficult in the midst of a busy clinical practice.

Countless printouts from our list circulate among brain tumor specialists. One list participant, a faculty member at a major U.S. brain tumor research center, routinely forwards list messages to forty-eight colleagues. Armed with our printouts, an oncologist in a developing country convinces colleagues to try new treatment options.

List members--layfolk and professionals alike--have moved beyond the old, obsolete mindset that holds that only certain "qualified" medical professionals may create and disseminate medical information. We layfolk are learning that we are

qualified through our experience, our knowledge, and our concern. We now see that we are capable of contributions no professional can make, and that by linking our efforts in a
coordinated team, we can advance the well-being of all.
    By breaking down the rigid social boundaries between doc-
tors, patients, and researchers, the Brain Tumor Network is
pointing the way toward a new type of participatory medicine
in which *all* those concerned with a given health problem
can work together as colleagues.

Samantha J. Scolamiero
Founder and facilitator
BRAINTMR mailing list
samajane@sasquatch.com

As Ed Madara wrote in a recent e-mail, "Samantha's work epitomizes what online self-help is all about."

**Health Online Distinguished
Achievement Award**

To: Samantha J. Scolamiero

For: The BRAINTMR mailing list

Weights

Another interesting example of a health-oriented support-group mailing list is the daily e-mail letter *Weights*. The list is owned by Mike Sullivan (sullivan@fa.disney.com), a serious recreational bodybuilder who does the newsletter "at break times, lunch time, and as I'm getting ready to leave in the evening. Since the newsletter consists entirely of incoming postings by other list members, it takes very little time to do."

Many of the postings sound like conversations you might overhear in a bodybuilding-oriented health club. Here's the heading and table of contents from a recent issue:

```
From: weights@fa.disney.com
X-From: sullivan@fa.disney.com
Reply-to: weights@fa.disney.com
To: weights-list@fa.disney.com

   Weights, Number 969

Today's Topics:

14 year-old needs help gaining weight?
Aesthetics
Bench Shirt & Squat Suit?
Gyms and training partner in the Cupertino area?
Gyms in Atlanta?
Re: Increasing Bench and Squat
Leg Presses vs. Squats?
Re: Lower Back Blues
Met-Rx
Reactions to Scott's Articles
Re: SHOULDER INJURY
Scott Carrell's Mailings
Sound BB Nutrition?
Re: Tendonitis?
Training Software for an Atari?
Ultimate Diet Book Update
WA/OR show
Re: Workout Schedules
chest help?
Re: freak show or health show
```

Here is one representative exchange from the *Weights* newsletter:

```
Q. When I work my chest, I can never get a pump, let alone a
burn, it seems my triceps give out too soon. Is there anyway
I can continue working my chest after my arms give out?

A. You are probably *overtraining*! I do biceps once every
other week for about 8 TOTAL exercises and they are pretty
big. And I can't move my arms when I leave the gym. I can't
even take my sports bra off! Your biceps and triceps get
worked whenever you do back, chest/shoulders, respectively.
So remember, MORE IS NOT ALWAYS BETTER!!!!!!!!!
```

To sign up for *ALS Digest*, *BRAINTMR*, or *Weights*, consult the alphabetical listings later in this chapter.

On Moderated and Unmoderated Lists

One nice thing about both Bob Broedel's list (the ALS Interest Group-ALS Digest) and Michael Sullivan's list (Weights) is that they are *moderated* lists; i.e., they're edited by a person, not a computer program. That means that Bob and Michael personally receive postings from list members and place them (edited or not) in the outgoing newsletter or digest. Irrelevant items are edited out. So as a list member, you see only worthwhile postings.

Many Internet mailing lists are operated not by human beings but by computer programs called *mail servers*. The most widely used mail server program is called Listserv, usually displayed in all-caps: LISTSERV. Other popular mail server programs include Listproc, Mailbase, Mailserv, and Majordomo.

The directions for signing up differ from list to list, as you'll see in the listings that follow. When you sign up for a mailing list, you will frequently receive a more extensive set of commands and directions you can use to make the mail server perform certain functions, e.g., subscribe, unsubscribe, switch to a digest, suspend mailings, or to obtain a list of subscribers or other files via e-mail.

While these automated programs can doubtlessly save much human labor, the machines are not able to distinguish between the wheat and the chaff. If no human editor intervenes, they will automatically send *everything* they receive forward to the entire list.

Some lists operated by a mail server therefore contain many irrelevant, off-topic, or carelessly produced postings. A few contain angry or abusive messages that a human list keeper might edit or omit. When computer-managed lists drift in the direction of a high proportion of negative or irrelevant postings, list members typically post increasing numbers of complaints. The whole business can proceed to the point where the negative messages far outnumber the useful ones. Flame wars may break out. Then, typically, most or all of the members will abandon the list. An active moderator can prevent that from happening.

Some automated lists work just fine and none of these problems seem to arise. But in browsing through the lists I visited for this chapter, I frequently found myself wishing that more of them saw the kindly, beneficial hand of a human moderator.

Netiquette for Mailing Lists and Newsgroups

Here's an exceptionally levelheaded posting I found on one mailing list in the midst of a pretty bad flame war. The author clearly has a good deal of experience and knows what she's talking about.

```
Subj: tips and hints for mailing list users...
Most of you have probably seen the recent series of flame-
filled messages and all the wonderful sentiments they con-
tained. As a veteran of many Internet mailing lists and
newsgroups, I'd like to offer some personal guidelines I've
found useful:
1. First of all, don't flame. A flame is a violent verbal
attack by someone who's angry, insensitive, insecure, or hos-
tile. Some formerly excellent lists have become scorched
plains because of the all-too-public flames. Not only is this
bad "netiquette" but it's a damned shame. Flaming is for
losers. Don't flame. Don't say anything that hurts.
2. Treat everyone on the list like friends and colleagues.
That means don't pump people for information unless you're
giving them something in exchange. If you have a personal
gripe or kudos for someone, write them personally. Don't sub-
ject the whole list and waste tons of bandwidth with "Way to
go!" or "I agree!" or the ever-dreaded "Ditto!" Arrrrgh!
3. Internet mailing lists are places for smart, caring people
to come together to share news, views, tips, hints, and expe-
riences of all types. Many lists encourage users to lurk for
a while before posting. Others encourage new users to jump
right in. No matter what list you're on, it *is* a good idea
to lurk for at least a few days, then jump in with a self-
introduction, which should include your name, your geographic
area, and your interests, along with what brings you to the
group.
4. If you find you don't like a list, simply unsubscribe
without comment. And if you want to unsubscribe (or to give
any other commands on the way you want your email to come to
you) WRITE TO THE LISTSERV, not to the list! And for God's
sake please don't write directly to the list and then say
"unsubscribe."
5. Remember that all these online resources are like virtual
babies--and all babies need lots of nurturing, stimulation
and care... ;-)
Cheers,
Katie Lindsey (952lindsey@alpha.nlu.edu)
```

Your Mailing List Master File

Before you start signing up for the lists in this chapter, please consider this suggestion: Set up a new folder on your hard disk where you'll keep the essential information about *all* the mailing lists you've subscribed to (or are considering subscribing to). I call mine "Mailing Lists Master." The contents of that file currently look something like this:

```
ALS Digest (On)
CancerNet (Off)
Couples-L (On)
Health Matrix-L (On)
I-Net Happenings (Off)
McLuhan List (On)
New List (On)
Self-Help List (On)
Stock-Picking (Off)
Weights (On)
```

The purpose of your mailing list master file is to keep a copy of the vital information for each list you subscribe to, including *how to unsubscribe from the list*. It's especially important to keep this kind of information for a list run by a mail server, as the server will accept your command to unsubscribe to the list only *if you have it exactly right*, and it may not be easy to contact the list keeper directly.

Your mailing list master file is a good place to save other useful information about the lists you are interested in as well, e.g., interesting quotes from the list, instructions for getting back issues or FAQs, a list of commands that work with that mail server, and guidelines for retrieving files via gopher, ftp, or the World Wide Web.

You can also use your mailing list master file to keep track of lists that you have currently turned on or off. Turning off a list is a good way to handle high-volume lists when you'll be away from your computer or when you're preoccupied by other projects. (Turning off most of my lists helped me get this book done.) If you note on or off for each list, a glance at your mailing list master file directory will provide a quick view of the lists you currently subscribe to.

Mailing List Overload

I'm writing this on a rickety bedside table in an obscure motel in southwestern Colorado. I've been trying to log on to my computer network to get my e-mail. But it's taking a long, long time.

The problem is, just before starting out on this trip, I signed up for a couple of new mailing lists. I didn't realize they were so active. There's so much traffic from these lists that it's taking forever for my e-mail to make its way through my modem. It's got my system all tied up.

The moral: Be careful in signing up for new Internet mailing lists. You may get flooded. Be careful not to sign up for new lists when you'll be away from your computer for several days. And be sure you've saved the unsubscribe information for the list in the mailing list master file you were clever enough to set up. Otherwise, you may find yourself stuck for hours in a crummy motel somewhere in the Rocky Mountains—as I am right now.

Representative Self-Help Mailing Lists

There are thousands of self-help mailing lists, with dozens more being added every day. The very selective listing below gives some of the best I found in my explorations, but don't stop with these. Ask other online self-helpers to recommend their favorite mailing lists. And consider starting your own (see p. 198). A later section of this chapter offers some suggestions for finding additional lists.

When you subscribe to most of these lists, you'll receive a welcome packet containing more information about the list. Save it in your mailing list master file for future reference.

AIDS and HIV

ABBS: Worldwide AIDS BBS Mailing List

ABBS is a worldwide list of bulletin boards that carry AIDS-related files and conferences. It's a read-only list and is updated monthly.

To subscribe: Send the message "subscribe abbs" to abbs-request@tde.com.

To unsubscribe: Send the message "unsubscribe abbs" to the same address.

Owner: Norman Brown (norman.brown@tde.com).

Allergies

The Allergy Discussion List

The Allergy Discussion List covers all types of human allergies. General topics include how allergies influence our health and lifestyles, treatments for allergies, personal stories, self-help guidelines, prevention and management of allergy symptoms, allergy support systems, and basic facts about allergies. Specific topics include sinusitis, asthma, hives, itchiness, puffiness, nasal allergies, and respiratory difficulties. Friends and family of the allergic are also welcome.

To subscribe: Send the message "subscribe allergy" followed by your real name to listserv@tamvm1.tamu.edu.

To unsubscribe: Send the message "unsubscribe allergy" followed by your real name to the same address.

E-mail: relevance@immune.com.

Owner: Ballew Kinnaman (kinnaman@immune.com).

For more information: Contact allergy-request@tamvm1.tamu.edu.

Additional notes: Archives are available through the list's World Wide Web home page (http://tamvm1.tamu.edu/~allergy/). You can get a list of available files by sending the message "index allergy" to the LISTSERV address. Leave the subject line blank.

Alzheimer's Disease

ALZHEIMER

ALZHEIMER is an e-mail discussion group for patients, professional and family caregivers, researchers, public policy makers, students, and anyone with an interest in Alzheimer's disease or related dementing disorders in older adults. It is intended to give interested individuals from various perspectives an opportunity to share questions, answers, suggestions, and tips.

To subscribe: Send the message "subscribe alzheimer" to majordomo@wubios.wustl.edu.

To unsubscribe: Send the message "unsubscribe alzheimer" to the same address.

Owner: Alzheimer's Disease Research Center, Washington University School of Medicine, Saint Louis, Missouri (alzheimer-owner@wubios.wustl.edu).

Amyotrophic Lateral Sclerosis (ALS, Lou Gehrig's Disease)

The ALS Interest Group-ALS Digest

The ALS Interest Group-ALS Digest is devoted to the discussion of all aspects of amyotrophic lateral sclerosis. The focus is on support, information, current research, drug treatments, and just a bit of gentle social activism. Participants include a blend of ALS patients, their friends, family members, health professionals, and ALS researchers.

To subscribe: Send a message to list moderator Bob Broedel at bro@huey.met.fsu.edu.

To unsubscribe: Send a message to list moderator Bob Broedel at the same address.

Owner: Bob Broedel.

Attention Deficit Disorder (ADD)

ADD-PARENTS

ADD-PARENTS offers support, information, and discussion for the parents of children with attention deficit or hyperactivity disorder. Typical participants include parents, educators, and some older children with ADD.

To subscribe: Send the message "subscribe add-parents" to majordomo@mv.mv.com.

To unsubscribe: Send the message "unsubscribe add-parents" to the same address.

E-mail: add-parents-approval@mv.mv.com.

Additional notes: To find out more about the server and the commands it understands, send the message "help" to majordomo@mv.mv.com.

Bisexual Women

BiFem-L

BiFem-L is a high-volume, moderated, women-only mailing list for those who are bisexual or "bi-friendly." It provides a safe online community for those who would like to express their own opinions and share their experiences. The list may not be used to solicit sexual partners.

To subscribe: Send the message "subscribe bifem-l" followed by your last name, first name to listserv@brownvm.brown.edu.

To unsubscribe: Send the message "unsubscribe bifem-l" followed by your last name, first name to the same address.

Owner: Elaine Brennan (elaine@netcom.com).

Additional notes: Anonymous posting is available. Contact the list owner for details.

Bodybuilding

Weights

Weights offers discussion, support, and questions and answers on weight training and related topics for beginning, intermediate, and serious bodybuilders and for those interested in weightlifting.

To subscribe: Send a message to weights-request@fa.disney.com.

To unsubscribe: Send a message to the same address.

To post a message to the list: Send it to weights@fa.disney.com.

Owner: Michael Sullivan (sullivan@fa.disney.com).

Additional notes: For a copy of the FAQ, send the message "frequent" to weights-back-issues@fa.disney.com. Back issues are also available; see the FAQ for details.

The Women's Bodybuilding Forum

The Women's Bodybuilding Forum is a mailing list for muscular women, female bodybuilders, and their fans and admirers. The purpose of the list is to support those female athletes who have attained the goal of physical mass, definition, and strength. The list is open to female bodybuilders as well as other women athletes who seek to develop and exhibit their physical prowess.

To subscribe: Send the message "subscribe femuscle" to femuscle-request@lightning.com.

To unsubscribe: Send the message "unsubscribe femuscle" to the same address.

Bone Marrow Transplants

BMT-Talk

BMT-Talk is a moderated mailing list for the discussion of bone marrow transplants. List keeper Laurel Simmons writes: "I had a bone marrow transplant in 1987 for chronic myelogenous leukemia . . . and . . . I have a million stories, anecdotes, experiences, complaints, feelings, and thoughts about the transplant process. I believe that the more people know, the better they will be prepared for a very tough but very doable experience."

To subscribe: Send the message "subscribe" to bmt-talk-request@ai.mit.edu.

To unsubscribe: Send the message "unsubscribe" to the same address.

To post a message to the list: Send it to bmt-talk@ai.mit.edu.

Owner: Laurel Simmons (laurel@ai.mit.edu, http://www.ai.mit.edu/people/laurel/laurel.html).

Additional notes: Archives are available on the list's World Wide Web home page (http://www.ai.mit.edu/people/laurel/Bmt-talk/maillist.html).

Brain Tumors

BRAINTMR: The Brain Tumor Discussion List

BRAINTMR provides discussion, information, and support for people with all types of brain tumors, whether benign or malignant. Information and experiences are shared among brain tumor patients, their families and supporters, all kinds of concerned medical professionals, medical educators, and researchers who study brain tumor growth or treatment. Discussions include conversations among patients and families dealing with the same tumor type, bulletins on the latest brain tumor research, the emotional aspects of brain tumor diagnosis and treatment, and the impact of brain tumors on individuals, society, and the practice of medicine. The list is open to anyone concerned with these topics.

To subscribe: Send the message "subscribe braintmr" followed by your real name to listserv@mitvma.mit.edu.

To unsubscribe: Send the message "unsubscribe braintmr" to the same address.

To post a message to the list: Send it to braintmr@mitvma.mit.edu.

Owner: Samantha Scolamiero (samajane@sasquatch.com).

For more information: Send the message "help" to the LISTSERV address.

Cancer

BREAST-CANCER

BREAST-CANCER provides discussion and support for women with breast cancer and their friends, families, and helping professionals. The list serves as a safe forum in which breast cancer patients and their loved ones can share their frustrations and victories and can offer alternative strategies in dealing with the disease, their medical professionals, and their medical institutions and can develop insights into the psychosocial management of their lives. It is open to all issues relating to breast cancer, including mainstream and alternative treatments, recent medical advances, personal experiences, mutual support, and the work of various grassroots breast cancer advocacy groups worldwide. The list does not advocate for any particular therapies, but seeks to increase the information available on all options and choices.

To subscribe: Send the message "subscribe breast-cancer" followed by your real name to listserv@morgan.ucs.mun.ca.

To unsubscribe: Send the message "unsubscribe breast-cancer" to the same address.

To post a message to the list: Send it to breastcancer@morgan.ucs.mun.ca.

E-mail: jchurch@kean.ucs.mun.ca.

Owner: Jon G. Church, Ph.D., Terry Fox Cancer Research Labs, Memorial University of Newfoundland.

For more information: Send the message "information breast-cancer" to the LISTSERV address.

CancerNet

CancerNet provides a quick and easy way to obtain a wide variety of in-depth cancer information from the National Cancer Institute's Physician Data Query (PDQ) system. It's an invaluable resource for all self-helpers concerned with cancer.

To subscribe: Send the message "subscribe" to cancernet@icicb.nci.nigh.gov.

To unsubscribe: Send the message "unsubscribe" to the same address.

Additional notes: When you subscribe, you'll receive a listing of available files and their request codes. Selected information is also available in Spanish. Some files are quite long—many exceed 100K—so check your mailbox and storage capacity before submitting requests. If you have problems accessing CancerNet, call (301) 496-7403 or send the message "help" to cheryl@icicb.nci.nih.gov.

The Ovarian-Cancer List

The Ovarian-Cancer List provides support and discussion for woman dealing with ovarian cancer. It is also open to their friends and family and interested health professionals. Topics include personal experiences, information about the disease, treatments, surgery, drugs, current research, and whatever else its members want to discuss.

To subscribe: Send the message "subscribe ovarian-cancer" to listserv@ist01.ferris.edu.

To unsubscribe: Send the message "unsubscribe ovarian-cancer" to the same address.

Owner: Carol Fortune (cfortune@ist01.ferris.edu).

Celiac Disease (Celiac Sprue)

CELIAC: Gluten and Wheat Intolerance List

CELIAC is a discussion list for and about people with celiac disease, gluten intolerance, wheat allergy, and similar conditions. (Others interested in these conditions are also welcome.) Topics include reviews of the latest scientific research, information on gluten-free foods, recipes, mail-order suppliers, tips on eating while away from home, and guidelines for coping with these conditions.

To subscribe: Send the message "subscribe celiac" followed by your real name to listserv@sjuvm.stjohns.edu.

To unsubscribe: Send the message "unsubscribe celiac" to the same address.

To post a message to the list: Send it to celiac@sjuvm.stjohns.edu.

Owners: Michael Jones (michael.jones@cfcs.oau.org) and Evan A. C. Hunt (evanh@sco.com).

For more information: Send the message "help" to the LISTSERV address.

Additional notes: To obtain a list of files in the archives, send the message "index celiac" to the LISTSERV address.

Chronic Fatigue Syndrome (CFS)

Cathar-M

Cathar-M is a monthly magazine featuring personal insights, humor, and poetry by and about people who have or are involved with CFS. It welcomes submissions, particularly those focusing on long-term CFS. Topics include personal health, intellect, and creativity.

To subscribe: Send the message "sub cathar-m" followed by your real name to listserve@sjuvm.stjohns.edu.

To unsubscribe: Send the message "unsub cathar-m" to the same address.

To post a message to the list: Send it to cathar-m@sjuvm.stjohns.edu.

Moderator: Molly Holzschlag, editor and publisher (mollyh@indirect.com).

Additional notes: A multimedia version is available on the magazine's World Wide Web home page (http://www.indirect.com/user/mollyh/cath.html). Archives are available via gopher at gopher sjuvm.stjohns.edu.

CFS-L: Chronic Fatigue Syndrome Discussion List

CFS-L provides discussion of chronic fatigue syndrome, also known as myalgic encephalomyelitis (ME) and immune dysfunction syndrome (CFIDS). Most participants are people with CFS. It emphasizes support and the exchange of information.

To subscribe: Send the message "sub cfs-l" followed by your real name to listserv@list.nih.gov.

To unsubscribe: Send the message "unsub cfs-l" to the same address.

To post a message to the list: Send it to cfs-l@list.nih.gov.

Moderator: Roger Burns (cfs-l-request@list.nih.gov).

Additional notes: A daily digest is available—once you've subscribed, send the message "set cfs-l digest" to the LISTSERV address. For a list of archives available, send the message "get cfs-l filelist" to the LISTSERV address. The list can also be followed by reading the Internet newsgroup *alt.med.cfs*.

CFS-NEWS: Chronic Fatigue Syndrome Electronic Newsletter

CFS-NEWS is a monthly newsletter of medical news and other items of interest for the chronic fatigue syndrome community. Typical participants are people with CFS and medical professionals concerned with this condition.

To subscribe: Send the message "sub cfs-news" followed by your real name to listserv@list.nih.gov.

To unsubscribe: Send the message "unsub cfs-news" to the same address.

E-mail: cfs-news@list.nih.gov.

Moderator: Roger Burns (cfs-newsrequest@list.nih.gov).

Additional notes: For a list of back issues and articles, send the message "get cfs-news index" to the LISTSERV address.

CFS-WIRE: CFS Newswire Service

CFS-WIRE is a weekly collection of news articles about chronic fatigue syndrome. Most of the postings come from editors of CFS newsletters and CFS group coordinators.

To subscribe: Send the message "sub cfs-wire" followed by your real name to listserv@sjuvm.stjohns.edu.

To unsubscribe: Send the message "unsub cfs-wire" to the same address.

To post a message to the list: Use cfs-wire@sjuvm.stjohns.edu.

Moderator: CFS/ME Computer Networking Project (cfs-wire-request@sjuvm.stjohns.edu).

Additional notes: For a list of available archives, send the message "get cfs-wire filelist" to the LISTSERV address. For a help file describing other CFS resources on the Internet, send the command "get cfs-net txt" to the same address.

Couples

Couples-L

Couples-L offers discussion, information, and support for those wishing to explore their significant relationships. Frequent subjects include sex, love, romance, and partner dynamics. Recent topics included romantic getaways and special moments, long-distance relationships, the fair division of household chores, sex talk—what works for you and what doesn't, and issues raised in the television show *Mad About You*.

To subscribe: Send the message "sub couples-l" followed by your real name to listserv@cornell.edu. Leave the subject line blank.

To unsubscribe: Send the message "unsub couples-l" to the same address.

Owners: Chuck Goelzer Lyons and Gil Emery (couples-owners-l@cornell.edu).

Additional notes: This is a very active list. A daily digest is available.

Cystic Fibrosis (CF)

CYSTIC-L: Discussion of the Impact of Cystic Fibrosis

CYSTIC-L provides discussion and support for people with cystic fibrosis and their friends and families. It is a forum for CF patients to vent about difficult experiences with their disease and frustrating encounters with the medical profession and institutions, to discuss ways of countering bias that may exist in job or school-related activities, to talk about the myriad of factors that make the lives of people with CF quite different from those with functioning chloride channels, and to discuss new therapeutic and nutritional treatments.

To subscribe: Send the message "subscribe cystic-l" followed by your real name to listserv@yalevm.cis.yale.edu.

To unsubscribe: Send the message "unsub cystic-l" to the same address.

To post a message to the list: Send it to cystic-l@yalevm.cis.yale.edu.

Owner: Antony Dugdale (antdugl@minerva.cis.yale.edu).

For more information: Send the message "help" to the LISTSERV address.

Depression

The Walkers-in-Darkness Discussion List

The Walkers-in-Darkness Discussion List offers support, discussion, and community for those dealing with depression and associated problems. It is open to sufferers from depression or bipolar disorder and affected friends—both "novices" and experienced self-helpers who have learned to cope with these conditions.

To subscribe: Send the message "subscribe walkers-in-darkness" to majordomo@world.std.com.

To unsubscribe: Send the message "unsubscribe walkers-in-darkness" to the same address.

To post a message to the list: Send it to walkers-in-darkness@world.std.com.

Owner: David Harmon (dmh@world.std.com).

For more information: Send the message "help" to majordomo@world.std.com.

DEPRESS Mailing List

The DEPRESS Mailing List provides ongoing conversation and support for those dealing with depression. Inspired by the *Soundprint* public radio documentary program "A Suffering Mind: Depression," produced by Stephen Smith of Minnesota Public Radio, it is a busy list with many appeals for help and many wise and compassionate responses from self-helpers with many years of experience at self-management.

To subscribe: Send the message "subscribe depress" to listserv@soundprint.brandywine.american.edu.

To unsubscribe: Send the message "unsubscribe depress" to the same address.

Owner: Beth Lewand (beth@soundprint.brandywine.american.edu).

Diabetes

The Diabetic Mailing List

Information and support for people with type I and type II diabetes and their friends, families, and those who care for them. Most participants are diabetics; a few are medical professionals.

To subscribe: Send the message "subscribe diabetic" followed by your real name to listserv@lehigh.edu. Leave the subject line blank.

To unsubscribe: Send the message "unsub diabetic" to the same address.

To post a message to the list: Send it to diabetic@lehigh.edu.

Owner: Steve Roseman (lusgr@lehigh.edu).

Additional notes: To receive the digest version send the message "set diabetic digest" to the LISTSERV address.

Disabilities

DADVOCAT: Fathers of Children with Disabilities

A forum by and for the fathers of children with disabilities or other special needs. DADVOCAT is open to anyone who cares for children with disabilities or other special health needs. (Note: "DADVOCAT" rhymes with "advocate.")

To subscribe: Send the message "subscribe dadvocat" followed by your real name to listserv@ukcc.uky.edu.

To unsubscribe: Send the message "unsub dadvocat" to the same address.

To post a message to the list: Send it to dadvocat@ukcc.uky.edu.

Owner: Bob Moore (str002@ukcc.uky.edu).

MOBILITY

Mobility provides discussion and support to help disabled persons gain access and mobility. Topics include public transportation, communications, cellular phones, socializing and dating, and education and employment.

To subscribe: Send the message "subscribe mobility" followed by your real name to listserv@sjuvm.stjohns.edu.

To unsubscribe: Send the message "unsub mobility" to the same address.

To post a message to the list: Send it to mobility@sjuvm.stjohns.edu.

Owner: Robert Mauro (rmauro@delphi.com).

Endometriosis

WITSENDO

WITSENDO offers discussion and support for all aspects of endometriosis. Most subscribers are women who suffer from this condition, and the emphasis is on coping with the disease and exploring possible treatments. Professionals are welcome, but since the list is primarily for the women suffering from the disease, they're urged to avoid authoritarian attitudes and professional jargon.

To subscribe: Send the message "subscribe witsendo" followed by your real name to listserv@dartmouth.edu.

To unsubscribe: Send the message "signoff witsendo" to the same address.

Moderator: John Bullock (jbullock@sednet.mcd.on.ca).

Additional notes: Archives are available.

Grief and Loss

GriefNet

GriefNet is a discussion list for those dealing with grief and loss. Common topics include death, dying, bereavement, physical disabilities, and other major emotional and physical losses. Participants include both professionals and layfolk. The group maintains the Bereavement and Loss Resources Directory, which lists support groups and other organizations concerned with these issues; the Professional Resources Directory, which lists professionals offering services for people dealing with major losses; and the Annotated Bibliography, a list of books, periodicals, articles, movies, and audio and visual tapes.

To subscribe: Send the message "subscribe griefnet" followed by your e-mail address to subscribe@rivendell.org.

To unsubscribe: Send the message "unsubscribe griefnet" followed by your e-mail address to the same address.

E-mail: cendra@rivendell.org.

Health and Medical Resources on the Internet

HMATRIX-L: A Discussion of Online Health Resources

Originally established for medical librarians, researchers, and clinicians, HMATRIX-L features listings and discussions of a wide variety of professional and popular online health resources. It is open to medical professionals involved in academic, clinical, and research areas, medical librarians, patients, online self-helpers, and other interested lay persons and professionals. Most sources listed are targeted at medical professionals, but the sophisticated lay user will find much of interest here as well. I highly recommend the list to all online self-helpers. In addition to this list, Lee Hancock and his colleagues provide a number of other unique and useful Internet resources for the entire online health community (see p. 268).

To subscribe: Send the message "subscribe hmatrix-l" followed by your real name to listserv@kumchttp.mc.ukans.edu.

To unsubscribe: Send the message "unsubscribe hmatrix-l" to the same address.

To post a message to the list: Send it to hmatrix-l@kumchttp.mc.ukans.edu.

Owner: Lee Hancock (le07144@ukanvm.cc.ukans.edu).

For more information: Send the message "help" to the LISTSERV address.

Homosexuality and Medicine

GLB-MEDICAL: Homosexuality and the Medical Profession

GLB-MEDICAL provides discussion of a wide range of issues related to homosexuality and the medical profession. Topics include being out (or not) as a medical student or professional; discrimination as experienced by gay, lesbian, or bisexual physicians and patients; special considerations for gay and lesbian patients with respect to such issues as suicide, addiction, abuse, gay bashing, and sexually transmitted diseases; and anything else relating to the experience of being a homosexual or interacting with homosexuals and the medical or allied medical professions. Personal anecdotes, opinions, original research, news, and requests for information are welcome. Confidentiality will be respected regarding the user names on the mailing list.

To subscribe: Send the message "sub glb-medical" to mailserv@ac.dal.ca.

To unsubscribe: Send the message "unsub glb-medical" to the same address.

To post a message to the list: Send it to glb-medical@ac.dal.ca.

Owner: Kevin Speight (kevinsp8@ac.dal.ca).

Additional notes: Address queries concerning the list or requests for items to be posted anonymously to the moderator.

Inflammatory Bowel Diseases (Crohn's Disease and Ulcerative Colitis)

The IBD List Digest

The IBD List Digest provides information, discussion, and support for those suffering from inflammatory bowel diseases, including but not limited to Crohn's disease (an inflammatory condition of the small intestine), and ulcerative colitis. Participants include people with these conditions, their relatives and friends, and medical professionals.

As we went to press, the subscription information for this list was about to change. For more information, send e-mail to the list moderator, Thomas Lapp at thomas%mvac23@louie.udel.edu or lapptl@wmvx.dnet.dupont.com.

Low-Fat Diets

FATFREE

FATFREE provides discussion and support for extremely low-fat vegetarianism—the type of diet championed by John McDougall and Dean Ornish. The emphasis is on consuming less than 15 percent of your calories as fat. Recipes exclude all meat, fish, and poultry, but may include milk, eggs, or honey. Regular members receive individual messages throughout the day. Digest members receive just one e-mail message each day containing all the previous day's messages.

To subscribe: Send the message "add" to join as a regular member or "add digest" to join as a digest member to fatfree-request@hustle.rahul.net.

To unsubscribe: Send the message "remove" or "remove digest" to the same address.

Owner: Michelle Dick (artemis@rahul.net).

Lyme Disease

LYMENET-L

LYMENET-L is an e-mail newsletter with summaries of the latest news and information on Lyme disease, the fastest growing infectious disease in the United States. Topics include new treatment protocols, research news, and political events.

To subscribe: Send the message "subscribe lymenet-l" followed by your real name to listserv@lehigh.edu.

To unsubscribe: Send the message "unsubscribe lymenet-l" to the same address.

To post a message to the list: Send it to lymenet-l@lehigh.edu.

Owner: Marc Gabriel (a229@lehigh.edu).

Additional notes: You can receive the LymeNet Resource Guide by sending a message to resource-guide@lymenet.org. LYMENET maintains a gopher site at gopher://gopher.lymenet.org. File archives may be obtained using ftp at ftp://ftp.lehigh.edu/pub/listserv/lymenet-l/newsletters. This mailing list is echoed to the newsgroup *sci.med*.

For more information: Send the message "help" to the LISTSERV address.

Menopause

MENOPAUS

MENOPAUS is devoted to discussions of menopause, its symptoms, and treatments—both traditional and alternative. Most subscribers are 35- to 60-year-old women, but the list includes doctors who offer useful medical advice and answer questions too embarrassing to ask anyone else and a scientist who is doing research on osteoporosis. A warm, caring group of women helping other women. This is a very busy list, but there is a digest version. Archives also are available.

To subscribe: Send the message "subscribe menopaus" followed by your real name to listserv@psuhmc.hmc.psu.edu.

To unsubscribe: Send the message "signoff menopause" followed by your real name to the same address.

To post a message to the list: Send it to menopaus@psuhmc.hmc.psu.edu.

Owner: Judy Bayliss (jbayliss@psuhmc.hmc.psu.edu).

For more information: Send the message "help" to listserv@psuhmc.hmc.psu.edu.

Mental Health

MADNESS

A discussion list for people who experience mood swings, fright, voices, and visions ("People Who"), MADNESS creates an electronic forum and distribution device for exchanging ways to change political systems that touch People Who and for distributing any information and resources that might be useful.

A basic premise of science and research is also a value of MADNESS—to share your findings with others.

To subscribe: Send the message "subscribe madness" followed by your real name to listserv@sjuvm.stjohns.edu.

To unsubscribe: Send the message "unsubscribe madness" followed by your real name to the same address.

Owner: Sylvia Caras (sylviac@netcom.com).

Obsessive-Compulsive Disorder (OCD)

OCD-L: The Obsessive-Compulsive Disorder and Life Discussion List

OCD-L offers support and discussion for people who have or are concerned with obsessive-compulsive disorder. Questions or comments on any OCD-related topic are welcome. Most participants are people with OCD and their family and friends. Interested professionals are also encouraged to subscribe and share their knowledge with other participants.

To subscribe: Send the message "subscribe ocd-l" followed by your real name to listserv@vm.marist.edu.

To unsubscribe: Send the message "unsubscribe ocd-l" to the same address.

To post a message to the list: Send it to ocd-l@vm.marist.edu.

Owner: Chris Vertullo (jzid@maristb.marist.edu).

For more information: Send the message "help" to the LISTSERV address.

Additional notes: To obtain a list of files in the archives, send the message "index ocd-l" to the LISTSERV address.

Online Support and Counseling Services

dnet: Dignity Net

Dnet is a discussion group for those involved in facilitating online support and counseling services. Participants share experiences about setting up and maintaining a variety of types of online services that dignify and empower people through computer networking. New members are invited to post a short self-introduction. This is a particularly useful list for online self-helpers and health professionals seeking to learn more about online interactions with clients.

To subscribe: Send the message "subscribe dnet" to majordomo@laplaza.taos.nm.us. No subject line is necessary.

To unsubscribe: Send the message "unsubscribe dnet" to the same address.

Owner: Stewart S. Warren (treedog@laplaza.taos.nm.us).

Parkinson's Disease

PARKINSN

PARKINSN is an information exchange network for individuals interested in Parkinson's disease. Subscribers include persons with the disease, family members and friends, health care workers, researchers, and others wishing to know more about the condition. Any topic related to Parkinson's disease is appropriate for discussion.

To subscribe: Send the message "subscribe parkinsn" followed by your real name to listserv@vm.utcc.utoronto.ca.

To unsubscribe: Send the message "unsubscribe parkinsn" to the same address.

To post a message to the list: Send it to parkinsn@vm.utcc.utoronto.ca.

Owner: Barbara Patterson (patterso@fhs.csu.mcmaster.ca).

For more information: Send the message "help" to the LISTSERV address.

Additional notes: Archives and a digest are available.

Polio

POLIO

POLIO is a mailing list for persons who have polio or who live with or work with persons with polio. Topics include information about polio, how it affects people, how doctors treat it, new therapies, drugs and their side effects, and how to live with post-polio syndrome. The owner, Robert Mauro, contracted polio in 1951 at age 5. He uses a respirator and an electric wheelchair and does all his computing lying down. He has published four books and publishes PeopleNet, an international personals networking newsletter by and for disabled singles.

To subscribe: Send the message "sub polio" followed by your real name to listserv@sjuvm.stjohns.edu.

To unsubscribe: Send the message "unsub polio" followed by your real name to the same address.

To post a message to the list: Send it to polio@sjuvm.stjohns.edu.

Owner: Robert Mauro (rmauro@delphi.com).

Repetitive Strain Injury

RSI-UK: The Repetitive Strain Injury Discussion List

RSI-UK provides discussion and support to repetitive strain injury, tendonitis, tenosynovitis, thoracic syndrome, carpal tunnel syndrome, and other forms of upper-limb disorder. Topics include support groups, books and articles, health facilities, and suppliers of ergonomic equipment. Most contributors are British.

To subscribe: Send the message "subscribe rsi-uk" followed by your real name to listserver@tictac.demon.co.uk.

To unsubscribe: Send the message "unsubscribe rsi-uk" to the same address.

To post a message to the list: Send it to rsi-uk@tictac.demon.co.uk.

Owner: Ellen Mizzell (ellen@tictac.demon.co.uk).

For more information: Send the message "help" to listserver@tictac.demon.co.uk.

Self-Help Research

SLFHLP-L: The Discussion Group for Self-Help Researchers

SLFHLP-L is a scholarly forum primarily for researchers and academics interested in research on self-help and mutual aid. People from many different fields and backgrounds participate in the list: social workers, community psychologists, sociologists, community health workers, self-help clearinghouses, graduate students, and others. Topics include research ideas, designs and methodologies, study results, announcements of upcoming conferences, and professional networking for those in this field. Self-helpers interested in these topics are welcome to participate in the discussions, but the list is not designed to function as an on-line self-help group nor as a referral to self-help groups or organizations.

To subscribe: Send the message "subscribe slfhlp-l" followed by your real name to listserv@vmd.cso.uiuc.edu.

To unsubscribe: Send the message "unsub slfhlp-l" to the same address.

To post a message to the list: Send it to slfhlp-l@vmd.cso.uiuc.edu.

Owner: owner-slfhlp-l@vmd.cso.uiuc.edu.

For more information: Send the message "help" to the LISTSERV address.

Sexual Abuse Survivors

Recovery

Recovery, also known as Survivors Anonymous, provides discussion and support for survivors of childhood sexual abuse, their partners, and interested professionals. Typical participants are sexual abuse survivors from all walks of life. As the moderator writes: "Expressions of support and sharing of one's own experiences are encouraged; unsolicited advice is discouraged. This helps to keep the list a safe, supportive environment for people who may have no other safe forum in which to discuss sensitive abuse issues. The emphasis is on healing and recovery through the use of the Twelve Steps of Alcoholics Anonymous as adapted for our purpose."

To subscribe: Send a message to recovery@wvnvm.wvnet.edu asking to join.

To unsubscribe: Send a message to the same address.

Moderator: Jeff Brooks (jeff@wvnvm.wvnet.edu).

Additional notes: You'll be sent the address for posting messages to the list when you subscribe. All postings go into a digest that is distributed two or three times a week. Unless you request a pseudonym, identifying information is reduced to first name and last initial. Archives are available.

Smoking Cessation

SMOKE-FREE

SMOKE-FREE is a support list for people recovering from addiction to cigarettes. Anybody with an interest in quitting smoking or in helping others quit, including ex-smokers and helping professionals, is encouraged to join the discussion.

To subscribe: Send the message "subscribe smoke-free" followed by your real name to listproc@msstate.edu.

To unsubscribe: Send the message "unsubscribe smoke-free" followed by your real name to the same address.

To post a message to the list: Send it to smoke-free@ra.msstate.edu

Owner: Natalie Maynor (maynor@ra.msstate.edu).

Additional notes: Archives are available.

Stroke

STROKE-L

STROKE-L offers support and shared information, opinions, ideas, and inquiries relating to any stroke-related topic, ranging from interesting experiences to basic science issues.

To subscribe: Send the message "subscribe stroke-l" followed by your real name to listserv@ukcc.uky.edu.

To unsubscribe: Send the message "unsubscribe stroke-l" to the same address.

To post a message to the list: Send it to stroke-l@ukcc.uky.edu.

Owner: Bob Moore (str002@ukcc.uky.edu).

For more information: Send the message "help" to the LISTSERV address.

Stuttering

STUT-HLP

STUT-HLP is a self-help information and support list for people who stutter, their families, and their friends. Most participants are people who stutter, typically adults in their twenties and thirties. This is not an academic discussion list, and "admonitions" from academics and clinicians are discouraged. Professionals are invited to lurk before participating. A digest is available.

To subscribe: Send the message "subscribe stut-hlp" followed by your real name to listproc2@bgu.edu.

To unsubscribe: Send the message "unsubscribe stut-hlp" followed by your real name to the same address.

To post a message to the list: Send it to stut-hlp@bgu.edu.

Moderator: Bob Quesal (r-quesal@bgu.edu).

Wellness

LONGEVITY

LONGEVITY discusses a variety of different ways to extend human life. Topics include diet, vitamin supplements, and new discoveries in science.

To subscribe: Send the message "subscribe longevity" followed by your real name to listserv@vm3090.ege.edu.tr.

To unsubscribe: Send the message "unsubscribe longevity" to the same address.

To post a message to the list: Send all articles to longevity@vm3090.ege.edu.tr.

Owner: postmaster@vm3090.ege.edu.tr.

For more information: Send the message "help" to the LISTSERV address.

MAXLIFE: Positive, Healthy Lifestyles

MAXLIFE is a list for those working toward a positive, healthy lifestyle while at the same time choosing to avoid heavy consumerism. It is intended to offer helpful and healthful ideas, not to pressure people into adopting any particular lifestyle. If you like any of the following publications, you might like this list: *Voluntary Simplicity, One Circle Gardening, Your Money or Your Life, The Utne Reader, Vegetarian Life, Organic Gardening.*

To subscribe: Send the message "subscribe maxlife" followed by your real name to listserv@gibbs.oit.unc.edu.

To unsubscribe: Send the message "unsub maxlife" to the same address.

To post a message to the list: Send it to maxlife@gibbs.oit.unc.edu.

Owners: Sharon Gordon (gordonse@iris.uncg.edu) and Penny Ward (crunchy@email.unc.edu).

For more information: Send the message "help"to the LISTSERV address.

Additional notes: A digest is available—you'll receive instructions on how to receive it when you subscribe.

WELLNESSLIST

WELLNESSLIST provides wide-ranging discussions on nutrition, physical fitness, increasing your life expectancy, and other wellness-related subjects. Topics include healthy recipes, fitness-related product reviews and announcements, and discussions of the books, methods, tips, and solutions recommended by participants. The list is open to anyone interested in these topics. Health professionals, authors, nutritionists, and other experts are invited to share their knowledge.

To subscribe: Send the message "subscribe wellnesslist" to majordomo@wellnessmart.com.

To unsubscribe: Send the message "unsubscribe wellnesslist" to the same address.

To post a message to the list: Send it to wellnesslist@wellnessmart.com.

Owner: George Rust (george@wellnessmart.com or gwrust@crl.com).

For more information: Send the message "help" to majordomo@wellnessmart.com.

Additional notes: A digest is available.

Yeast Infections

YEAST-L

YEAST-L offers support and information for those "suffering from the very real yeast problems that a large part of the medical community is still skeptical about." Topics include yeast overgrowth and yeast allergies, remedies and treatments, and yeast-free recipes. The list is open to anyone interested in candida problems. Most participants have yeast allergies or yeast overgrowth problems. A digest and archives are available.

To subscribe: Send the message "subscribe yeast-l" followed by your real name to listserv@psuhmc.hmc.psu.edu.

To unsubscribe: Send the message "signoff yeast-l" followed by your real name to the same address.

Owner: Judy Bayliss (jbayliss@psuhmc.hmc.psu.edu).

How to Find More Self-Help Internet Mailing Lists

The preceding listings provide some valuable starting points for your explorations of the world of self-help Internet mailing lists. But they're just a representative sample of all the mailing lists that are out there—many good lists will be added or changed since this book went to print.

New lists are started every day, and established lists are often moved, discontinued, or merged into other lists. But don't worry. With a little practice you'll soon learn how to track down the lists (and other resources) you want with a minimum of hassle, even if they've changed or moved. (It can sometimes even be a benefit not to know the exact address of a desired list—while searching, you may come across equally valuable information that you never knew existed.)

Here are two World Wide Web home pages that can help you find additional self-help mailing lists in your areas of interest. (You'll find more on the Web and Web addresses in Chapter 11.)

- http://kuhttp.cc.ukans.edu/cwis/units/medcntr/lee/HOMEPAGE.html will take you to the Medical Matrix.
- http://home.mcom.com/home/internet-directory.html will take you to another good directory that includes self-help mailing lists.

Finally, here is one more mailing list, an extremely valuable one that I would never want to be without.

NEW-LIST

NEW-LIST provides news of new Internet mailing lists on a variety of topics, not just health and medical, and updates and announcements on existing lists. Subscribing is a good way to keep up to date on the rapidly changing world of Internet mailing lists.

To subscribe: Send the message "sub new-list" followed by your real name to listserv@vm1.nodak.edu.

To unsubscribe: Send the message "unsub new-list" followed by your real name to the same address.

Owner: Marty Hoag (hoag@vm1.nodak.edu).

For more information: Send the message "get new-list readme" to the LISTSERV address.

Additional notes: Several extremely useful files are also available. To obtain the document "How to Find an Interesting Mailing List," send the message "get new-list wouters" to the LISTSERV address. To receive a list of online directories of additional Internet mailing lists, send the message "get listsoflists" to the same address.

HOT TIP

In most cases, both commands sent to automated mailing lists and Internet addresses can be all caps, all lowercase, or any combination of the two.

Starting Your Own Mailing List

What if you still can't find a mailing list for your interest? For instance, imagine you're interested in horseback-riding programs for children with handicaps. You've met several people online with the same interest, yet you can't find a mailing list that covers the specific subject. The lists you've found about horses and about handicapped children bring too many messages on other topics to your e-mail box.

If you're faced with a situation like this, think about starting your own mailing list. It's easy and inexpensive, even on a commercial service, if your group starts small. Learn to use your e-mail address book. Many e-mail programs let you group a number of e-mail addresses. Create a group of the people who are interested in your topic. Send them all one message announcing that you'll organize and forward any information on the topic that anyone wants to share with the group. Ask them to spread the word to other people who share your interest.

Collect the material that your group members send you into one large message. Send it out weekly, monthly, or as you choose. Be sure to keep copies of past postings for new members. If the list grows too large to handle by hand, consider a more powerful e-mail manager or a mail server program. Running an electronic mailing list may sound like work, but you'll be surprised at how easy it is and what a powerful tool for online self-help it can be.

Chapter 10

Internet Newsgroups

No matter how bad life gets, there's always time to help someone.

A severely depressed online self-helper
posting on the newsgroup alt.support.depression

AN INTERNET NEWSGROUP is yet another type of electronic "place" where people with similar interests can exchange messages. Many of these groups are devoted to support, health, and medical purposes. Like the self-help mailing lists and the support forums on the commercial services, health- and support-oriented newsgroups offer a way to join an active network of self-helpers in an ongoing discussion of just about any imaginable health-related topic of special interest to you—from alcohol addiction and bulimia to yeast and Zoloft.

Internet newsgroups are also frequently referred to as USENET newsgroups, after the USENET network that makes the newsgroups possible. You may also hear these groups described as USENET news, Net news, network news, or Internet news.

To access the Internet newsgroups use the AOL keyword "Internet," on CompuServe use the command "Go USENET," and on Prodigy use "Jump Internet." If you have a direct Internet connection, you'll need to use a type of software called a newsgroup reader. Your service provider should be able to supply or recommend a suitable program.

"Read My Newsgroups"

To read the Internet newsgroups of your choice, you first need to select (subscribe to) them. You make your selection from a long list featuring *all* the newsgroups available through your service. (You may wish to put together a preliminary list from this chapter.) On later visits, simply click on "Read My Newsgroups" (or a similar command) to choose the groups you want to read from the list you've already selected. You can change the newsgroups on your personal list as your interests change.

Newsgroups are organized into "hierarchies" with a general subject or "category" at the top. The name of a newsgroup always starts with the name of the hierarchy, or category. The names and categories for the most common hierarchies are:

Name	*Hierarchy (category)*
alt	Groups set up using an "alternative" application procedure
comp	Computer-related topics
misc	Miscellaneous groups that don't fit elsewhere
news	Newsgroups and newsgroup software
rec	Recreation, entertainment, and the arts
sci	Scientific topics
soc	Social issues and specific social groups
talk	Current controversies for people who like to argue

HOT TIP

Contrary to a widespread popular belief, the *alt* newsgroups are *not* named for their alternative subject matter, but for the alternative application procedure the groups' originators went through to establish the groups in the first place: It requires a much simpler procedure to establish a new *alt* group than it does to start a group under the other hierarchies.

A Newsgroup for Every Interest

With thousands and thousands of newsgroups—and more coming online every day—there are groups for just about any topic you can think of. Many of the topics might never occur to you, e.g., *alt.tasteless*, *alt.whine*, *alt.devil.bunnies*, and *alt.sex.bestiality.barney* (don't ask). There are also such highly specialized scientific newsgroups as *bionet.genome.chrom22*—for all you fans of human chromosome number twenty-two.

Not all services carry all the newsgroups. If some of the groups you'd like to read don't appear on your system's newsgroup master list, ask your system's customer service representative if they can be added. In many cases, they'll be able to do so quickly and easily.

Here's a randomly chosen list of newsgroups:

Newsgroup	*Subject*
alt.support.depression	Self-help and support for depression
comp.databases	Computer databases
misc.consumers	Topics of interest to consumers
news.announce.newusers	Announcements for new newsgroup users
rec.arts.cinema	Movies and film making
sci.environment	Environmental issues and research studies
soc.culture.japan	Japanese culture
talk.politics.misc	Current political topics

Many of the self-help and support-oriented newsgroups are found under the *alt* hierarchy. And many have a name that looks like this: *alt.support.<topic>*—e.g., *alt.support.arthritis*, *alt.support.step-parents*, or *alt.support.grief*.

Many newsgroups post a periodic introductory message that describes the content, purpose, and customs of the group. Look for this welcome notice the first time you sign on to a new group.

Your First Newsgroup

Let's say you've been dealing with a longstanding low-grade depression, and you're feeling especially low today. You feel you could use a little support and understanding. So you decide to read the latest postings on the newsgroup called *alt.support.depression*.

You fire up your software, log on, click on the commands that take you to the appropriate area of your service, choose the groups you'd like to have on your personal newsgroup list, then click on *"alt.support depression."*

Next thing you know, you find yourself looking at a list of the topics currently under discussion in that newsgroup. The number that follows each subject tells you the number of postings currently available on that thread (a list of postings on a common subject). Let's say this is the topic list:

```
Subject                                          Number
Treatment with Paxil                                  2
Personal Names for Depression                        15
Ramblings Late at Night                               4
Zoloft                                               14
Questions for Dr. Goldberg                            5
What the Hell Am I Doing?????????????????             7
Hateful                                              10
Death of Pet                                         15
The Closet Illness                                   15
Who Cares?                                           10
Caffeine and Depression                               8
```

You find three of these threads especially interesting: "Personal Names for Depression," "Caffeine and Depression," and "The Closet Illness." So you click on each in turn and read the postings they contain. Here are (edited) exchanges you might find under "Personal Names for Depression":

```
Some of us have pet names for the state we get into when
we're depressed. So what do *you* call *your* depression?
```

```
I call it Egbert. It helps to personify it as some dopey
unwelcome house guest. (My apologies to anyone out there
named Egbert.)
```

```
I call mine "the garbage room" after that room in Star Wars
where the walls kept closing in. I think about that scene all
the time. It's a great visual metaphor for the big D.
```

```
Like Winston Churchill, I call my depression my 'black dog.'
Like many of us (your humble correspondent included)
Churchill discovered that if he kept busy all the time he
could hold his 'black dog' at bay.
```

Under "Caffeine and Depression," you might find these:

When I'm depressed I often use caffeine to give me an energy
boost and overcome my inertia. Whether it works or makes
things worse is another question. Do you use caffeine as a
tool for dealing with your depression?

Yes, I do. I sometimes see it as an antidote to my
sorrows--others use exercise or food--and often wonder, as
I'm sipping my coffee, what I'm really trying to wash down:
My sadness? My tears? Some painful old experiences I no
longer remember?

When I'm down, I step up my caffeine intake (and I mean WAY
UP). A typical day might look like this: 8 cups of filter-
brewed coffee, 4 shots of espresso, 1 can of Jolt Cola and a
six-pack of Diet Coke. It means lots more trips to the toilet
and I do feel wired, but it gives me the energy to 'get up
and go' on those days when I might otherwise just sit around
feeling sorry for myself.

You might find these postings under "The Closet Illness":

I don't usually tell people I'm depressed. Only my closest
friends and family know what I'm going through. Maybe it
would be better if I spoke more openly about my depressed
feelings. How do others handle this?

I never tell anyone I'm seeing a therapist or taking Prozac.
I'm ashamed that I have the luxury of popping a pill instead
of just gritting my teeth and getting on with my life.

I do sometimes tell people I trust (e.g., my dad, my boss,
and a couple of close friends) that I'm depressed and on medication. When I first tried this I found that they obviously
didn't understand. But over time I've learned how to explain
my depression in a way they can really hear. Here are the
three keys on how to do this:
1. Let them see how bad you feel when you're *without* your
antidepressant.
2. Let them see you're not artificially 'up' when on your
meds--in fact you're often still pretty far down.
3. Most people can't conceive of any feeling beyond what
they've felt themselves. So you must explain that most nonde-
pressed people have *never* felt anywhere near as low as
someone with clinical depression feels all the time.

> I used to hide my depression. Then I bought a t-shirt that reads "Beyond Prozac: ZOLOFT!" with a drawing of the chemical structure of Zoloft. I started wearing it to work and around town. I get all kinds of great comments from passersby like, "Right on, Bro!" and "Hey, I take Zoloft, too." It starts a lot of conversations, so wearing it has helped me feel more at ease 'coming out' about being depressed. If others can't handle it, it's their problem, not mine.

The first time you visit a newsgroup, see if they have a list of frequently asked questions (FAQ). If so, obtain a copy and read it. It's not considered good form to post questions that have already been answered in the FAQ. For more on FAQs, see p. 225.

What to Do After You've Read a Newsgroup

After you've read the postings on a newsgroup, you have several choices:

- You can add an additional public comment to an existing thread.
- You can start a new thread with a new subject heading on a different topic.
- You can send an e-mail message to anyone who posted to the newsgroup. Only the person who wrote the original posting will see your message.
- You can, of course, read the messages without responding at all.

Think (and proofread) before you post. Don't forget that hundreds or thousands of newsgroup readers across the Internet may be able to read and respond to your message.

A Dozen Exemplary Self-Help Newsgroups

Trying to describe the immense world of self-help newsgroups feels a little like trying to describe the *Encyclopedia Britannica* after skimming through its voluminous pages for an hour or so. While my faithful newsgroup researcher, Jayne Butler, and I can't claim to have read every posting on every health-related newsgroup, we've dipped into quite a few of them. And we've put together our own very subjective list of groups that are well worth your attention.

misc.kids.health

The *misc.kids.health* newsgroup is made up of parents concerned with their kids' health. Contributors share experiences and offer practical guidelines on dealing with various types of childhood illness. Most messages request or offer information and support for managing a wide range of situations involving sick kids.

```
I'm a stay-at-home mother of two. I've had a cold for the
past three days. I've tried everything to keep my kids from
getting it, but now the whole household is experiencing cold
symptoms. What do you do when one or both parents get some-
thing contagious to keep from passing it on to your children?
And how do you find the time to take care of yourself when
you're running around after the kids?
```

```
I just got over a bout with bronchitis & my husband was too
busy with work and school to help. I found that canned soup
with fruit on the side can be perfectly nutritious for
a few days. I also shamelessly abused TV and read stories on
the couch. Somehow, it works out. You muster just the energy
you need. (On Friday, my son had a febrile seizure and seri-
ous adrenaline kicked in to get me to the ER.) Good luck!
Believe me, a lot of us can sympathize.
```

```
The cold virus infects your body by three access points: the
nose, mouth, and eyes. The best way to prevent a cold, in the
company of those that have one, is to (1) keep your hands away
from these areas and (2) wash your hands very frequently.
```

```
I'm looking for the 800 number of a group in Vienna, VA.
Their name is the National Vaccine Information Center and/or
Dissatisfied Parents Together. Can anybody help?
```

```
We received a lot of good information from this group,
related to our concern over whole-cell pertussis in DPT
[diptherial pertussis tetanus](our son had a bad reaction).
The National Vaccine Information Center can be reached at
(800) 909-SHOT or (703) 938-DPT3. You will probably get a
recording--they are understaffed & get a lot of calls. Snail
mail is: 512 W. Maple Ave. #206, Vienna VA 22180.
```

alt.support.grief

The *alt.support.grief* group focuses on the personal experiences of loss and grief and the psychological processes involved in grieving and healing from losses of various kinds. Contributors give and receive support from one another as they share and compare their experiences of loss—e.g., fear of impending death, the death of family and friends, violent death, and sudden infant death. Other common topics are loneliness, missing a departed loved one, expressions of sympathy, and difficulties in talking with other family members about issues of loss, death, and grief.

> The nights are still the hardest. That's when Ken and I would have our best and deepest conversations. Just the two of us, with nothing else to distract us. It still hurts so much. I guess it always will.
> So many times I've felt numb with grief--only vaguely aware of the pain somewhere deep down inside, but it couldn't and wouldn't surface. I guess the body will only allow us to feel so much pain. Then it just turns off the feeling button.
> You've got to find a way to express the pain. Or your body will just bottle it up inside and you will never heal. Crying and posting to this group are the best ways for me. They allow me to howl and cry and release a lot of the heartache. And after I do it, I can feel the healing starting its long, slow journey.

> I lost my 17-year-old son in a stupid car accident about a year ago. I am still not doing real well.
> Losing a child is different from any other loss. We're supposed to protect our children. We're supposed to die before they do.
> Facing each day without S. is the hardest thing I've ever done. It feels as if all happiness, joy, and fun have been permanently banished from my life. I keep plugging away, trying to be a good mom for my other kids and hoping that someday it won't be so hard.
> If you haven't already found them, the support group The Compassionate Friends can be a tremendous help for those of us who have lost a child. They understand what you are going through and will listen to you and help you begin the healing.

alt.support.cancer

A lively, compassionate newsgroup, *alt.support.cancer* covers a wide range of cancer-related concerns. Many of the threads revolve around the difficult issues a person with cancer must face: dealing with a new diagnosis, deciding whether to try chemotherapy, coping with the loss of physical and mental abilities, and accepting the changes in relationships and the loss of control that may result from a serious illness.

Many requests are for information on specific types of cancer and on specific treatments. The information shared ranges from highly technical medical research news to intimate stories of personal experiences. Here are two typical postings:

```
Yes, I'll eventually have to get around to going to the doc-
tor's again but right now between cancer, viruses, rashes,
etc., etc., I have that "I'm all doctored out" feeling. Has
anyone else been through this?
```

```
Many surgeons will try to talk men with prostate cancer into
surgery, arguing that it is really important to reduce the
tumor burden, even though your cancer has already metastasized.
Don't let them do it! If my experience is any guide, you will
feel like hell afterward, even worse from the radiation.
    I am still asymptomatic from the cancer, but am still
dealing with many of the side-effects of the treatments.
```

In addition to a great deal of wise advice, the group's FAQ includes an extensive list of online and offline cancer resources. See "FAQs Available by E-Mail" (p. 228) for guidelines on getting the FAQ.

alt.support.crohns-colitis

The *alt.support.crohns-colitis* newsgroup is a forum where people with ulcerative colitis, Crohn's disease, and irritable bowel syndrome can share their experiences with these illnesses, and discuss medicines, treatments, surgery, diet, health care providers, and other topics. Discussions cover all types of medicine, from conventional to alternative, from state-of-the-art research to your Aunt Harriet's home remedies.

The FAQ covers symptoms, medications, treatments (including surgery), and coping strategies. As diet plays such a key role in this condition, nutrition is a particularly common theme.

> The book purports to control Inflammatory Bowel Disease through diet alone, but I think it's fair to say there is no consensus among doctors and readers of this newsgroup that this book's methods work any better than placebos. I hope they work for you, but I hate to have newcomers to the group think that all of a sudden there is this secret cure that their doctors have withheld from them.

> I'm happy to say that Crohn's disease is an almost completely ignorable part of my life these days. It did take quite a while for it to go into remission (nearly 8 years) but it *has* mostly gone away now, and it *is* mostly staying away. I now feel that unless I abuse myself either physically, dietarily, or stress-wise, I'll probably never have a serious recurrence again.

alt.support.depression

An active, compassionate group, *alt.support.depression* has a heart as big as the Internet. Postings include frequent responses to cries for help—both from professionals and from self-helpers who have made their own journeys into the dark world of chronic depression:

> Can someone please help me? I am sinking quickly and continue to reach a new low every day. If this continues, I'll soon be buying myself a gun.

> It doesn't sound like you've got the right medication yet. But don't worry, two tries isn't very much. (Many of us had an even harder time finding a med that worked.) You should talk to your MD about this, and if he/she is unresponsive, forget the gun and spend that extra money on a second opinion. Then there's the ultimate safety net, the hospital, which (as those of us who've been there can tell you) is really not so bad. Just think of it as a kind of extended rest cure.

> Please don't apologize for taking up space on the planet! As for your feelings of low self-esteem, we've all gone through that. Depression seems to make one focus on all the bad things about oneself, rather than the good things. Just because you can't see the good things about yourself doesn't mean they aren't there. I know we can't see you in person, but that doesn't mean we don't care. Hey--after just a couple of days and a couple of postings, people on this group are really getting to like you!

Some of the frank postings on this and other support newsgroups may be a bit of a stretch for those not intimately familiar with the extremities of the conditions under discussion:

> If you are depressed and feel like cutting yourself, but are afraid that some authority figure will notice the cuts and be unreasonable with you, buy a bag of clothespins. Attach the pinchy clothespins to your arms or legs, then knock them off. If you leave them on for a while before knocking them off, it hurts a whole lot. Very satisfying in a twisted sort of way.

> When I cut myself, I'm not just into it for the pain. In fact, I usually use ice cubes or (better yet) anbesol to numb my wrists before I do it.
>   During the summer, when I was severely depressed, I would cut to make myself bleed. I bled very carefully into plastic cups (which was also convenient for figuring out how much blood I'd lost and being sure I didn't bleed too much). During one two-week period, in three separate cuttings, I lost five pints of blood. But once my medications kicked in, the cutting became a lot less frequent. Now, on the rare occasions when I still do it, it's not for blood or for pain but just for sheer destructiveness. So I don't think clothespins wouldn't be a viable alternative for me.
>   Apparently cutting is not that uncommon. An article in Health magazine said that something like 1,400 people per 100,000 cut themselves. It gave the name of a Chicago hospital that has a 30-day in-patient program designed to deal with self-mutilation. Their number is 1-800-DONT-CUT (1-800-366-8288). They can provide referrals to help cutters as well as friends and relatives of people with an urge to self-injury.

alt.support.diet

The *alt.support.diet* group offers emotional support, encouragement, and practical advice to those who want to improve their health, appearance, or self-image through a weight loss or weight maintenance program. As the FAQ makes clear, the name of the group, *alt.support.diet*, is somewhat unfortunate because: (a) exercise is just as important as diet in weight loss, and (b) the word "diet" is often interpreted as 'a temporary regimen that's somehow expected to lead to permanent weight loss,' rather than its original meaning of 'how one eats thin.' The group's focus includes these deeper aspects. Here are some sample postings:

> I've always hated exercise, not because it's hard, but because it takes so much time & gets so boring. I just can't stand that long period of exasperation. Any suggestions?

> I've noticed that the people who do a sport they enjoy are far more successful at losing weight than those who hate it but exercise because they *must.* Almost any activity will do--cycling, ice skating, racquetball, horseback riding, etc. The people I know who are in the best shape don't fuss over how much aerobic vs. anaerobic exercise they do. They just get out there and enjoy themselves.

> We all sometimes have to do things we don't like: I had to pay my bills this morning, and it didn't exactly give me mul-tiple orgasms. I won't pretend that stepping up and down on my stair climber is the world's next designer drug. But I do it--because it's a price I'm willing to pay to stay in shape.
>   I too went through a period of doing only exercises I liked--and I didn't lose an ounce for years. Then I decided "I'm gonna do what it takes, whatever it happens to be," and lost 50 pounds of fat in 14 weeks. Excuse me now, but I'm going to go do my second (boring) aerobic workout of the day.

misc.health.arthritis

The *misc.health.arthritis* newsgroup is devoted to the discussion of arthritis and related autoimmune disorders (e.g., lupus and scleroderma). Anyone with an interest in these conditions, including patients, friends, family, and health professionals, is welcome. Typical topics are symptoms and causes, conventional and alternative treatments, overcoming practical problems, and as community and online resources.

> I'm looking for others who (like me) have Lupus (SLE) [Systemic Lupus Erythematosus]. I'd be happy to offer any help and support I can to people who are newly diagnosed and others who have questions. I was diagnosed 14 years ago and have dealt with all sorts of doctors, medications, life expe-riences, etc.

> I was diagnosed with SLE a year ago and am currently being
> weaned off of prednisone--A month or so ago my intake was
> 40 mg daily. It's now 12.5 mg. Over the last month I've expe-
> rienced symptoms of what I call "brain freeze." Like when you
> drink a slurpee too quickly and feel that unmistakable frozen
> sensation in your head. (I also feel the "icy" sensation in
> my chest, and my teeth have become cold sensitive for the
> first time in my life.) I've also experienced a tingling sen-
> sation on the right side of my scalp, near my hairline--like
> a slight electrical current. I'm wondering if you could pro-
> vide any possible insight into these strange symptoms.

alt.recovery

Devoted to the discussion of alcohol and drug addictions, *alt.recovery* is also a good place to look for announcements on a wide range of recovery-related resources and the latest on other, more specific recovery-related newsgroups. But it is *not* a Twelve Step group, and many of the people who post messages here don't go to Alcoholics Anonymous, Narcotics Anonymous, or other Twelve Step groups. Those seeking ongoing support in terms of the Twelve Step model would do better going directly to *alt.recovery.aa,* for Alcoholics Anonymous, *alt.recovery.na,* for Narcotics Anonymous, or another Twelve Step group.

Here is a good example of the support the group provides:

> I'm terrified of the telephone, yet one of the first things
> my sponsor asked me to do was to start calling other people
> in the program. I have no problem asking for numbers (in per-
> son) but just can't seem to find the nerve to use them. I'm
> not a shy person, but I get very anxious when I think of
> calling--especially when it's someone I don't really know. It
> brings back all those fears of not fitting in, boring other
> people to tears, bothering other people, etc. Am I the only
> addict that has difficulty using the phone to reach out?

> I share your phone phobia. It's amazing how heavy those darn
> telephones can get--virtually impossible to pick up sometimes.
> I just try to push on through & make myself do it. I figure
> that if I can get in the habit of calling people when I don't
> need help, it will be much more comfortable when I do.

> I know exactly how you feel. I too simply *hate* calling peo-
> ple I don't know on the phone. (Though I love it when people
> call me.) Two quick tips that have worked for me: (1) I usu-
> ally make my "most-hated" phone calls first thing in the
> morning. Once I get them out of the way, I can feel good for
> the rest of the day. (2) Keep the phone call short by saying,
> "Look, I can only talk for a minute," or something similar.
> Part of my fear of phoning comes from my worry that the call
> will drag on for ages.

alt.recovery.aa

The Twelve Step–oriented *alt.recovery.aa* is a discussion group for those recovering from alcohol addiction. Most regulars attend face-to-face AA meetings
and know the basic guidelines of the AA Twelve Step approach to recovery as
presented in the frequently cited "Big Book." Members use the Twelve Step
framework to discuss their problems and successes as they support one
another with their experiences and insights, and many of the postings are in
AA lingo (e.g., "I'm still working on Step Three"). There is also much discussion comparing AA with other methods of recovery:

> I was in Alcoholics Anonymous (AA) for over a year: I loathed
> it. I felt like I was in a mind-control cult that tried to
> tell me I was insane, and religious salvation was the only
> cure. Luckily I found a group called Rational Recovery (RR)
> which suits my needs much better.
>
> Whereas AA promotes "powerlessness," RR promotes self-
> empowerment because "surrender" only relieves guilt and does
> not get at the root of the problem. I am now leading a
> happy, productive life and I have RR to thank for that.
>
> The Rational Recovery headquarters is in New York City,
> listed under The Institute for Rational Emotive Therapy.
> There are probably meetings in your area.

> I'm a stone cold atheist, raised in an atheist family. Never
> had much use for religion of *any* kind. Not the traditional
> forms, nor the touchy-feely new-wave stuff that came later.
> But what I found in AA was people who had been where I'd
> been: To alcoholic hell. They showed the solution on their
> faces and in their actions. I took the Twelve Steps out of
> desperation, believing in the usefulness of only about four
> of them. But I'm still sober, five years later.

> The idea that we are powerless over all kinds of crap is not part of the official AA program, just one opinion from the back of the book. AA *gave* me power. It saved this atheist's life.
>
> If RR works for you, fine and good. Me, any time I hear the politically correct new-wave term "empower" I get nauseated. Sorry, but I get defensive when people find it necessary to knock AA, which is the only thing in this world with enough juice to give me and other last-gaspers a life.

alt.recovery.na

The *alt.recovery.na* group follows the Narcotics Anonymous (NA) Twelve Step format. Contributors often start their postings with their name and the statement that they are addicted to a particular drug. Comments are generally empathic and supportive, with contributors sharing what has and hasn't worked for them. There are many questions and comments from newly "clean" group members, as well as from those who are still using. They're usually answered by self-helpers who have abstained from their drug for many months or years:

> Smoking a hit of crack feels like coming. There's nothing remotely like it. Nothing at all. It feels *so* great. And hey, ain't I free to use my drug of choice? So you tell me,.na dudes, why I should ever *want* to quit?

> You're absolutely right, my friend. Smoking crack feels totally orgasmic. Oh man, the memories. Just thinking about it makes me want to light up.
>
> But hey, just for fun let's walk through the rest of the feelings that inevitably follow, OK? Like paranoia about the cops busting you and ending up in jail. That sickening feeling when you're desperate for another hit and the rock's all gone. The bitter, stupid fights with your best buddies. The way you end up f***ing over your closest beloved family members and friends just to cop another stupid score. Fear and trembling as you realize that your whole life is coming apart and you've ended up hungry, alone, broke, homeless, and friendless, hanging out with other selfish scumbags who've traveled the same path.
>
> You're right. There's nothing remotely like it. Nothing at all.

> Any time you want help in stopping, write me back. Even
> if you *don't* want to quit right now, write me back. You
> remind me of my younger self. I'd like to keep up on what's
> happening with you.

alt.adoption

Much information on almost any conceivable adoption-related topic is to be found in *alt.adoption*. Postings include messages from parents wanting to adopt children and from adoptees trying to locate their birth parents. Birth mothers share their experiences. So do adoptees. Parents searching for their birth children and children searching for their birth parents seek advice from others who have been successful. Occasionally there are flames from militant adult adoptees who are anti-adoption. (Another newsgroup called alt.adoption.agency is geared to adoptive parents and features lists of children available for adoption from various adoption agencies.)

Here's a sample of a posting that isn't about adoption, but is related:

> Of course infertility is a disability. It prevents you from
> functioning in a normal way. And it scars you for the rest of
> your life. The best you can hope for is to adapt to it, as
> you would do to any disability.

> I disagree. Infertility is not covered under the Americans
> with Disabilities Act. You don't need vocational rehabilita-
> tion, education assistance, or adaptive technologies to per-
> form the skills of daily living or perform your job. You
> don't face housing or employment discrimination by virtue of
> infertility. Some people consider their infertility a benefit
> because they don't *want* to have children. Others accept it
> as a limitation no different than other limitations (short
> stature, big nose, lack of perfect pitch, etc.). Many infer-
> tile people are happy, well adjusted and lead full (though
> childless) lives. Others choose to use infertility as a way
> to give themselves to children in a way they may not have had
> the resources for if they were raising a family--foster par-
> ents, child care workers, special ed. teachers, etc. And some
> people, like us, choose to adopt.

alt.infertility

Much of the discussion in *alt.infertility* focuses on the various treatments available for both male and female infertility. Contributors share their successes and failures in trying to get pregnant as they support and encourage one another. Clinic resources for specific parts of the country, insurance coverage, and information resources are also frequent topics of discussion.

Here's one note of success and thanks:

> Great news: After two ectopic pregnancies followed by two attempts at in-vitro fertilization, B. (my wife) and I are at last pregnant. We're thrilled. And we're very grateful to our fellow-participants on alt.infertility.
>
> We were so eager to make our infertility program succeed, but before joining this group, we didn't have a clue as to how to do it. The discussions here helped us put everything in perspective: You taught us what was important and what wasn't, what signs to look for, and what questions to ask. We visited our doctors as highly informed, responsible consumers. And we learned to think of our infertility as a biological problem, not a personal failure. We hope you all get back lots of good luck and blessings for all the kind assistance you've given us.

alt.support.sleep-disorder

Postings to *alt.support.sleep-disorder* request and offer information about insomnia, snoring, sleep apnea, sleep monitoring, narcolepsy, and other sleep problems. Contributors share experiences and offer practical guidelines on dealing with various types of sleep disturbances. Other common topics are sleeping pills and other medications, sleep clinics, current sleep research, informational resources, and conventional and unconventional approaches to a wide variety of sleep disorders.

> I'm thrilled to be on Prozac. My depression is gone, my craving for alcohol is gone, and I am more the person I always wanted to be. I do have one problem, however: I keep waking up during the night. (This never happened before I started on P.) I've been taking it for about 90 days, and take 40 mg every day. Altering the dosage doesn't help. We already tried that. Any suggestions?

> My doc told me that about 5 percent of Prozac users develop a
> sleep problem. According to numerous posts on
> alt.support.depression, adding a once-a-day dose of trazodone
> (Desyrel) at bedtime will often take care of this SSRI-
> insomnia effect. Trazodone is a hybrid antidepressant with a
> short half-life and sedating properties. It weakly blocks
> reuptake of serotonin as well as blocking serotonin receptors.

sci.med

The *sci.med* group is a forum for questions and answers on a wide range of
medical conditions. Postings cover practical guidelines on self-treatment, diagnosis, referrals to an appropriate medical specialist, etc. Many of the answers
are contributed by medical professionals.

Here are two questions and their answers:

> Does anyone know how ginger helps to prevent motion sickness
> and does it really work? Does it have to be fresh ginger?

> Question 1: No. Question 2: Yes. 3. No, Ginger Beer works fine
> (not "Ginger" Ale, but real traditional cloudy Ginger Beer).
> And has anyone tried that pickled ginger you get at a Sushi
> bar? I'd guess it should work, and it sure tastes great.

> I'm looking for information on atrial septal defect and would
> appreciate any help or suggestions.

> I'm only a lowly medical student, so take anything I say with
> a mountain of salt, but here's what I know from my lectures
> and my medical textbooks: An atrial septal defect is a hole
> between two of the chambers of the heart. The hole is in the
> wall separating the two atria (plural for atrium). This wall
> is called the septum. The hole allows blood to flow "in the
> wrong direction"--from one atrium into the other.
>
> Patients who have uncomplicated atrial septal defects
> without pulmonary hypertension and shunt ratios exceeding 1.5
> should undergo repair electively, preferably during child-
> hood. Pulmonary hypertension is not common in this congenital
> illness. Your physician should be able to help determine the
> appropriateness of surgery in your situation.

sci.med.diseases.cancer

Featuring questions and answers on a wide range of cancer-related conditions, *sci.med.diseases.cancer* is oriented to research studies and searches of the medical literature, whereas *alt.support.cancer* (see p. 209) emphasizes support and personal experience, but there is much overlap. Many of the postings here include referrals to information sources on and off the Net:

```
Call 1-800-4CANCER for free literature and general info from
nationally recognized cancer treatment centers. This service
is run by the National Cancer Institute. Most of the informa-
tion available there can also be found over the Net.
```

```
Yes, but the most valuable thing you can get via 800-4CANCER,
clinical trial searches, cannot be obtained over the Net--at
least not for free. You can get into the clinical trials
database on some of the high-priced commercial services, but
this is *not* part of CancerNet. Good as CancerNet is, you'll
still want to call 800-4CANCER for a customized search of
current clinical trials (experimental treatments) for your
type of cancer.
```

HOT TIP

The Web page *Psych Central: Dr. John Grohol's Mental Health Page* provides an extensive and constantly updated listing of self-help newsgroups (see page 242).

Health- and Support-Oriented Newsgroups

Here's a selected list of health-and support-oriented newsgroups:

Group	Purpose
alt.abuse.recovery	Support for those recovering from all types of abuse
alt.adoption	Support and discussion for those interested in or involved with adoption (see p. 216)
alt.backrubs	Discussion of massage as a stress reliever and a healthful nonsexual activity

alt.food.fat-free	Discussion and support for those attempting to eat an extremely low-fat diet
alt.health	Discussion of miscellaneous health issues (this is a good place to post a query if you haven't been able to find the group you're seeking)
alt.health.ayurveda	Discussion of ayurvedic medicine
alt.hypnosis	Discussion of hypnosis
alt.infertility	Support for those dealing with infertility, including discussion of the causes and treatments of infertility (see p. 217)
alt.med.allergy	Support and information for those suffering from allergies, their friends and families, and health professionals
alt.med.cfs	Support and information for those dealing with chronic fatigue syndrome (CFS)
alt.med.fibromyalgia	Support and discussion for those dealing with fibromyalgia or fibrosis
alt.meditation	Discussion and support for meditation
alt.parents-teens	Discussion and support for the parents of teenagers
alt.psychology.help	Discussion and support for those seeking help with psychological problems
alt.psychology.personality	Discussion of personality-related topics
alt.recovery	Discussion of a wide variety of topics relating to recovery (see p. 213)
alt.recovery.aa	Support and discussion for members of Alcoholics Anonymous (see p. 214)
alt.recovery.addiction.sexual	Support and information for those recovering from sexual addictions
alt.recovery.catholicism	Support for those recovering from the negative effects of Catholic religious training or experiences
alt.recovery.codependency	Support and information for those recovering from codependency

alt.recovery.na	Support and discussion for members of Narcotics Anonymous (see p. 215)
alt.recovery.religion	Support for those recovering from the negative effects of religious training or experiences
alt.self-improve	Support and discussion for those interested in various types of self-improvement
alt.sexual.abuse.recovery	Support and information for those recovering from sexual abuse
alt.shenanigans	Discussion of practical jokes and other kinds of benign silliness in which no one gets hurt
alt.society.mental-health	Discussion of various mental health issues
alt.support	Discussion of miscellaneous support-related topics
alt.support.abuse-partners	Support for partners of sexual abuse survivors
alt.support.anxiety-panic	Support and discussion for those dealing with anxiety and panic disorders
alt.support.arthritis	Support and discussion for those dealing with all aspects of arthritis
alt.support.asthma	Discussion and support for those dealing with all aspects of asthma
alt.support.attn-deficit	Support and discussion for those dealing with attention-deficit disorder and their friends and family
alt.support.big-folks	Support and discussion for those interested in fat-acceptance (no dieting talk)
alt.support.cancer	Support and information for people with cancer and their friends and families (see p. 209)
alt.support.cancer.prostate	Support and information for men with prostate cancer and their friends and families

alt.support.cerebral-palsy	Support and information for people with cerebral palsy and their friends and families
alt.support.crohns-colitis	Support for people with Crohn's disease, ulcerative colitis, or irritable bowel syndrome (see p. 209)
alt.support.depression	Support and information for those dealing with depression and mood disorders, their friends and families, and health professionals interested in depression (see p. 210)
alt.support.depression.manic	Support and discussion for those with manic depression or bipolar disorder
alt.support.dev-delays	Support for parents and patients dealing with all types of developmental delays
alt.support.diabetes.kids	Support for parents and family of children with diabetes
alt.support.diet	Support and information for those attempting to lose weight (see p. 211)
alt.support.dissociation	Support for people with dissociative disorders (e.g., multiple personality disorder)
alt.support.divorce	Support for those going through a divorce or other disrupted relationships
alt.support.eating-disord	Support for people with eating disorders (anorexia, bulimia, etc.)
alt.support.epilepsy	Discussion and support for all aspects of epilepsy
alt.support.ex-cult	Support and discussion for former cult members and their family and friends
alt.support.foster-parents	Support and discussion for foster parents
alt.support.grief	Discussion of issues of grief and loss (see p. 208)

alt.support.headaches.migraine	Support for those dealing with migraines or related headache ailments
alt.support.learning-disab	Support for learning disabilities (e.g., dyslexia)
alt.support.loneliness	Support for those suffering from loneliness
alt.support.mult-sclerosis	Support and discussion of multiple sclerosis
alt.support.non-smokers	Support for non- or ex-smokers and discussion of the effects of second-hand smoke
alt.support.obesity	Support for people dealing with obesity
alt.support.ocd	Support for those dealing with obsessive-compulsive disorder (OCD)
alt.support.ostomy	Support for people who have had ostomies
alt.support.personality	Support and discussion for those with borderline personality disorder or other personality disorders
alt.support.post-polio	Support for those with postpolio syndrome
alt.support.prostate.prostatitis	Support and discussion for men with prostatitis
alt.support.social-phobia	Support and discussion for those with social phobias (e.g., performance anxiety, fear of crowds)
alt.support.sleep-disorder	Support for those dealing with sleep disorders and problems sleeping (see p. 217)
alt.support.spina-bifida	Support and discussions of spina bifida
alt.support.step-parents	Support for being a stepparent
alt.support.stop-smoking	Support for stopping or quitting smoking
alt.support.stuttering	Support for those dealing with stuttering or other speaking difficulties

alt.support.tinnitus	Support and discussion for those dealing with ringing in the ears (tinnitus) and other head noises
alt.support.tourette	Support and discussions of Tourette's syndrome
alt.transgendered	Support and discussion for persons who identify themselves as belonging to the opposite sex and those interested in sex-change procedures
comp.risks	Discussions of the health hazards of computer use (e.g., repetitive stress injuries, exposure to radiation, computer addictions)
misc.fitness	Discussion of fitness and exercise training
misc.handicap	Discussion of all types of handicaps
misc.health.aids	Discussion of issues relating to AIDS and HIV
misc.health.alternative	Alternative and holistic health approaches
misc.health.arthritis	Discussion of arthritis and related conditions (see p. 212)
misc.health.diabetes	Discussion of diabetes and hypoglycemia
misc.kids	Discussion of parenting and other issues relating to children
misc.kids.health	Discussion of health issues of kids (see p. 207)
misc.kids.pregnancy	Discussion of issues relating to pregnancy and childbirth
rec.food.veg	Discussion of vegetarian diets
rec.pets.cats	Discussion for cat fanciers
rec.pets.dogs	Discussion for dog owners
rec.sport.running	Discussion and support for runners (you'll find groups for many other sports under *rec.sport.* *)
sci.med	General questions and discussions on health, illness, and the practice of medicine (see p. 218)

sci.med.aids	Discussion of AIDS and HIV
sci.med.diseases.cancer	Discussion of cancer (see p. 219)
sci.med.informatics	Discussion of computer applications in medical care (e.g., computerized medical records, clinical information systems, diagnostic software)
sci.med.nutrition	Discussion of nutrition research and practical aspects of nutrition
sci.med.vision	Discussion of eye problems and conditions
sci.psychology	Discussion of psychology
soc.support.fat-acceptance	Self-acceptance for fat people with no guilt-tripping or diet talk
soc.support.transgendered	Discussion and support for transgendered and intersexed persons (see *alt.transgendered*)
soc.support.youth.gay-lesbian-bi	Discussion and support for young people concerned with gay, lesbian, or bisexual issues

HOT

TIP

Postings are kept on most newsgroups for only a limited time—usually a few weeks. As a result, you'll sometimes find yourself reading a thread in which it's clear that the originating posting has been dropped. If you're lucky, you may happen upon a later posting that quotes the message, so you'll get to see the original posting that people are responding to.

Frequently Asked Questions (FAQs)

"Frequently Asked Questions" is a wonderful online genre that grew out of the experiences of regular members of some early Internet newsgroups. Because of the rapid growth of the Internet, thousand of new users are now coming onto the newsgroups every week. And many of these newsgroup newbies ask questions that the regulars on these groups have seen and answered many times before.

At some point, some insightful newsgroup veterans decided to record a list of frequently asked questions, with answers, and to make them available to new users. The practice caught on quickly. Other newsgroups developed their own lists of frequently asked questions—or FAQs for short—and the rest is Internet history. Today you'll find FAQs nearly everywhere—on Internet mailing lists, on the commercial networks, on Web pages, even in the pages of *Time* magazine—as well as on thousands of newsgroups.

What does a FAQ look like? Here are some brief samples from two outstanding FAQs. The first is from the *alt.support.diet* FAQ.

```
Q. What do the terms "overweight" and "obese" mean?

A. Physicians usually define "overweight" as a condition in
which a person's weight is 10 to 20 percent higher than "nor-
mal," as defined by a standard height/weight chart. "Obesity"
is usually defined as a condition in which a person's weight
is 20 percent or more above normal weight. "Morbid obesity"
means that a person is 50 to 100 percent or more, or more than
100 pounds over their normal weight, or sufficiently overweight
to severely interfere with health or normal functioning.

Q. Are there any other ways (other than regular weighing or
having my body fat measured) to find out whether I'm over-
weight or overfat?

A. Waist-to-hip ratio is a useful indicator and is simple to
calculate: Stand in front of a full-length mirror so that you
can easily see the areas you are measuring. Use a tape mea-
sure to measure your waist circumference at the level of your
navel. Next, measure your hip circumference at its widest
point. (Don't pull the tape measure too tightly.) Divide your
waist measurement by your hip measurement to determine your
waist-to-hip ratio. For example, if your waist measures 26"
and your hip measurement is 36", your waist-to-hip ratio is
0.7. For men, a waist-to-hip ratio of 0.95-1.0 or greater
indicates an increased risk for heart disease. Women should
have a ratio of 0.8 or less.
Another useful measurement is your Body Mass Index (BMI). To
determine your BMI, multiply your weight in pounds by 703,
then divide by the square of your height in inches. For exam-
ple, if you weigh 130 pounds and are 5'4"(64") tall, your BMI
is (130 x 703)/(64 x 64) = 22.3. A BMI of 25 or less indi-
cates that you are at low risk for heart disease; 30 or
higher suggests that you are at moderate to very high risk.
```

The next is from the *alt.support.depression* FAQ:

Q. What is depression?

A. Being clinically depressed is very different from the down type of feeling that all people experience from time to time. Occasional feelings of sadness are a normal part of life, and it is unfortunate that such feelings are often colloquially referred to as "depression." In clinical depression, such feelings are out of proportion to any external causes. There are things in everyone's life that are possible causes of sadness, but people who are not depressed manage to cope with these things without becoming incapacitated.

As one might expect, depression can present itself as feeling sad or "having the blues". However, sadness may not always be the dominant feeling of a depressed person.

Depression can also be experienced as a numb or empty feeling, or perhaps no awareness of feeling at all. A depressed person may experience a noticeable loss in their ability to feel pleasure about anything. Depression, as viewed by psychiatrists, is an illness in which a person experiences a marked change in their mood and in the way they view themselves and the world. Depression as a significant depressive disorder ranges from short in duration and mild to long term and very severe, even life threatening.

Depressive disorders come in different forms, just as do other illnesses, such as heart disease. The three most prevalent forms are major depression, dysthymia, and bipolar disorder.

Q. What is major depression?

A. Major depression is manifested by a combination of symptoms (see symptom list below) that interfere with the ability to work, sleep, eat, and enjoy once-pleasurable activities. These disabling episodes of depression can occur once, twice, or several times in a lifetime.

Q. What is dysthymia?

A. A less severe type of depression, dysthymia involves long-term, chronic symptoms that do not disable, but keep you from functioning at "full steam" or from feeling good. Sometimes people with dysthymia also experience major depressive episodes.

> Q. What is bipolar depression (manic-depressive illness)?
>
> A. Another type of depressive disorder is manic-depressive illness, also called bipolar depression. Not nearly as prevalent as other forms of depressive disorders, manic-depressive illness involves cycles of depression and elation or mania. Sometimes the mood switches are dramatic and rapid, but most often they are gradual. When in the depressed cycle, you can have any or all of the symptoms of a depressive disorder. When in the manic cycle, any or all symptoms listed under mania may be experienced. Mania often affects thinking, judgment, and social behavior in ways that cause serious problems and embarrassment. For example, unwise business or financial decisions may be made when in a manic phase.

Finding the FAQs You Need

How do you find the FAQs you're looking for? Newsgroups will typically post their latest FAQ to the group at regular intervals (e.g., every week or two), or you may find a message on the list telling you how to find the latest version.

There are other ways to get FAQs as well: There are special newsgroups called *alt.answers, misc.answers, soc.answers*, etc., where you can find the FAQs of many different newsgroups. The FAQ from a given group is sometimes posted to another group as well (e.g., the vision and eye care FAQ from *sci.med.vision* can also be found on *sci.med*). You can obtain FAQs from many support newsgroups by a simple e-mail request (see the list below). And if all else fails, you can always post a brief, courteous message to the newsgroup itself asking whether there is an FAQ and, if so, where to find it.

FAQs Available by E-Mail

Here is a list of FAQs available by e-mail.

Adoptive parents FAQ

Newsgroup:	*alt.adoption*
Request from:	annette@acm.org (Annette Thompson)

AIDS FAQ

Newsgroup:	*sci.med.aids*
Request from:	aids-request@cs.ucla.edu

Asthma FAQ

Newsgroup: *alt.support.asthma*

Request from: wrean@cco.caltech.edu (Patricia Rose Wrean)

Cancer Information Sources FAQ

Newsgroups: *alt.support.cancer, sci.med.diseases.cancer*

Request from: snydere@ucsub.colorado.edu (Steve Dunn)

Chronic fatigue syndrome FAQ

Newsgroup: *alt.med.cfs*

Request from: camilla@netcom.com (Camilla Cracchiolo)

Depression FAQ

Newsgroup: *alt.support.depression*

Request from: cf12@cornell.edu (Cynthia Frazier)

Diabetes FAQ

Newsgroup: *misc.health.diabetes*

Request from: ed@titipu.resun.com

Dissociation FAQ

Newsgroup: *alt.support.dissociation*

Request from: tina@tezcat.com (Tina Sikorski)

Ear infections/tubes FAQ

Newsgroup: *misc.kids*

Request from: lcheap@u.washington.edu (Laurel Cheap)

Fibromyalgia syndrome FAQ

Newsgroup: *alt.med.fibromyalgia*

Request from: camilla@netcom.com (Camilla Cracchiolo)

Inflammatory bowel diseases FAQ

Newsgroup: *alt.support.crohns-colitis*

Request from: holmes@mrx.webo.dg.com (Christopher Holmes)

Migrane FAQ

Newsgroup: *alt.support.headaches.migraine*

Request from: schaffer@mopac.amd.com

Organ transplants FAQ

Newsgroup: *sci.med*

Request from: mhollowa@epo.som.sunysb.edu (Michael Holloway)

Suicide FAQ

Newsgroup:	*news.answers*
E-mail address:	greyham@research.canon.oz.au (Graham Stoney)

Vaccinations FAQ

Newsgroup:	*misc.kids*
Request from:	gazissax@netcom.com (Lynn Diana Gazis)

Vision and eye care FAQ

Newsgroup:	*sci.med; sci.med.vision*
Request from:	grants@research.canon.oz.au (Grant Sayer)

HOT TIP

For an excellent file containing a considerably more extensive and up-to-date guidelines for finding self-help FAQs—and additional medical FAQs available by e-mail—send a request for the file "Medicine-Related FAQs" by Bruce C. McKenzie to bruce-m@cyber-tas.demon.co.uk.

Once you become a newsgroup regular and really know your way around, remember: When a newsgroup newbie logs on and posts a question you and your online buddies have repeatedly heard and answered and you're tempted to post a curt response, take a deep breath instead, think back to your early days online, then send him or her a nice note with information on how to obtain your newsgroup's FAQ—or even better, a copy of the FAQ itself.

Newsgroups FAQ

Here's my own FAQ about newsgroups:

Q *Why are they called "newsgroups?"*

A No one I've talked to seems to know. It doesn't really make much sense, since the postings on the newsgroups are, in most cases, not about news at all, but ongoing discussions of a topic of common interest.

Q *How many newsgroups should I sign up for at first?*

A The world of newsgroups can be overwhelming, so it's probably wise to start small. I'd suggest you sign up for no more than half a dozen at first. You can always add more later. And you'd be well advised to pick one or two for your first session.

Q *What is a "moderated" newsgroup?*

A Most newsgroups are unmoderated: All messages sent to the list can be read by all. That sometimes means that newsgroup regulars will be subjected to dozens of trivial, off-topic, abusive, or misdirected postings. As such postings can be extremely distracting (and can repel participants or give rise to flame wars), some news groups have chosen to keep the discussion focused by appointing a group member to edit all postings. On these moderated groups, the moderator reads all incoming messages, edits out irrelevant or offending comments, and posts the "approved" messages to the newsgroup to be read by all.

Q *How do I know what to put for a subject heading when I post a message to a newsgroup?*

A Good question! A little thought on the subject heading can make your post ing much more effective.

Think back to the example earlier in this chapter, when we selected three threads from the newsgroup *alt.support.depression*. We chose to read the messages we did because the subject headings sounded interesting. Similarly, most newsgroup participants first scan the subject headings, then choose to read only those postings of special interest to them. So if you want your message to be read, think of a subject heading that will (1) sound interesting or intriguing and (2) also clearly represent what the reader will find in your posting. It always helps to be as specific as you can.

Suppose, for instance, that your daughter was just diagnosed with Crohn's disease and you were trying to help her find an online support group. Which of these headings do you think would work the best?

Group Wanted
Daughter Needs Group
Crohn's Disease
Help!
Online Crohn's Disease Support Group?

The last heading would probably be the best. It would let the reader know exactly what you were looking for.

Q *How can I start a self-help newsgroup?*

A Starting a newsgroup is quite complicated, so I would recommend starting a mailing list first. For a newsgroup, you may need to convince at least 200 Internet users to vote for its creation, and your members will need to convince the people who run their Internet sites to carry it. The complete process is beyond the scope of this book, but you can find more information about it in *The USENET Book* by Bryan Pfaffenberger (Addison-Wesley, 1995).

Sample Subject Headings from Popular Self-Help Newsgroups

alt.adoption

4/6/64 female, Bakersfield, ISO birth father
Are all a-parents the "bad guys"?
Baby girl, Oct 8, 1946, in Washington, DC
How to get FAQ & other Net resources
New "how to" adoption search book
Philippine adoption
Single foster parents
Tom Cruise has adopted another one
Transracial adoption
Why do people want kids?

alt.psychology.help

alt.support.dissociation FAQ
Anger management
Cyber psychology
Emotional support on the Internet
Jealousy
Jungian archetypes
Lack of sex drive
Lithium/alcohol interactions
Morbid sexual fantasies
Online group therapy
Schizophrenia info, please
Women with no maternal instincts

alt.recovery

4th-step/self-esteem game
Clutterers Anonymous
Gamblers Anon.
IRC recovery channel #12steps
Living with a gambler
Meetings in Florida

Music heals

Naltrexone works—Part 4

Overeaters Anonymous

Queers in recovery

Theories of alcoholism

Web page on recovery

alt.recovery.aa

AA and antidepressants

Books, tapes, movies for recovery

Can AA help an atheist?

Doing the first step for fifth time

Getting a sponsor

Getting the Big Book on the Net

My fear

Newcomer intro

On stuffing your feelings

Recovery bulletin boards

Seven Deadly Sins: The alcoholic's version

This group cracks me up

alt.support.arthritis

Advice on gout

Devil's claw root for rheumatoid arthritis?

FAQ for *misc.health.arthritis*

Fibromyalgia--any suggestions?

Hand surgery--personal experiences

Herbal therapies

Knee-replacement surgery

Pain in fingers & toes

Rheumatologist vs. orthopedic docs?

What else "looks" like RA?

WOW! Great support

Yawning causes facial cramps

alt.support.diet

Birth control pills & fat

How to take it off & keep it off

Hypnosis—does it work?

Low-fat diet makes me the bitch from hell

Managing the midnight munchies

Sick of being fat!

Slimfast—does it work?

Surgical options

The nature connection

Water & weight loss

Weight loss computer programs

Weight Watchers vs. Jenny Craig

alt.support.infertility

Can a good diet improve sperm?

Conferences on infertility

Egg donation

Hysteroscopy

Infertility resources

Internet adoption services

OB/Gyns in the DC area?

Picking a sperm donor

Stress as a cause of infertility?

Surgery for blocked fallopian tubes

Surrogate parenting

Underwear & infertility

Vasectomy reversals

alt.support.sleep-disorder

Best beds for insomniacs

Do I have a sleep disorder?

Do-it-yourself sleep lab

Night terrors

Nightmares & post-traumatic stress disorder

Phantom sleep apnea and snoring archive

Restless leg syndrome

Sleep apnea monitor keeps me awake

Sleep problems with prozac

Sleeping too much

Snoring

Talking in your sleep

misc.health.alternative

Alternative health insurance

Bell's palsy

Vitamins by mail

Chinese medicine

Enlarged prostate?

Garlic tablets

Ginseng

Harmful herbal remedies

Homeopathic remedies for ADD

How much niacin?

Natural menopause

What the heck is Reynaud's syndrome?

misc.kids

Barney sucks!

Bilingual families

Child leashes

Dealing with grandparents

Dealing with kids who tell lies

Godparent etiquette

Losing temper with kids—help!

Losing weight after childbirth

Pierced ears (7-year-old)

RTSS (ridiculous things strangers say)

Teaching toddlers to understand "No"

Terrible Twos

misc.kids.health

Still wetting the bed (7-year-old)

Are uncoated aluminum pots bad?

Babies & epilepsy?

"Cafe-au-lait" spots and neurofibrumatosis?

Daycare center dilemma

Dust mite allergy

Ear infections and garlic treatment

Heat lamp for fluid in ear?

Hepatitis A vaccine

How long should we sleep with our newborn?

Tongue-tie surgery info wanted

Weaning from nighttime bottle

sci.med

ABO & Rh factor

Aftereffects of steroids

Ankle problems

Beta blockers and hypertension

Chelation therapy

Eapsicin cream

Endometrial ablation vs. hysterectomy

Flaming doctors on the Net

Methadone maintenance

Personal experiences with Accutane

Question re: pacemaker

When limbs "fall asleep"

Chapter 11

The World Wide Web

I recently brought my mother to my office and turned her loose on the Web while I finished some work. When I was ready to go, it took me half an hour to pry her away.

John Bell
(my editor for this book)

—————◆—————

THE *WALL STREET JOURNAL'S* Walter S. Mossberg, one of our sharpest-eyed observers of cyberspace, recently wrote, "The Web is so compelling that within a year I expect it to subsume most old-style textual Internet services." By the time his piece appeared in print a few weeks later, his prediction had already pretty much come true. The World Wide Web has become the de facto standard for providing text and multimedia information on the Internet. The former producers of many earlier Internet services are now scurrying to put their information on easy-to-access World Wide Web sites.

That's very good news indeed. It means that new online users can explore the Net without mastering the intricate protocols of gopher, telnet, file transfer protocol, and other technical functions their online forefathers were forced to struggle with. They can simply point and click their way around the Internet with their handy Web browser.

The rapid development of new health resources on the World Wide Web has been nothing short of phenomenal. And not only has the Web become the most essential Internet service for the online traveler in search of textual information, it's one of the most visually sophisticated as well. Graphically speaking, Web sites are to the rest of the Internet as spiffy full-color Mac and Windows screens are to the old monochrome DOS interface.

Each site on the Web consists of a so-called home page (often written as "homepage"), a sort of colorful electronic magazine-article-cum-extended-table-of-contents that can be accessed through the commercial services or via a direct Internet connection by using Web browser software such as Netscape Navigator or Mosaic. If that was all, it would be enough. But the Web offers even more: network-wide hypertext.

A Web document can have built-in links to other Web documents and other Internet sites. The other documents linked to your home page may be on your own hard disk, on the university server down the street, or on a computer in Australia or Japan, half a world away. So in addition to the graphics, text, and multimedia applications supplied by the home page's creator, Web home pages can contain hyperlinks to any other Web site.

Consider this fictional example: Suppose you were to access Judy Jones's Web page for the parents of newborns with Down's syndrome. You not only might see the text, images, and multimedia clips that Judy has created (diagrams, illustrations, family photos, her kids' artwork, videos of a recent birthday party, etc.) and the files she has composed or collected (a database of family members, minutes of a local PTA meeting), but you also could use Judy's home page as a jumping-off place for visiting all of Judy's other favorite Web sites. Just click on any hot link on Judy's home page—a block of underlined or colored text—and, zap, you're on your way.

In addition to speeding you around the Web itself, most Web browsers can also take you to most of the other important types of Internet resources: gopher, ftp (see Glossary, p. xxv), and other ways of accessing the other more esoteric parts of the Internet.

The Web already contains vast amounts of useful health and medical information, and dozens of new sites are being added daily. Fortunately, because anything on the Web can be linked to anything else that's related, you'll be able to find the best new entries—even those that came online after this book went to press—by using the Web sites listed in this chapter as starting places. But before we begin visiting Web sites, let's step back and review a few important things the Web is only beginning to do.

The Web: Limitations

Web sites are best at providing easily accessible information in text form, with some graphics and audiovisual clips tacked on. But to date, most Web sites contain essentially one-way information produced by the providers and read by the users, with very limited conversation between the two. Partly because of technical limitations and partly because of the way Web site creators have used these technologies, most Web sites aren't highly interactive. You can usually send e-mail to a Web site's creators, and on some pages you can fill in certain kinds of forms. But for a self-helper accustomed to the interactive groups and networks described in earlier chapters, this leaves much to be desired.

The Web in its present state thus offers a powerful platform for a single individual or organization to offer a fascinating menu of text and multimedia to a worldwide audience. But although it's technically possible, Web pages are rarely used as a platform for live chat groups or as a forum for presenting a number of different perspectives. Like most of the solicitations you receive via old-fashioned snail mail, most Web sites are more interested in either marketing certain products or expressing a single point of view.

Don't get me wrong. I think the Web is an exciting and powerful new tool for online health. But an alarmingly small number of the sites I reviewed in researching this book provided the invaluable kind of multiperson discussion you routinely find in the commercial forums, the newsgroups, and the Internet mailing lists. And I came across a few Web home pages that didn't even include the creator's e-mail address, a shocking oversight. Interaction, after all, is the life's blood of support communities in cyberspace.

How do you make a Web site more interactive if you're a producer? Invite and display user input. Include a constantly evolving database of questions from people who have previously visited the site, with answers from you or other knowledgeable experts (see Go Ask Alice, p. 245). Offer live chat groups with the Web page's creator (see Psych Central, p. 242). Be a facilitator, not an authority. Create an open-ended self-help ethos, rather than remaining stuck in the old top-down model of health education.

The Web, in its current incarnation, provides a dazzling, easy-to-use new platform for transmitting information. As this exciting new technology evolves, more and more Web page producers will find more powerful ways to make the Web a more interactive, and thus genuinely transformative, vehicle for community.

All the major commercial services now offer their members personal home pages at little or no additional cost. This makes it easier than ever to create your own online self-help resource.

My Web Hotlist

This section contains most of the health-related Web sites on my personal hotlist. These are the pages I most frequently refer to, recommend to others, and use in demonstrations of health-oriented Web sites.

Yahoo/Health

Yahoo/Health is a powerful Web site that provides easy access to hundreds of other health and medical Web sites. It's a great starting place for exploring health sites on the Web, an outstanding directory that lists thousands of health-related home pages and provides a search tool to help you find what you're looking for. The master Yahoo menu (at http://www.yahoo.com) provides similar Web site directories for other topics as well—art, computers, politics, science, etc.

The placement of topics on the Yahoo/Health directory is somewhat arbitrary (Yahoo lets home page creators list their sites as they choose) and there is little quality control (all comers are welcome), but Yahoo's search engine works very nicely. So if you're looking for a specific topic, just click on "search" and enter a keyword or two. Yahoo will list all the home pages whose titles, keywords, or addresses contain your chosen terms.

If you're just browsing, start out by clicking on the subdirectories for your favorite topics. But beware: This is Web surfing at its most addictive—so you may want to set an alarm so you don't forget to eat dinner or go to bed.

When I last visited, the Yahoo health directory had information on more than 2,000 health sites. The top-level directory for Yahoo/Health lists the following topics:

Alternative Medicine	Medicine
Commercial Health Products	Mental Health
Companies	News
Conferences	Nursing
Dentistry	Nutrition
Disabilities	Occupational Safety and Health
Education	Pharmacology
EMF Health Issues	Public Health and Safety
Environmental Health	Public Interest Groups
Fitness	Sexuality
General Health	Support Groups
Health Administration	Travel
Health Care	Women's Health
Institutes	Weight Issues
Insurance	

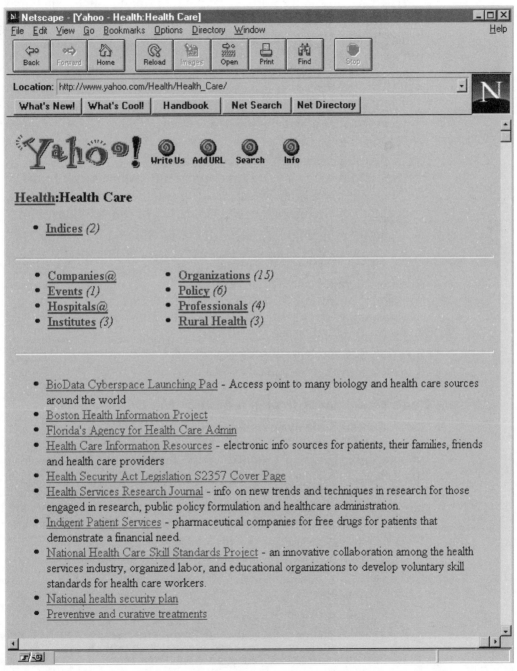

This is one page from Yahoo's vast index of World Wide Web pages. Clicking on any of the underlined phrases will take you to another Web page—either a more specific Yahoo index or the listed Web page itself. (Design © Yahoo and Netscape)

For the more adventurous Web surfer, Yahoo offers what may be the wildest ride in cyberspace: Click on "A Random Link" and it will spin you out to a randomly chosen site on the Web, selected from the thousands of home pages in its master directory. It's a surprisingly fascinating (and time-consuming) way to explore the Net. During one recent random-link session, I had the following adventures:

- Took an online tour of Web servers in Iceland (all three of them)
- Learned a lot about the life of a Canadian college student from Sri Lanka
- Listened to sound clips by a South African singer
- Visited the New York Yankees home page
- Browsed through a list of every university gopher server in the world
- Was sent to an extensive database of Internet consultants
- Cruised the home page of the University of Osaka in Japan

According to Yahoo impresarios David Filo and Jerry Yang, the self-deprecating young Stanford grad students who have unexpectedly become Web superstars almost overnight, the unusual name is an acronym for "Yet Another Hierarchically Officious Oracle."

Yahoo and Yahoo/Health are two online directories anyone with a Web browser simply must visit. This may well be the Web's most remarkable site on any topic. "Yahoo" indeed.

http://www.yahoo.com/health
E-mail: info@netscape.com

Psych Central: Dr. John Grohol's Mental Health Page

Psych Central is a truly comprehensive one-stop guide to psychology, support, and mental health issues, resources, and people on the Internet. The page includes an extensive, frequently updated guide to the best newsgroups, mailing lists, and Web pages offering psychological and emotional support.

Psychologist John Grohol has done just about everything right: The interface is clean and easy to use, the resources are extensive, the lists are updated regularly, and users are invited to join the proprietor in an online chat session each Wednesday evening—at which he will:

```
. . . gladly answer questions about mental health, provide
caring words of wisdom, point you in the right direction for
support online, and offer informative opinions about psycho-
logical issues of importance in today's ever-changing
world.... And when I'm not around [you're invited to] drop in
to discuss psychological and mental health issues with others
there; it is open to consumers and professionals alike. Best
yet, it is entirely anonymous and your identity is not seen
if you just want to join in to watch.
```

Dr. Grohol's best friend took his own life while they were both graduate students, and John has taken a strong interest in helping people find online mental health support groups ever since —"to prevent tragedies like this from happening again and to reduce the stigma of depression and other mental health problems." This Web site is dedicated to his late friend.

Psych Central may well be the best mental health resource on the Net. Don't miss it.

**Health Online Distinguished
Achievement Award**

To: John Grohol

For: Psych Central—Dr. John Grohol's
Mental Health Page

http://www.coil.com/~grohol/
E-mail: grohol@coil.com

OncoLink

OncoLink was created by Loren Buhle, Ph.D., editor of an outstanding cancer FAQ, in early 1994. Buhle tracked down just about every significant online cancer resource. You could browse through the directory, search OncoLink's extensive online database for your topic of choice, click your way through a variety of other useful home pages having to do with cancer, or read the wisdom of dozens of experienced self-helpers writing about self-managing and about coming to terms with their cancer.

Buhle included information from many sources and encouraged patients and other layfolk to share their experiences. As a result, he was charged with putting potentially "medically dangerous information" on the site and was eventually removed from his faculty position at the University of Pennsylvania. The control of OncoLink was turned over to two physicians.

The power struggle that resulted in Buhle's ouster was apparently a battle for power and glory that contained elements of the old M.D. versus Ph.D. conflict. Although many of the files that made this site unique have been removed by the current editors, no medically dangerous information was ever found on OncoLink.

OncoLink is still a useful site for people with cancer—and their friends and family, featuring continually updated information from the National Cancer Institute for those moving through the process of diagnosis, treatment, and cancer survivorship. There is useful material on the emotional aspects of cancer and helpful guidelines for family caretakers and professionals. The graphics still include a gallery of full-color art by kids with cancer. But to those who knew it in its prime—when it was hands-down the best health site on the Web—the current resource is a sad shadow of its former self.

OncoLink was just slightly ahead of its time. The conservative culture into which it was born was unable to accept something so revolutionary. But Loren Buhle is still pursuing his dream of a truly empowering, self-help-oriented Web page for people with cancer. To read Buhle's incredibly detailed cancer FAQ, go to http://www.cis.ohio-state.edu/hypertext/faq/usenet/cancer-faq/faq.html, or e-mail him for a copy at buhle01@mcrcr6.med.nyu.edu or buhle@rdz.stjohns.edu.

http://cancer.med.upenn.edu/
E-mail: editors@oncolink.upenn.edu

Information about Alcoholics Anonymous: A Guide to AA-Related Literature

An extremely valuable and nicely done self-help Web site, Information about Alcoholics Anonymous provides an extensive list of AA-related books, catalogs, conferences, and upcoming events. It also has a good list of other recovery-related Web sites and useful support materials for those who are beginning to wonder about their drinking, for problem drinkers, and for alcoholics who have been dry for a considerable period of time. There's also introductory information about AA and alcoholism for the general reader.

Among other goodies, you can read about the latest activities of AA's newly formed Living Cyber interest group, which seeks to develop online AA services and to link existing online AA networks together. You can even view digitized photos of AA's original cofounders, the revered "Dr. Bob" and "Bill W."

http://www.moscow.com/Resources/SelfHelp/AA/
E-mail: philw@moscow.com

The Recovery Home Page

While its alcohol-oriented listings overlap somewhat with the preceding AA site, the Recovery Home Page carries much additional useful information and listings for other recovery-related groups and concerns: Cocaine Anonymous, Overeating Anonymous, Adult Children of Alcoholics, other Twelve Step recovery sources, sex and love addictions, marijuana addiction, Christians in recovery, food addictions, and many more. It includes a list of commercial recovery centers and programs.

http://www.shore.net/~tcfraser/recovery.htm
E-mail: tcfraser@shore.net

The Al-Anon Home Page

The Al-Anon Home Page is a Web site for the families and friends of alcoholics. If you're concerned about someone else's drinking or were raised in an alcoholic home, Al-Anon (or Alateen) may be for you.

The site includes *The 12 Steps of Al-Anon, The 12 Traditions of Al-Anon*, a simple, self-scored questionnaire that will assist you in determining whether or not Al-Anon is for you, a listing of phone numbers you can use to find local groups around the world, and much more. As page owner Dan R. explains:

> Al-Anon offers a self-help recovery program for families and friends of alcoholics whether or not the alcoholic seeks help or even recognizes the existence of a drinking problem. Members give and receive comfort and understanding through a mutual exchange of experiences, strength and hope. Sharing of similar problems binds individuals and groups together in a bond that is protected by a policy of anonymity.
>
> Al-Anon is not a religious organization or a counseling agency. It is not a treatment center and is not allied with any other organization offering such services.... No dues or fees are required. Membership is voluntary, requiring only that one's own life has been adversely affected by someone else's drinking problem.

http://solar.rtd.utk.edu/~al-anon/
E-mail: odat@ccnet.com

For additional recovery-related sites, go to http://yahoo.com and do a search for "alcoholism."

Go Ask Alice

Ever wondered what's on the minds of college students these days? Alice knows! Go Ask Alice contains a database of questions asked by students at Columbia University and the answers supplied by a team of health educators at the school's Student Health Service.

You'll find lots on sex and relationships, as well as the problem of no boyfriend or girlfriend. The result reads as a sort of combination discussion with the family doctor, Dear Abby column, and conversation from a late-night slumber party.

You can also access Alice's database by browsing through questions on the following topics:

Sexual Health & Relationships   Drug and Alcohol Concerns
Nutrition & Healthy Diet   Emotional Well-Being
General Health

Reading the questions and answers on Go Ask Alice makes it clear that effective health education can't be separated from the other vital and complex issues of a person's life.

The "Ask Alice" format—a Web page built around an evolving database of user questions—has become an important model for self-care–oriented Web page designers.

http://www.columbia.edu/cu/healthwise/all.html
E-mail: consultant@columbia.edu

(A similar list of college students' health questions can be found at the Healthy Devil Web site, produced by the Duke University Student Health Service: http://h-devil-www.mc.duke.edu/h-devil/interact/answers.htm.)

"Collected Writings of Ivan K. Goldberg" (Ivan Goldberg's Home Page)

For the last two years, New York–based psychiatrist and psychopharmacologist Ivan Goldberg has served as an adviser and resource person for the Walkers-in-Darkness mailing list, a support network for people dealing with depression (see p. 185). His home page, "Collected Writings of Ivan K. Goldberg," lists the responses he's given to the hundreds of queries posed to him by members of the list.

The result is a searchable, browsable database of his answers. Keywords in the database range from attention deficit disorder, agoraphobia, anger, and anxiety; to Pamelor, panic, paranoia, and Prozac; to Wellbutrin, withdrawal, Xanax, and Zoloft.

This site thus provides the user with in-depth access to one very sophisticated clinician's knowledge about depression and the drug treatments for the condition. A wide range of related topics is also covered.

Dr. Goldberg understands the skills of effective online facilitation. He presents complex information in a frank, low-key style that assumes a high level of self-responsibility and competence in his correspondents. He treats the lay members of the network with the same respect and trust he would extend to a professional colleague. He's never condescending. And he does his best to share his considerable knowledge without reservation.

The mutually respectful, authoritative but nonauthoritarian relationship that has developed between Dr. Goldberg and the members of the Walkers-in-Darkness list is a fine example of supportive and collaborative online work by a health professional. Thus the site is not only an invaluable resource for those dealing with depression; it's also an important model of one very effective way in which health professionals can support online self-help networks.

Here are a few gems from Dr. G's database:

> It's not at all rare for depressed people to mistake one of the early symptoms of depression--memory loss--for the signs of early Alzheimer's. Here's one simple way of telling Alzheimer's from depression: When you ask someone a question, a depressed person will often say they don't know, or give up in the middle of giving a correct answer. A person with Alzheimer's will typically give a grossly incorrect answer--and will then be completely unaware that the answer is inappropriate.
>
> A number of studies show that sleeping more than eight hours out of twenty-four increases depression, while sleep deprivation tends to relieve depression and increase mania. In light of these findings, depressed people would be well-advised to limit their time in bed to a maximum of eight hours per day.
>
> Major mood swings are almost always more obvious to others than to you yourself. The earliest indications of both hypomania (low-level mania) and depression are typically noticed first by those around you. It's thus very useful to ask one or two close friends or family members to serve as your "early warning network" for mood changes.
>
> The incidence of sexual side effects with seratonin-specific reuptake inhibitors (e.g. Prozac) is about 40 to 50 percent at the usual doses (20 to 80 mgs. per day). At the higher doses needed by many people (e.g. 160 mg per day) the incidence of sexual side effects approaches 100 percent.

avocado.pc.helsinki.fi/~janne/ikg/
E-mail: psydoc@netcom.com

The Cansearch Home Page

The Cansearch Home Page, sponsored by the National Coalition for Cancer Survivorship, is an excellent first stop for people newly diagnosed with cancer who are new to the Web. Cancer survivor Marshall Kragen guides you through your first visits to CancerNet (see p. 267) and OncoLink (see p. 243)—both can be a bit overwhelming to the new user—and offers some gentle advice on how people with cancer can use the Net to find the medical information they need. Kragen writes:

As a twelve year survivor of colon cancer helping others I am
frequently called upon by survivors seeking information on
their specific type of cancer. When I do so I use certain
valuable sources.... This guide will take you step through
step through an orderly stop at each of the principal store-
houses of cancer information...

Before you begin...you should...know the type of cancer
you have and the stage it is in.... On CancerNet...you should
get both the physician's and patient's versions [of the files
for your type of cancer].... You will then be able to ask
more informed questions and be more aware of what is being
done for you and should be done for you....

One of the most important pieces of information you need
to know is whether there are any clinical trials being conducted for your type of cancer. If you are eligible for these
you will be at the cutting edge of medicine, often being done
by leading physicians at leading institutions. (These experimental treatments will often be provided at no cost to you.)
You can find this information on OncoLink under Clinical
Trials.

Cancer patients need lots of support and indeed I don't
think I would have survived without it... You need to talk to
those who can help you spiritually and mentally and can be a
strong source of support--other cancer survivors.

http://www.access.digex.net/~mkragen/cansearch.html
E-mail: mkragen@access.digex.net (Marshall Kragen)

DeathNet: An International Library Specializing in All Aspects of Death and Dying—With a Sincere Respect for Every Point of View

DeathNet includes a wide range of materials on the legal, moral, medical, his-
torical, and cultural aspects of human mortality. Most of these materials are not
readily available from any other sources on or off the Internet.

The resources listed here cover a wide range of end-of-life issues, from pal-
liative care to suicide and from conscious dying to euthanasia. There's information on bereavement, caregiving, and guidelines for providing emotional
support and counseling for the dying. Other topics include specific illnesses
and severe disabilities, living wills, choices in dying, and efforts to humanize
the last months and days of life.

There's also a special archive for journalists and an online obituary service offering personal home pages honoring the deceased. There are more than a hundred online links to medical libraries and other online services dealing with similar and related topics.

Founder John Hofsess encourages us to take as much responsibility for our dying as we do for the other aspects of their lives. He writes:

```
Many people with terminal illnesses find candor in rare sup-
ply from their doctors. They are not told honestly what is
likely to happen to them nor are they advised that they have
*any* options except to suffer whatever misery their imper-
sonal illness may inflict upon them as it runs its course.
```

DeathNet was recently honored as the Best Health/Medical Web Site by the Canadian Internet Awards.

http://www.islandnet.com/~deathnet/
E-mail: rights@islandnet.com

Re-evaluation Counseling (Co-counseling)

The Re-evaluation Counseling home page contains a wealth of information about re-evaluation counseling, also known as co-counseling. It is produced by the Re-evaluation Counseling community, of which I am a member. The group is a national network of self-helpers who support each other to work on emotional issues and engage in peer counseling, or co-counseling, sessions. Co-counselors support each other by working together in self-therapy sessions in which two people take turns counseling and being counseled: The active client directs the process, talking, discharging, and reevaluating old experiences, while the supportive co-counselor draws the other out and permits, encourages, and assists emotional discharge while constantly providing continuing and mostly silent attention and support.

Co-counseling assumes that everyone is born with tremendous potential, zest, and lovingness, but that those qualities may become blocked in adults as the result of accumulated distress experiences. Effective co-counseling often leads to a natural and healing emotional discharge—often evidenced by crying, trembling, laughing, or other sounds or bodily movement—through which our hurts can be healed. When such healing occurs, we can also become free of the rigid patterns of behavior and feeling we adopted to defend ourselves.

http://www.deltanet.com/rc/
E-mail: ircc@halcyon.com

The Emotional Support Guide: Internet Resources for Physical Loss, Chronic Illness, and Bereavement

The Emotional Support Guide is an extremely useful directory of resources on the Internet for emotional support for those battling a physical challenge or loss, for those who have lost a loved one, for friends and families of those going through such challenges, as well as for caregivers. It lists resources for physical loss (amputation, blindness, traumatic brain injury, etc.), chronic illness (Alzheimer's, Parkinson's, stroke, etc.), and bereavement (death of a family member, miscarriage, suicide, etc.). The resources include electronic discussion groups, directories of face-to-face support groups nationwide, and documents in which people share their personal experiences. The tone is friendly, understanding, respectful, and kind.

http://asa.ugl.lib.umich.edu/chdocs/support/emotion.html
E-mail: support-guide@umich.edu

Psychology Around the World

Psychology around the World is an extensive guide to psychology resources on the Internet, produced by psychology professor Joe Plaud of the University of North Dakota. It includes a rich collection of links to Web resources covering almost every possible aspect of psychological, emotional, and psychiatric health. While some of the materials are of academic interest, there is a great deal for self-helpers as well. A special bonus is a photo of the author with his idol, psychologist B. F. Skinner.

http://rs1.cc.und.nodak.edu:80/misc/jBAT/psychres.html
E-mail: plaud@badlands.nodak.edu

Steve Dunn's CancerGuide

I highly recommend Steve Dunn's CancerGuide. Steve is a cancer survivor. Faced with a life-threatening cancer with a bad prognosis using the standard medical remedies, he decided that if he wanted the best possible treatment, he would have to find it himself. Topics on Steve's home page include:

> The Pros and Cons of Researching Your Cancer
> Cancer and Statistics (Highly Recommended!)
> Understanding Cancer Types and Staging
> Recommended Books on Cancer
> Steve's Guide to Clinical Trials
> My Approach to Alternative Therapies
> How to Research the Medical Literature
> How to Find and Use a Medical Library
> Online Cancer Information Sources

There also are valuable links to a number of regional and local organizations (e.g., Oregon Alliance for the Mentally Ill and the Sleep Disorders Center of San Francisco). Steve writes:

```
I bumbled and stumbled my way through researching my
options....
In the end I found the right information, asked the right
questions, enrolled in the right trial, and it saved my life.
After I recovered, I decided that I wanted to help others
learn to do what I'd done...
```

The information here reflects solid knowledge and is highly personalized. This page is one lucky cancer survivor's no-holds-barred guide to how to find cancer-related information on the Internet and what to do once you've found it. Start out with Steve's tour of the site.

http://bcn.boulder.co.us/health/cancer/cancerguide.html
E-mail: dunns@bcn.boulder.co.us

Natural Medicine, Complementary Health Care & Alternative Therapies

The Natural Medicine, Complementary Health Care & Alternative Therapies home page, produced by a group of naturopaths at the Alchemical Medicine Research and Teaching Association (AMRTA), provides information on the benefits of a wide variety of natural products. Topics include nutritional supplements, herbs, homeopathic remedies, health foods, aromatherapy, Bach flower remedies, oriental medicine, massage, and other natural therapies. The site includes an excellent list of other Web sites on alternative and natural medicine. It also provides information on AMRTA's IBIS software for alternative practitioners and on the PARACELSUS mailing list for health professionals interested in complementary approaches to health.

Be sure to check out the subpage Understanding Ourselves under the heading "Health Information and Tools for Wellness." It includes a list of thought-provoking articles on body/mind medicine: "A Stress-Hardy Profile," "Emotional Tone Scale," "The Shadow and Physical Symptoms," "Holographic Consciousness," "Converting a Symptom to a Signal," and several pieces on guided imagery.

http://www.amrta.org/~amrta/
E-mail: amrta@amrta.org

The Weaver

The Weaver is a monthly Web-based magazine on psychology, spirituality, and holistic health with a New Age perspective. Recent articles cover ancient healing wisdom, Eastern spiritual approaches, personal development, and individual growth. The lead quote on the home page is destined to be copied and taped up on the monitors of many a net bunny:

> We did not weave the web of life, we are merely a strand in it. Whatever we do to the web, we do to ourselves.
>
> —Chief Seattle

http://tito.hyperlink.com/index.htm
E-mail: weaver@hyperlink.com

Dr. Bower's Complementary Medicine Home Page

Dr. Bower's Complementary Medicine Home Page provides a good overview of alternative health resources on the Internet. It covers acupuncture, body/mind medicine, chiropractic, energy medicine, flower remedies, herbs, homeopathy, reflexology, Chinese medicine, yoga, and much more. Of special interest is a section on current research into complementary medicine approaches, which includes a list of complementary practitioners by state and a selection of links to other Web sites on complementary medicine.

http://galen.med.virginia.edu:80/~pjb3s/ComplementaryHomePage.html
E-mail: pbower@virginia.edu

Self-Help Psychology Magazine

Written by mental health professionals, *Self-Help Psychology Magazine* is devoted to the in-depth discussion of issues in psychology as they affect our daily lives. Recent articles, columns, and reviews include "Should You Be Concerned about Your Drinking?" "Working with Difficult People," "Transforming Your Relationships," "Spicing Up Your Sex Life," "Avoiding Workaholism," and "Codependency or Kindness?" An unusually practical, readable, and empowering Web site, *Self-Help Psychology Magazine* is also available by e-mail.

http://www.well.com/www/selfhelp/
E-mail: selfhelp@well.com

Internet Vet

Internet Vet is a free weekly electronic newsletter in which a veterinarian answers readers' questions. The home page includes current and back issues, and you can send your own questions to the e-mail address below. *Internet Vet* also appears on the *rec.pets.cats* and *rec.pets.dogs* newsgroups. You can subscribe for free by sending the message "subscribe internet-vet-column" to listserv@netcom.com.

http://io.com/user/tittle/ivc/home page.html
E-mail: internet-vet@netcom.com

Traveler's Choice

Traveler's Choice, produced by the International Travelers Clinic, Department of Medicine, Medical College of Wisconsin, is a great source of information about the diseases and immunizations you need to be concerned with when traveling to foreign countries. Diseases listed include cholera, dengue fever, diphtheria, giardiasis, hepatitis, malaria, meningitis, poliomyelitis, plague, rabies, and typhoid. It also has guidelines for avoiding altitude sickness, auto accidents, and motion sickness—and links to more than a dozen other Web sites dealing with healthy travel.

http://www.intmed.mcw.edu/travel.html
E-mail: barnas@post.its.mcw.edu

Interactive Frog Dissection: An Online Tutorial

Miss your chance to dissect a real live frog in high school or college? Don't despair. You can now dissect a full-color virtual frog at the Interactive Frog Dissection. This nifty Web site, produced by the Curry School of Education at the University of Virginia, was designed for use in high school biology classrooms. It makes a great demo for those unfamiliar with the Web. Impress your children and amuse your friends. It's amazingly like the real (gulp!) thing.

http://curry.edschool.Virginia.EDU:80/~insttech/frog/menu.html

Good Medicine Journal

The *Good Medicine Journal* offers an interesting selection of articles on alternative health practices, with an emphasis on integrating alternative approaches into mainstream medical practice. One recent article featured the newly introduced guided imagery program at Marin (California) General Hospital. And while you're at the site, check out the other health and fitness resources at Coolware, which contains this journal. You'll find it up one menu, at http://www.coolware.com/health/info.html.

http://www.coolware.com/health/good_med/
E-mail: webmaster@coolware.com

The Weightlifting Home Page

An impressive and useful collection of links to a wide variety of information about weight training and bodybuilding, the Weightlifiting Home Page offers glamorous but tasteful pictures of some elaborately muscled males. It also includes full access to the newsgroup *misc.fitness*, the *misc.fitness* FAQ, the Weights mailing list FAQ, an abdominal training FAQ, and links to the Training Nutrition home page.

http://www.cs.odu.edu/~ksw/weights.html
E-mail: ksw@cs.odu.edu (Kyle Wilson)

PharmInfoNet

PharmInfoNet offers an extensive assortment of information on prescription drugs, including an excellent FAQ. While much of what you'll find here was designed for health professionals and those in the pharmaceutical industry, consumers too will find much useful drug information. The page includes drug-related research bulletins, a drug information database (DrugDB), an archive of discussions from the *sci.med.pharmacy* newsgroup, and links to other drug-related Web sites.

To use DrugDB, you can either browse by brand name or search alphabetically. Click on one of the hotlinked articles and you'll get a detailed explanation of the drug, including its mode of action and in most cases a nifty molecular diagram.

http://pharminfo.com/pin_hp.html
E-mail: pialtd@ix.netcom.com

Quantum Medicine

A Budapest-based cyberspace source for naturopathy, homeopathy, acupuncture, and other areas of natural medicine, Quantum Medicine includes useful links to other worldwide online resources for these topics. For example, clicking on the homeopathy link leads you to a brief introduction to what homeopathy is and provides links to everything from allergies to cancer to hypertension to smoking. These links enable you to download graphs as well as text-based information on these topics. There is also a disease dictionary that will soon be available in shareware. For more information on this knowledge base, send a message to genesis@usa.net.

http://usa.net/qmed/
E-mail: qmed@usa.net

The Breast Cancer Information Clearinghouse

An excellent resource for women with breast cancer, the Breast Cancer Information Clearinghouse is extensive, fairly attractive, and easy to use. I particularly liked the search capabilities. The graphics give the site a friendly feel, and the information provided is very useful. The site includes a link to CancerNet, a list of support groups around the country, and articles from the *National Alliance for Breast Cancer Newsletter.*

http://nysernet.org/bcic/
E-mail: kennett@nysernet.org (Terri Kennett)

Women's Health Resources on the Internet

A 22-page list, Women's Health Resources on the Internet covers emotional health (body image, eating disorders, relationships, stress management, support groups), physical health (diseases, drugs, alcohol, medical tests, gynecological exams, fitness, nutrition), and sexual health (AIDS, birth control, menopause, menstruation, pregnancy, sexually transmitted diseases, sexuality). It's a nicely done guide to an important health topic.

http://asa.ugl.lib.umich.edu/chdocs/womenhealth/womens_health.html
E-mail: women-health@umich.edu

HabitSmart

Offering practical approaches to changing addictive behavior, HabitSmart is an impressive, useful page and a good starting place for those dealing with addictions. Topics covered include:

Self-Scoring Alcohol Checkup
Coping with Addiction
Coping with Adolescents
How Kids Learn to Drink
Understanding Blood Alcohol Level
Changing Addictive Behaviors
Recent Addiction Research
Coping with Urges
Smoking Reduction
Self-Scoring Drinkers' Checkup
A User-Friendly Model of Change
Links to Other Addiction-Related Web Sites

http://www.cts.com/~habtsmrt/
E-mail: wstrmyr@cts.com or habtsmrt@cts.com

The Sleep Medicine Home Page

The Sleep Medicine Home Page provides good information, including eye-opening facts, about sleep, sleep apnea, insomnia, restless sleepers, sudden infant death syndrome, dreams and dreaming, and a variety of other common sleep problems and concerns. It also includes links to related Web sites, a list of sleep-related newsgroups (*alt.dreams*, *alt.support.sleep-disorder*, etc), a sleep apnea FAQ, and a collection of articles (e.g., "Everything You Always Wanted to Know about Caffeine"). The site is operated by the National Sleep Foundation.

http://www.cloud9.net/~thorpy/
E-mail: thorpy@aecom.yu.edu

Mood Disorders

A nice site that, like Ivan Goldberg's home page (see p. 246), provides fairly comprehensive coverage of depression and manic depression, Mood Disorders contains a terrific list of resources for these difficult yet common problems. It includes links to the excellent Walkers-in-Darkness and Pendulum mailing lists, the *alt.support.depression* FAQ, a good annotated list of books on depression, a number of other valuable resources on depression (e.g., self-scoring scales, and information on seasonal affective disorder and antidepressant drugs), and a long list of other valuable mental health resources on the Internet.

http://avocado.pc.helsinki.fi/~janne/mood/mood.html
E-mail: janne@avocado.pc.helsinki.fi

The Virtual Heart

The Virtual Heart is part of the Franklin Institute's virtual science museum, a successful example of using the Web to provide access to textbook-type health information. For self-care tips, be sure to check out the section "How to Have a Healthy Heart."

http://sln.fi.edu/biosci/heart.html
E-mail: webmaster@slnfi.edu

Roger Burns' Chronic Fatigue Syndrome

An extensive collection of information and links to the world of online resources for chronic fatigue syndrome, Roger Burns' Chronic Fatigue Syndrome home page includes CFS-related discussion groups, access to several CFS electronic newsletters and magazines, a chronic fatigue syndrome FAQ, a guide to dealing with doctors, and an extensive list of CFS-related Web sites and other electronic resources.

Q. What is CFS?
A. Chronic fatigue syndrome (CFS) is an emerging illness characterized by debilitating fatigue (experienced as exhaustion and extremely poor stamina), neurological problems, and a variety of flu-like symptoms. The illness is also known as chronic fatigue immune dysfunction syndrome (CFIDS), and outside of the USA is usually known as myalgic encephalomyelitis (ME). In the past the syndrome has been known as chronic Epstein-Barr virus (CEBV).

The core symptoms include excessive fatigue, general pain, mental fogginess, and often gastro-intestinal problems. Many other symptoms will also be present, however they will typically be different among different individuals. These include: fatigue following stressful activities; headaches; sore throat; sleep disorder; abnormal temperature; and others.

http://metro.turnpike.net/C/cfsnews
E-mail: cfs-news-request@list.nih.gov

Other Health-Related Web Pages Worth Checking Out

Here's a list of other health-related Web home pages that provide a good starting place for their topic:

Abdominal Training (http://www.dstc.edu.au:80/staff/nigel-ward/abfaq/abdominal-training.html)

Abuse Survivors (http://www.tezcat.com/~ting/psych.shtml)

Addictions (http:www.well.com/users/woal)

AIDS (http://actwin.com:80/aids/vl.html) and (http://the body.com)

Allergies (http://www.sig.net:80/~allergy/welcome.html)

Alternative Health and Self-Managed Care (http://www.healthworld.com)

Alternative Therapies (http://werple.mira.net.au/sumeria) and (http://www.sky.net/~ngt/welcome.html)

Alzheimer's Disease (http://werple.mira.net.au/~dhs/ad.html) and (http://teri.bio.uci.edu)

Aromatherapy (http://www.dircon.co.uk:80/home/philrees/fragrant/aroma1.html)

Attention Deficit Disorder (http://www.seas.upenn.edu:80/~mengwong/add/) and (http://wwwchadd.org)

Ayurvedic Medicine (http://www.protree.com:80/Spirit/ayurveda.html)

Balance Magazine: Fitness on the Net
(http://tito.hyperlink.com/balance/)

Be Your Own Therapist Newsletter (http://www.slip.net/~purplepp/)

Bone Marrow Transplants (http://www.ai.mit.edu/people/laurel/
Bmt-talk/maillist.html)

Breast Cancer (http://www-med.stanford.edu/CBHP)

Cancer (http://bcn.boulder.co.us/health/cancer/canguide.html and
http://asa.ugl.lib.umich.edu.chdocs/cancer/cancerguide.html)

Carpal Tunnel Syndrome (http://www.cyberport.net:80/mmg/cts/
ctsintro.html)

Chiropractic (http://www.mbnet.mb.ca:80/~jwiens/chiro.html)

Chronic Fatigue (http://huizen.dds.nl:80/~cfs-news/)

Cool Medical Site of the Week (http://hooked.net/users/wcd/cmsotw.html)

Crohn's Disease and Ulcerative Colitis (http://qurlyjoe.bu.edu:80/
cduchome.html)

Cybercise–Fitness and Health (http://www.cybercise.com)

Depression Resource List (http://earth.execpc.com/~corbeau/)

Diabetes (http://www.niddk.nih.gov:80/NIDDK_HomePage.html and
http://www.biostat.wisc.edu/diaknow/index.html)

Digestive Problems
(http://www.niddk.nih.gov:80/NIDDK_HomePage.html)

Drug and Alcohol Abuse (http://www.health.org:80/)

Drug Information (http://www.pitt.edu:80/~mbtst3/druginfo.html)

Eating Disorders (http://ccwf.cc.utexas.edu:80/jackson/UTHealth/
eating.html)

The Emotional Development of Children
(http://www.med.umich.edu:80/ aacap/facts.index.html)

Emotional Support on the Internet (http://fiona.umsmed.edu/
~sturges/support.text)

Exercise Log (http://www.sweatnet.com)

Food Diary (http://www.nutribytes.com)

Herbal Medicine (http://sunsite.unc.edu:80/hrf/) and
(http://www.cri.com/~robbee/herbal.html)

Home Test Kits Homepage
(http://kerouac.pharm.uky.edu:80/KitsHP.html)

Homeopathy (http://www.dungeon.com:80/home/cam/homeo.html)

Inline Skating (http://www.xs4all.nl:80/~lowlevel/skate/inline-skating.html)

Medscape Medical News Service (http://medscape.com)

MedWeb Mental Health Index
(http://www.cc.emory.edu:80/WHSCL/medweb.mentalhealth.html)

Mental Health Net (http://www.cmhc.com)

Mental Health Problems of Children
(http://www.psych.med.umich.edu/web/aacap/factsFam/)

Multiple Myeloma (http://www.comed.com/IMF/imf.html)

Multiple Sclerosis (http://www.infosci.org)

Naturopathy
(http://www.sims.net/organizations/naturopath/natuopath.html)

Nicotine Anonymous (http://www.slip.net/~billh/nicahome.html)

Noodles Panic-Anxiety Page
(http://frank.mtsu.edu/~sward/anxiety/anxiety/html)

Nutrition (http://128.196.106.42:80/nutrition.html)

Obsessive-Compulsive Disorder
(http://mtech.csd.uwm.edu/~fairlite/ocd.html)

Osteopathy (http://www.demon.co.uk:80/osteopath/index.html)

PMS Information (http://www.ccnet.com/~diatribe/pms.html)

Qigong (http://www.protree.com:80/spirit/qigong.html)

Quit Net–Stop-Smoking Information
(http://csc6203s.mgh.harvard.edu/QuitNet/index.html)

Shrynk BBS–Mental Health and Wellness (http://shrynk.com/)

Sleep Apnea
(http://www.access.digex.net:80/~faust/sldord/osa.faq.html)

Strescape Alternative Health Page (http://stresscape.com)

Tai Chi (http://www.protree.com:80/Spirit/tai-chi.html)

Weight Training
(http://www.bigdipper.umd.edu/healthfitness/index.html)

Wellness Web (http://wellweb.com/wellness)

Women's Health Topics
(http://www.mit.edu:8001/people/sorokin/women/index.html)

Your Health Information Resource
(http://www.coolware.com/health/joel/ health.html)

How to Find More Web Home Pages

As I suggested at the beginning of this chapter, my own favorite way to look for health Web sites is via Yahoo/Health (http://www.yahoo.com/health). Here are some other good directories and search engines that can help you find the Web sites that are right for you:

Aliweb
(http://web.nexor.co.uk/public/aliweb/search/doc/form.html)

All-in-One Search Page (http://albany.net/~wcross/all1srch.html)

InfoSeek (http://www.infoseek.com)

Internet Sleuth (http://www.intbc.com/sleuth/)

Lycos (http://lycos.cs.cmu.edu/)

Multimedia Medical Reference Library
(http://www.tiac.net/users/jtward/multimed.html)

Open Text Web Index
(http://opentext.uunet.ca:8080/omw/html)

Point (http://www.pointcom.com/text/home/)

SavySearch
(http://www.cs.colostate.edu/~dreiling/smartform.html)

Spry Internet Wizard
(http://compuserve.com.wizard/wizard/html)

WebCrawler (http://webcrawler.cs.washington.edu/WebCrawler/WebQuery.html)

Whole Internet Catalog/Health (http://www.gnn.com/gnn/wic/med.toc.html)

World Wide Web Worm
(http://www.cs.colorado.edu/home/mcbryan/WWWW.html)

Yanoff Connection/Medical
(http://www.uwm.edu/Mirror/inet2.html#MEDICAL)

Chapter 12

Other Online Resources

When historians look back at this early period of online self-help, they'll conclude that this was the time humankind finally found a way to use high tech to escape the pervasive isolation of modern society.

"MarshHawk"
Online self-helper

———————— ◆ ————————

THIS CHAPTER LISTS a number of valuable online resources, health information brokers, books, and people that didn't quite fit into any of the earlier chapters.

Health-Oriented Computer Bulletin Boards

Computer bulletin boards systems (BBSs) are like small computer networks, a sort of miniversion of AOL, Prodigy, or CompuServe. There are thousands to choose from, including a considerable number devoted to health and self-help topics.

Accessing a BBS is a bit more complicated than logging on to a commercial computer network. You'll need a computer, a modem, and telecommunications software capable of accessing dial-up computer bulletin boards. You'll also need the log-in or modem phone number of the BBS you want to access. You'll receive log-on instructions on screen when you call.

Health-oriented BBSs range from the Nerve Center in Maryland (modem: [410] 655-4708) to the Virtual Medical Center in Montana (modem: [406] 994-2564) and from the Nursing Network in Connecticut (modem: [203] 237-1131) to the Cardio Board in Washington State (modem: [206] 328-7876) and Med Help International on Long Island (modem: [516] 423-0472).

Many of these BBSs belong to an international exchange network called Fidonet, which allows them to share postings on more than three hundred special health-related sections. Many also carry newsletters, news items, and educational programs. A few self-help organizations have developed boards of their own, e.g., NAPWA-Link, run by the National Association of People with AIDS (modem: [202] 898-0414). Also of special interest is a bulletin board that specializes in providing resources to those with handicaps, Handicapped News (modem: [203] 926-6168) and another for hospital administrators, health care executives, vendors, professional health care organizations, consultants, other health care professionals, and futurists: Health Online (modem [415] 356-4300; e-mail: info@healthonline.com).

The Black Bag BBS
(modem: [610] 454-7396)

Of special note is the remarkable online health resource, Black Bag Bulletin Board, where sysop-physician Ed Del Grasso (ed@blackbag.com) maintains an up-to-date national list of more than three hundred health-related BBSs. A printed copy of the Black Bag List is available by snail-mail for a minimum donation of $5.00 from Ed Del Grasso, PO Box 632, Collegeville, PA 19426, or simply call the Black Bag BBS to download a free copy.

In addition to maintaining its list of health BBSs, the Black Bag BBS is itself a terrific resource, providing access to a huge assortment of other valuable health-related support networks. And although he provides a great deal of free access and performs a vital service on a volunteer basis, Del Grasso depends on donations to support the board's continuing existence. So if you end up using the board, please consider a generous donation.

Discussion Groups and Message Areas on the Black Bag Bulletin Board

12 Steps to Recovery	Attention Deficit Disorder
AIDS/HIV	Blindness
Alcoholic Families	Cancer Survivors
Alcoholics Anonymous	Caregiver Support
Alcoholism	Cerebral Palsy
Alternative Medicine	Child Abuse
Alzheimer's	Chronic Fatigue Syndrome
Amputees	Chronic Pain
Anxiety	CVA/Stroke

Deafness	Occupational Injury
Diabetes	Overeaters
Disabled	Post-Polio
Disabled Children	Problem Child
Drug Abuse	Rare Conditions
Fibromyalgia	Respiratory Disease
Gender Identity	Seizure Disorders
Hearing Loss	Spinal Injury
Incest Survivors	Spouses of Sexual Abuse Survivors
Mental Health	Stop Smoking
Multiple Personality	Stress Management
Multiple Sclerosis	Survivors of Ritual Abuse
Narcotics Anonymous	Tourette's Syndrome

**Health Online Distinguished
Achievement Award**

To: Ed Del Grasso

For: The Black Bag BBS and
The Black Bag List
of Health-Related Bulletin Boards

How to Learn More about Computer Bulletin Boards

If you'd like to learn more about computer bulletin boards, a good source of up-to-date information is *Boardwatch* magazine. (Call [303] 973-6038 for subscription information.) You can also learn a great deal by perusing the Internet newsgroups devoted to this topic:

- *alt.bbs.lists.d* features discussions of computer bulletin boards and related subjects.
- *alt.bbs.lists* carries lists of bulletin boards on a variety of topics.
- *alt.bbs.ads* contains advertisements for a huge number of diverse bulletin boards.

Internet Relay Chat (IRC)

Internet relay chat is a kind of worldwide online version of CB radio. IRC is organized into hundreds of channels. The names of the channels always begin with a pound sign ("#"). Typical IRC channels include #asap (abuse survivors and partners), #Arthritis, and #Recovery. The titles of the channels are specified by the user and may change daily. If you don't find the channel you want, you can start your own.

IRC is not currently available through the commercial services. If you have a direct Internet connection, you should ask your provider to supply or recommend the software you need to participate.

One online self-helper who frequents the self-help channels of IRC wrote:

> I'm a 35-year-old woman who's had a challenging life, three kids, and a lot of experience in working through my own difficulties. As an IRC self-helper, I constantly find myself comforting and counseling online friends--most are much younger than me, e.g., a depressed 14-year-old boy, who thinks he'll never be loved, a young man, 20, who cuts himself, and a young woman, 24, who's facing a reproductive crisis that's tearing her apart.
>
> I've gotten pretty good at reading their words, feeling what lies behind them, and offering my support and what help I can. A group of us from one IRC channel recently kept a young woman who'd attempted suicide on the phone until help arrived, then spoke to her doctor about her problems. Many IRCers are seriously troubled, but can't or won't seek professional help, sometimes because their parents deny the problem, sometimes for financial reasons.
>
> There are *lots* of channels devoted to self-help support groups, though they're always changing, and many people like me, who see their friends' pain and do what we can to help. I limit my input to that of an online friend, offering comfort and advice, never stepping over the line into providing a professional role.
>
> Hope this helps...come say hello on #arthritis some time. (My IRC screenname is deadrose@irc.)
> Heidi (sonata@eskimo.com)

For more on IRC, see the Web page at http://www.cyberspace.com/~elric.

Gopher Sites

Gopher is a special type of software designed for searching for and retrieving documents on the Internet, especially text documents stored at gopher sites (sometimes called gopher servers). Gopher sites are like World Wide Web sites, except that they contain text-only files without graphics or hyperlinks. Gopher sites can be accessed by typing the gopher address into your Web browser, just as you would with a Web page address. A gopher site address looks like this: gopher://gopher.health.state.ny.us/11/.consumer.

Gopher sites are what we used to have before the World Wide Web was widely used. Many universities and government agencies that formerly offered gopher servers are now switching over to Web pages, but many interesting gopher sites still remain. A good example is the Library of Congress's Medical Resource List (gopher://marvel.loc.gov/11/global/med/med). This site gives you access to all the principal gophers at all U.S. medical centers. The top-level directory for the gopher site lists these topics:

```
Medical Journals
Guides to Medical Resources on the Internet
Medical Sources Arranged by Discipline or Disease
Health Sciences Resources (Medical College of Georgia)
Academic Physician and Scientist
Albert Einstein College of Medicine
American Medical Student Association
American Physiological Society
Anesthesiology Resources
Cancer & AIDS Resources
Center for Advanced Medical Informatics at Stanford (CAMIS)
College of Optometry (Ohio State University)
Comprehensive Epidemiological Data Resource Gopher
Continuing Medical Education (CME) Resources
Drug Information Center
Food and Drug Administration FDA BBS
GASNET Anesthesiology Gopher
Harvard University Medical Gopher
Health Care Reform
Health and Clinical Information (+Bioethics Online Service)
Human Genome Resources
Institute for Child Health Policy (University of Florida)
International Center for Genetic Engineering & Biotech...
```

```
Medical Research Council of Canada
Medical Resource Directory from UC Irvine
NIH National Institutes of Health Gopher System
NYU Medical Center, Hippocrates Project gopher
National Institute of Allergy and Infectious Disease (NIAID)
National Library of Medicine (NIH)
National Micropopulation Simulation Resource
National Toxicology Program (NTP)
New York State Department of Health
Nursing Resources
Physicians' GenRx International (Prescription Drugs)
RuralNet Rural Medicine Gopher (Marshall U. Sch. of Med.)
Safety and Health, US Dept. of Energy
Society for Neuroscience
The American Heart Association
Toxicology and Environmental Health Info Gopher
World Health Organization (WHO)
```

Gopher sites can also contain lists of other gopher sites, so you can click your way through the libraries and databases of some of our most august medical centers. For example, here's the top-level directory for the Harvard Medical gopher site (gopher://gopher.med.harvard.edu:70/1):

```
About the Harvard Medical Gopher
Countway Library of Medicine: Resources & Services
Harvard Medical Area Information
Basic Science Resources
Clinical Resources
Public Health Resources
Medical Education Resources
Government and Statistical Resources
Grants and Funding Resources
Libraries and Literature Resources
Harvard University and Other Local Information
News and Publications
Virtual Reference Desk
Internet Resources
NEW AND NOTEWORTHY AT THIS GOPHER SITE
Comments and Suggestions
```

CancerNet
(gopher://gopher.nih.gov:70/11/clin/cancernet/pdqinfo)

CancerNet is the National Cancer Institute's database of professional and patient files for many types of cancer (see p. 181). The top-level directory of the CancerNet gopher site looks like this:

PDQ Treatment Statements for Physicians

Extensive information files for approximately eighty different types of cancer, from AIDS-related lymphoma to Wilm's tumor, written for physicians

PDQ Treatment Statements for Patients

Extensive information files for approximately eighty different types of cancer, from AIDS-related lymphoma to Wilm's tumor, written for layfolk

PDQ Supportive Care Statements

Practical guidelines for managing a variety of problems that people with cancer may face, from constipation and fatigue to sleep disorders and superior vena cava syndrome

PDQ Screening/Prevention Statements

Guidelines for preventing and screening for cancer

PDQ Drug Information Statements

A guide to experimental drugs for cancer

Other PDQ Information

Information on experimental treatments for cancer

Other Interesting Health-Related Gopher Sites

Here are a few more interesting health-related gopher sites:

Rice University's Healthinfo Service (gopher://riceinfo.rice.edu/11/Safety/HealthInfo)

Purdue's Mental and Physical Health Resources (gopher://oasis.cc.purdue.edu:2525/)

University of Illinois' McKinley Health Center (gopher://vixen.cso.uiuc.edu:70/11/UI/CSF/health/heainfo)

The New York State Department of Health's Consumer Information Gopher (gopher://gopher.health.state.ny.us/11/.consumer)

Medical Matrix

The Medical Matrix is one of the best directories of professional medical resources on the Internet. This unique database comes in four different configurations:

1. Medical Matrix (a Web page)
2. The Medical List: A Guide to Internet Clinical Medicine Resources (a gopher site)
3. H-Matrix (an Internet mailing list)
4. *Physician's Guide to the Internet* (a book)

An older version of this database, which at the time was usually called Lee Hancock's List (from the days when most people assumed that "Internet" probably had something to do with stockings or thermal underwear) was the first online list of medical resources I ever saw. I immediately wanted to compile a similar guide for layfolk. So in a sense, Lee's list was an early inspiration for this book. (For more on Lee, see the Author's Notes.)

These guides are necessary reading for all health professionals seriously interested in medical resources on the Internet. The lists include online resources for radiographic imaging, medical case studies, clinical guidelines and treatment protocols, product information, conference announcements, and state-of-the-art research and advanced discussion in virtually every medical field.

Some of the resources require a high level of technical competence. Others are for professionals only. But if you're seeking clinical medical information, this database is an excellent place to look.

Here's how to use each of the four resources.

Medical Matrix (http://kuhttp.cc.ukans.edu/cwis/units/ medcntr/Lee/homepage.html)

The Medical Matrix home page, with hypertext links to many of the listed resources, is best for online browsing. It was compiled by medical librarian Lee Hancock and family physician Gary Malet. Lee and Gary's lists on specific medical topics (e.g., AIDS, cancer therapies) provide access to state-of-the-art research bulletins. Much of the information here is more current than anything in the printed literature. Some of the professional sites listed include a selection of lay health education materials. The top-level directory looks like this:

```
Introduction to Medical Matrix
News and New Resources
Featured Programs
Disease Categorized Information
Specialty Categorized Information
Medical Education
Healthcare Policy
Clinical Practice Issues
Medical Literature Searches
Images and Multimedia
Allied Health Worker Resources
Patient Education and Support
Medical Institutions, Schools, and Libraries
Electronic Journals
Resource Guides and Miscellaneous Programs
Clinical Medicine Documents
Introduction to Medical Internet Resources
How to Access Internet Medical Resources
WWW Search Engines
```

The Medical List: A Guide to Internet Clinical Medicine Resources (gopher://una.hh.lib.umich.edu/00/ inetdirsstacks/medclin%3amalet)

The Medical List gopher site is the best place to download the entire document (or parts of it.) You can then either read it at your leisure on screen or print out selected parts or the whole thing.

H-Matrix

The H-Matrix mailing list provides continuing updates of the lists and discussion about the resources listed and related matters. To subscribe, send the message "Subscribe Hmatrix-L Your_Name" to listserv@www.kumc.edu.

Lee and Gary update the lists regularly and would be happy to hear about additional or updated listings for future editions. You can contact Lee at LE07144@kumc.wpo.ukans.edu and Gary at gmalet@surfer.win.net.

**Health Online Distinguished
Achievement Award**

To: Lee Hancock. and Gary Malet

For: Medical Matrix

Physician's Guide to the Internet

The Physician's Guide to the Internet, by Lee Hancock (Lippincott-Raven, New York, 1995, ISBN 0-397-51634-7), contains much the same material in a handy, reference-book format. It also has introductory chapters and technical information on accessing the listed resources.

Other Useful Online Resources

Even though the following resources were designed primarily for health professionals, they contain many resources that will be of interest to the self-helper.

MedWeb: Electronic Newsletters and Journals (http://www.emory.edu/WHSCL/medweb.html)

Med Web is a free medical library on the Net. It contains a spectacular collection of hundreds of online medical sites—including medical journals and newsletters—as well as some popular health publications—many with downloadable full text.

IHP Net Health Resources (http://www.interaccess.com/ihpnet/health.html)

An extensive directory of medical resources for professionals, IHP Net Health Resource includes lists by medical specialty and a useful list of the home pages of health-related international and U.S. agencies.

Medscape (http://www.medscape.com/)

A medical textbook online subtitled "The Online Resource for Better Patient Care," Medscape provides peer-reviewed, practice-oriented information edited by leading clinicians. Topics currently covered include AIDS, infectious diseases, urology, and surgery. There's also a quiz that lets you test your knowledge of medical facts. Hypertext articles and full-color graphics are supplemented with archival literature searches and annotated links to relevant Internet resources.

The EINet Galaxy Medicine Page
(http://galaxy.einet.net/galaxy/Medicine.html)

A good list of resources by medical subspecialty, from allergies to urology, the EINet Galaxy Medicine Page also contains useful information for medical students and those applying to medical school.

The Multimedia Medical Reference Library
(http://www.tiac.net/users/jtward/index.html)

The Multimedia Medical Reference Library is another extensive and attractive guide to professional medical resources on the Internet.

The National Wellness Institute (nwelli@wis.com)

The National Wellness Institute sponsors a workshop each July entitled "Wellness Goes Online," taught by NWI Chairman Bill Hettler, M.D., and myself. It covers the areas described in this book, plus issues of special interest to health, wellness, and computer professionals. The NWI is also the home of the National Wellness Association, an organization for wellness and health education professionals. Send a message to Anne Helmke at the address above for further information.

Using a Health Information Broker

Here's another useful way to use online services to access the best available medical information on a topic of special concern: Hire a health information broker to do it for you. You may choose this route whether or not you have access to a computer linked to the Net.

Here's how it works: You call in by phone, describing your current medical concern in considerable detail. The broker will then put together a customized search of the popular and professional medical literature. Within a few days, you'll receive a fat packet of printed information on your topic of interest.

According to consumer health information specialist Patty Phelan (prp@well.com) in Sausalito, California, who is in the process of setting up her own health information broker service, Direct Medical Knowledge, the two best U.S. health information brokers are:

The Health Resource, Inc.
564 Locust Street
Conway, AR 72032
(800) 949-0090

Prices: $195 for a comprehensive search on topics other than cancer, $295 for a comprehensive cancer search

Notes: The staff is friendly, easy to work with, and highly professional in all respects. They'll send you a nicely bound report. Express delivery is available.

Planetree Health Resource Center
2040 Webster Street
San Francisco, CA 94115
(415) 923-3680

Prices: $35 for basic information, $100 for a comprehensive search
Notes: The staff is friendly and pleasant to work with but sometimes hard to reach. Reports consist of a loose packet of carefully selected but unbound printouts and articles.

Here's another online information broker that can provide medical information via e-mail. This nonprofit organization appreciates donations of $35 and up per information request to help cover their costs.

Med Help International
Suite 130, Box 188
6300 North Wickham Road
Melbourne, FL 32940
(407)253-9048

http://medhlp.netusa.net/index.html
E-mail: staff@medhlp.netusa.net

The American Self-Help Clearinghouse

It's only fitting that we end this book with one of the most valuable and important resources in the field, the New Jersey–based American Self-Help Clearinghouse. A telephone-based service ([800] 367-6274 or [800] FOR-MASH [Mutual Aid Self-Help]), it can help you find information on more than 750 self-help organizations across the country. Many, though not all, of these groups currently offer online resources.

Depression has recently become the leading call-in category at the clearinghouse, narrowly displacing the former number one, alcohol-related problems. If the clearinghouse can't match you up with a satisfactory existing group or network, it will help you start one of your own.

The first state-financed self-help clearinghouse in the country, it has since become a model for twelve others in the United States and abroad. Clearinghouse staffers have helped to set up similar clearinghouses in California, New York, and Texas, as well as in Argentina, Japan, and Croatia.

**Health Online Distinguished
Achievement Award**

To: The American Self-Help Clearinghouse

For: Their Information and Support Services for Self-
Helpers in New Jersey, across the United States, and
around the World

In addition to his important work at the clearinghouse, founder and executive director Ed Madara has been a key facilitator of the growth of online self-help networks. There are few places in self-help cyberspace I visited where Ed hadn't been long before, and his name was by far the most frequently cited when I asked self-helpers about online contacts who had been most helpful to them.

If his busy schedule hadn't prevented it, Ed would have been a co-author of this book. As it was, he give me invaluable information and an unwavering flow of advice and support.

Ed kindly provided the first words in this book. I'd like him to have the last as well. When I asked him to suggest a few key points I could use to end this chapter, I received the following message:

```
Dear Tom,
The most important points to end your book with might well be
these:
(1) We often fail to realize that most of the health-related
associations, societies, and online networks we have today
were started by individuals much like ourselves, faced with
an illness or that of a family member, who didn't want others
to go through that hell alone. Online systems make it easy
for us to express our natural altruism, bringing the isolated
together, and providing 'you are not alone' support.

(2) In addition to what we can do to support each other, self-
help networks can do much to help our society at large: by
providing critical feedback to medical professionals, by help-
ing citizens become involved in local health decisions, and by
providing grassroots input for medical research, professional
education, and state and national health policy issues.

(3) The self-help process can't begin until one or two or
three individuals muster the courage to begin. That's why I'm
especially interested in helping those who are seeking to
start new types of self-help support networks (either face-
to-face or online) that don't yet exist on the planet. I've
```

```
made it a personal priority to help these first-timers get
going, so I'd be happy to hear from any *Health Online* read-
ers seeking to take these crucial first steps.

Take care and hope,

Ed Madara
EdMadara@aol.com
70275.1003@compuserve.com
```

Essential Reading

The Self-Help Sourcebook: Finding and Forming Mutual Aid Self-Help Groups

Compiled and edited by Barbara J. White and Edward J. Madara

The Self-Help Sourcebook is a guide for those seeking to find or form mutual aid self-help groups in their local communities. Up to date, well written, and invaluable, it includes a section on electronic self-help. It is available for $10.00 postpaid from:

The American Self-Help Clearinghouse
Attn: Sourcebook
Northwest Covenant Medical Center
25 Pocono Road
Denville, NJ 07834
(800) 367-6274

Epilogue

The Healing Computer

*The future of health care in these troubled times requires cooperation
between organized medicine and self-help groups to achieve the best care for
the lowest cost.*

C. Everett Koop, M.D.
Former U.S. Surgeon General

It ALWAYS SURPRISES ME when people speak of the information superhighway as
something that belongs to the distant future. The online revolution has
already begun.

The self-care movement goes back at least to the early 1970s. But today a
new generation of electronic tools makes it easy to do what only the most dedicated and diligent could do before. It now seems clear that later generations of
online and on-disk systems will allow us to build a new Information Age health
care system around the health-savvy, health-responsible layperson. With the
support of such systems, a person with a health concern or problem should be
able to manage it at the highest possible level of the following hierarchy.

The Six Tiers of Information Age Health Care

1. **Individual Self-Care.** When we become aware of a health concern, we
   will first attempt to prevent, diagnose, manage, or treat it on our own,
   with the help of printed, online, or on-disk resources. In most cases, we'll
   be able to do so.

2. **Friends and Family**. If individual self-care doesn't solve the problem, we'll turn to family, friends, and neighbors for advice, information, and support. The telephone and e-mail will frequently be used for such requests. Much additional care will be provided at this level as more lay-folk are encouraged to see themselves not only as consumers of health care, but as key providers of care to their friends and loved ones.

3. **Self-Help Networks**. When the help above is not sufficient, we'll turn to experienced self-helpers, mutual-aid networks, face-to-face self-help groups, and other "natural helpers" outside our immediate circle of family and friends. The emerging online links described in this book make it much easier to reach those with the appropriate expertise.

4. **Health Professionals as Facilitators**. Many unnecessary clinical visits occur because consumers can't obtain the information or advice they need by phone or e-mail. Facilitating electronic communication between layfolk and health professionals will help cut medical costs while improving access to professional care. This development will require health professionals to step out of their accustomed role as unquestioned authorities and to learn to serve as coaches, advisers, facilitators, and supporters of self-provided care. Resolving issues of legal liability would make health professionals more comfortable with this new role.

5. **Health Professionals as Partners**. When serious or chronic problems require occasional or regular contacts between patients, families, and health professionals, layfolk and clinicians will increasingly work together as client-professional teams guided by computerized medical systems and relying on computer databases—rather than the professional's memory—for access to current medical knowledge. These contacts will include more and more electronic communications and fewer face-to-face clinic and hospital visits.

6. **Health Professionals as Authorities**. When all else fails, in emergency situations, when the person needing care is unconscious or incapacitated, and in cases where the client chooses certain high-tech interventions (e.g., surgery), we may ask our health professionals to step in and make the key medical decisions—at least temporarily. But they will do so only when we request it. And even in such extreme situations, the person and the family will be considered a vital part of the medical team. They will be kept up-to-date on all developments, will be asked to make key decisions, and will be encouraged to do everything they can.

The New Health Care System

Here are some other key points to keep in mind as we move toward Information Age medicine:

- The Industrial Age "map" of health care, developed nearly a century ago, divided health care into three categories: primary (front-line health professionals), secondary (community hospitals and specialists), and tertiary care (academic medical centers). The whole realm of lay medicine was literally left off the map. We have thus habitually overlooked (and often actively discouraged the use of) the biggest health resource of all—our ability as informed layfolk and experienced self-helpers to prevent and manage our own health problems.

- Online systems are beginning to make the grand database of professional medicine accessible to everyone. Layfolk will soon have access—many already do—to most of the same information professionals rely on. This is the medical equivalent of the removal of the "Berlin Wall" that has traditionally separated lay health care from professional medicine.

- We need to provide all our citizens—especially our children—with the tools, skills, information, and support they will need to play the role of primary caretakers in the emerging new heath care system. Community-based clinical skills—from the skills of the physical exam and the process of diagnosis and treatment to the skills of using and creating self-help networks—should be taught in school, along with geography and math.

- Preliminary studies suggest that online health systems can reduce costs while actually improving the quality of health care. The sidebar on page 278 shows the benefits reported by members of the Better Health and Medical Forum on America Online.

- In Information Age health care, it will be the health-active consumer, the concerned and supportive family caretaker, the neighborhood natural helper, the corporate wellness professional, the online self-help group facilitator, the newsgroup coordinator, the network sysop, the Web page creator, and perhaps other key players yet to evolve—working in cooperation with a new generation of supportive health professionals—who will serve as the real primary practitioners.

Benefits of a Health-Oriented Online Support Forum

5.9% for whom the question was applicable reported 1 or more unnecessary emergency room visits were saved, with an average of 10 visits saved per 100 responses.

26.1% for whom the question was applicable reported 1 or more unnecessary doctor visits were saved, with an average of 50 visits saved per 100 responses.

50% indicated increased medical self-care skills.

55% indicated increased confidence in their ability to talk with health professionals about the benefits, risks, and costs of alternatives, including medications.

63% reported increased confidence in their ability to control decisions that affect health and well-being.

68.2% for whom the question was applicable indicated increased ability to live successfully with a chronic or disabling condition.

73% indicated increased understanding of factors (lifestyle, risks and benefits of medical care, etc.) that influence health and well-being.

86% indicated increased understanding of health and medical information specific to their needs and interests.

From Martin Luther to Self-Managed Care

There are some instructive parallels between what's happening in health today and what happened in religion in Martin Luther's time. About four centuries ago, Luther and his contemporaries realized that priests did not have a monopoly on God. About two decades ago—I would date this from the early days of the women's health movement—the American medical consumer began to realize that physicians and other health professionals do not have a monopoly on health care.

The Reformation of Luther's time transformed Christianity and established the legitimacy of free choice and self-determination in religious matters. Our current medical reformation is establishing the legitimacy of free choice and self-determination in health matters.

At a time when the demand for professional health care services outpaces what the nation can afford to supply, online health networks which connect layfolk to clinicians and self-helpers to each other will increasingly be recognized for their unique ability to transform patients into providers and problems into resources.

As we move into the new millennium, I wouldn't be terribly surprised if online self-help, electronic communications between clinicians and consumers, and other online health systems turned out to be important links in a long-term process of successful health care reform. I would suggest that such reform will succeed only to the extent that we're able to encourage and support self-managed care by giving lay health care the same level of attention, respect, and support we have traditionally given to professional care.

How You Can Help Update This Book

I hope you've enjoyed reading this book just half as much as I've enjoyed writing it. I must say that despite a tight deadline and the usual fuss over checking innumerable details, I really had a ball on this one.

I did my best to put myself in your shoes and deliver the kind of information you'd find most enjoyable and most useful. But I'm sure there are many important online health resources I missed and others that have come into existence since this book went to press.

Now it's your turn: I'd like to hear about your experiences in the world of online health. How has it helped most in your life? What advice would you give to a new user? How can we improve the next edition? Your answers to the following questions—and any other comments on this book you'd care to make—would be extremely helpful.

Please respond in the most convenient way: e-mail, fax, or snail mail. (See the addresses below.) Thanks in advance for your help. See you online.

—Tom Ferguson

My Feedback on Health Online

Dear Tom,

  1. Here's what I liked best about *Health Online*:

  2. Here's what I liked *least*:

  3. Here are my suggestions for improving the next edition:

  4. Other comments:

Please send feedback by your preferred route:

E-mail: DrTomHO@aol.com

Fax: (512) 472-1345

Snail mail: Tom Ferguson, PO Box 5307, Austin TX 78763

Thanks again.   —TF

A Note to Health and Computer Professionals

Online, computer-assisted communication...promises to replace a substantial amount of care now delivered in person.

Jerome P. Cassirer, M.D., Editor
The New England Journal of Medicine

Up to this point I've chosen to emphasize the consumer's point of view. As a result, the preceding chapters describe only one aspect of online health resources. The role of health and computer professionals in developing, improving, and maintaining effective consumer health information systems is equally important.

Within the next few years we'll see major changes in the way health care is practiced:

- Layfolk will find an increasing amount of health information and support online. We need to be thinking about how we can help them do it.
- Our clients will soon be reading and writing in their own online medical records. We need to be thinking about how those systems will operate.
- More and more communications between health professionals and their clients will take place online—eventually including videoconferencing between the doctors in their offices and layfolk at home. We need to be thinking about how those systems will work and what we can do now to build the necessary infrastructure.

- Medical facilities will soon be expected to provide their customers with online resources, including consumer interfaces for their in-house computer systems. We need to be thinking about what those interfaces should look like and how patients will be able to interact with hospital and clinic-based medical information systems.

The Computer as Patient's Assistant

Let's look at how one typical patient might use online health resources. A woman who suspected that her symptoms were due to an undiagnosed ulcer could take the following steps:

- She might review the diagnostic guidelines for ulcers, talk with experienced self-helpers on an ulcer support forum, and read an online FAQ for people with ulcers.
- She could view an online video illustrating the key anatomy, physiology, and pathology of her condition. She could make a customized lifestyle assessment to identify likely risk factors. She could learn about nutritional and stress management guidelines and other preventive measures.
- She could obtain information on local doctors and hospitals that treat ulcer patients and could check on the preferred treatments, success rates, and consumer satisfaction ratings for each.
- She could check her online medical record to review earlier symptoms and drugs she had used in the past. She could document her findings and her plans in the "Patient's Notes" section of her medical record.
- After reviewing a decision support video that reviewed her available options, she could collaborate with her doctor of choice in choosing a treatment plan.
- She could monitor her response to the chosen therapy, entering her observations in her online medical record.
- She could continue her participation in an online self-help group for people with ulcers, obtaining continuing support while sharing her knowledge and expertise with others.

The Emerging Field of Consumer Health Informatics

I've been very lucky to have had the opportunity to coordinate and speak at a continuing series of professional meetings and workshops on *consumer health informatics* (CHI), a new field devoted to the study, development, and implementation of computer and telecommunications applications designed to be used by health consumers.

These mixed gatherings of health and computer professionals and online self-helpers have been highly rewarding experiences for all involved. Those of us who seek to create and participate in computerized systems for consumer health have much to learn from each other.

Notable demonstrations at recent meetings have shown a home health workstation for people with AIDS (from the University of Wisconsin's CHESS project), an interactive system that helps men with enlarged prostates decide whether to have surgery (from the Foundation for Informed Medical Decision Making in Hanover, New Hampshire), a psychological spreadsheet for people experiencing stressful life events (from Interactive Health Systems in Santa Monica, California), and a voicemail-based system for creating local self-help networks (from Dr. Farrokh Alemi at Cleveland State University).

Meeting participants have discussed doctor-patient e-mail and voice mail links, patient interfaces for computerized medical records, bedside computer terminals for patients in hospitals and at home, and a variety of other online self-help networks, databases, bulletin boards, and CD-ROMs. Here are some of the tentative conclusions that have come out of those meetings:

- Online health resources will replace some face-to-face clinical interactions. Patients will be able to avoid unnecessary emergency room or doctor's office visits—and the associated inconvenience and long waits—because they'll be able to get the information or advice they need through online systems.
- CHI systems will change the relationships between patients and providers. We will see more client-provider teamwork and fewer "doctor's orders."
- Clinicians will spend less time "delivering" professional services to passive patients. They will spend more time helping and guiding health-responsible consumers as they provide high-quality care for themselves and their families.
- Use of these systems won't be limited to computer wizards wielding sophisticated hardware. One present consumer health informatics system serves drug-abusing, pregnant women in inner-city Cleveland. They connect with the system via touch-tone telephone.
- Issues of liability must be solved as quickly as possible. Failure to do so could impede the full development of effective CHI systems.
- Some CHI systems will need to guarantee strict confidentiality to be used at all. Patients asked about sensitive issues have repeatedly refused to use CHI systems unless strict confidentiality was ensured.
- These systems will improve the quality, availability, and cost-effectiveness of health care. These goals, already achieved in pilot projects, require continued progress in several major areas: technology, program content, regulation, and involvement, acceptance, and support by both providers and consumers.

- Major barriers to consumer health informatics systems include:
  —lack of access to computers for populations in need
  —fee-for-service funding (no professional incentives)
  —professional resistance to new technologies
  —professional resistance to empowered medical consumers
  —liability concerns
- Major factors favoring the development of consumer health informatics systems are:
  —consumer demand
  —the substantial potential for cost savings
  —the increasing availability of computers for populations in need
  —the increase in HMOs and other capitated funding
  —competitive market advantage for professionals offering online contact and services
  —the potential for increased quality of care

What CHI Will Mean to Health Professionals

The growing availability of online self-help networks and computer-accessible medical information is just one of many forces which will elevate clients to a much more responsible and central role in managing their own health care in the years to come. Other factors include government cutbacks, market forces, managed care, assertive health consumers, and other deep cultural changes of the Information Age.

The health consumer of the twenty-first century will play a far more active role than the passive patient of the past. This change will be so dramatic that it may not be long until the very term "patient" falls out of use. In one Texas clinic, staffers have moved from calling their customers *patients* to *consumers* to *clients* to just plain *people*. They are now considering an ever further step: calling the customer *"boss."*

In most respects, this will be a positive trend for both clients and providers. As these new systems permit consumers to take on more and more medical responsibility, health professionals will be able to admit their uncertainty and to share the burdens they have long carried alone. Information Age health care will offer providers less need to memorize and less need to keep up with current research. Our computers will do these things for us on a "as-needed" basis. There will be less need to play the authority at all times. But it will require a major role adjustment: Doctors will need to learn to share their power with their clients.

This may be a difficult adaptation for some. But there will be a thousand opportunities for the "early adopters" who become involved in this field while it is still in its early stages. As one enthusiastic physician told me, after a talk I gave to a recent professional meeting, "Consumer health informatics is like a train moving faster and faster. We clinicians have a choice: We can jump on early. Or we can remain on the track."

For those of us who suspect that our highest medical calling may be to join with others—colleagues and layfolk—to create, improve, and operate effective consumer health informatics systems, the future looks bright indeed.

I hope you'll join us. And I'll look forward to crossing paths with you at a future consumer health informatics meeting.

How to Learn More about Consumer Health Informatics

For information on upcoming consumer health informatics meetings, workshops, and publications, send a request with the subject line "Prof. Info Please" to DrTomHO@aol.com. Please include your name, mailing address, and phone and fax numbers. If you don't currently have e-mail access, send this information with a self-addressed, stamped envelope to *CHI Info*, P.O. Box 5307, Austin TX 78763.

Author's Notes

Introduction: How to Use This Book

P. xvii. "When Sara Styles...": The stories of Sara, Tracy, and Stan are composites combining the experiences of two or more online self-helpers. As with many of the case histories recounted in this book, names have been changed to protect the privacy of those involved.

P. xix. "a quarter of a million online 'hits' per month": Personal communication from Elin Silveous (ESilveous@aol.com), sysop of the Better Health & Medical Forum, America Online, April 17, 1995.

Chapter 1: Going Online the Easy Way

P. 4. "roughly half of those surveyed...": Rosalind Resnick, "Despite Cyberphobia, Opportunities Growing," *Miami Herald Online* Column, Jan. 2, 1995. Rosalind Resnick (rosalindharrison@win.net) is a freelance writer specializing in business and technology. You can write to her in care of Business Monday, *Miami Herald*, Herald Plaza, Miami, FL 33132.

Chapter 2: What You'll Find When You Get There

P. 11. "One cannot travel...": Peter H. Lewis, "Strangers, Not Their Computers, Build a Network in Time of Grief," *New York Times*, March 8, 1994.

P. 11. "Support groups in slow motion...": Like many of the ideas in this book, I owe this description of online self-help forums to Ed Madara.

P. 15. "In an earlier draft I had included...": In the end I figured out a way to have my cake and eat it too. Here's the original excised passage:

```
From: Jack Redmond
To: All
   My son recently strangled himself trying to make a
Halloween haunted house in our garage. I'm not all that sure
that I can talk about this here, so don't be surprised if I
disappear. I'm having a hard time typing. I look at the screen
and see my son dying. No one knows exactly what happened, but
my brain has made up a scene that keeps flashing into my mind.
```

I had never let myself realize just how much I loved him, and now he's gone. I never ever would have thought that this could hurt so much, or that I would miss him so badly. My wife and I have been seeing a therapist and from what she says, after almost three weeks, we may still be operating in shock and this could get worse before it gets better.

I'd like some insight into this shock business: how do you know if you *are* in shock, how do you know if it's wearing off, and what does it feel like when it does wear off?

We've been told to take it easy and let this go at it's own pace, but I can't help wondering if there isn't there something I can do to speed up the process?

Any help would be much appreciated.

P. 17. "Let's say you're a 43-year-old leukemia survivor...": This example is adapted from the transcripts of several sessions on America Online's Better Health & Medical forum. It has been edited to serve as a general example of a typical online visit. "Lois" is a pseudonym while Glenna Tallman ("GlennaT") is real. She was a legendary host on AOL's Living with Cancer forum. She died a few months after she wrote these words.

P. 20. "A group of Barbie doll collectors...": The quote and the other information on the Barbie doll collectors' group is from Phyllis Phlegar, "Barbie Doll Collectors Meet Online," *Boardwatch*, October 1994, pp. 54–55.

P. 21. "when Brendan Keho, the 24-year-old author...": The quote and the information on Keho and his online friends is from Peter H. Lewis, "Strangers, Not Their Computer, Build a Network in Time of Grief," *New York Times*, March 8, 1994.

Chapter 3: The Human Side of E-Mail

P. 24. ". . . most people feel more comfortable being candid via e-mail. . . ": This is from an article in *On-line Access*, May 1994, page 19.

P. 29. "Hank" is a pseudonym for my online friend. Other identifying characteristics have been changed to protect the privacy of my online correspondent and his or her family.

P. 31. "Dysthymia is simply...": The names and other identifying characteristics in this message have been changed to protect the privacy of the online self-helpers.

Chapter 4: Cyberspace Friends and Online Angels

P. 40. "professional meeting on online self-help": For more about such meetings, see "A Note to Health and Computer Professionals," p. 283.

P. 41. "Online self-help networks are like surrogate families...": Parts of this section are adapted from the article "Finding or Forming Your Own Self-Help Network (Face-to-Face or Online)" by Edward J. Madara and Tom Ferguson, M.D., which first appeared in *The Millennium Whole Earth Catalog*, HarperSanFrancisco, San Francisco, 1994, p. 172.

P. 41. "available for free": Not literally, of course, since access charges may apply. The point here is that self-help support is performed on a voluntary basis.

P. 42. "7 PM and 1 AM": Personal communication, Ed Madara, October 10, 1995.

P. 43. "Research studies are beginning to show...": For a useful review of this area, see David Spiegel, "Social Support: How Friends, Family, and Groups Can Help," in *Mind/Body Medicine: How to Use Your Mind for Better Health*, edited by Daniel Goleman and Joel Gurin, Consumer Reports Books, Yonkers, NY, 1993.

P. 47. "Some months ago, the great love of my life...": This quote is from John Perry Barlow, "Is There a 'There' is Cyberspace?" *Utne Reader*, March-April, 1995, p. 56. Reprinted with the author's kind permission.

Chapter 5: America Online

P. 58. DACLilly's real name is Lilly Ann Roth. She's been hosting this forum since January 1991. She writes: "I have watched a lot of growth and many changes in the online community. If your readers would like to discuss any aspect of the disability community online further, they should feel free to contact me at DACLilly@aol.com."

P. 74. "SeniorNet members can receive a special deal...": The SeniorNet membership fee is $35 for the first year and $25 for each subsequent year. New members, receive a copy of the *SeniorNet Sourcebook* (a guide to more than twenty-five creative computer projects developed by SeniorNet members), a subscription to the SeniorNet quarterly newsletter, and a SeniorNet Catalog of computer-related products with a special discount to SeniorNet members. You can take computer classes exclusively for seniors at SeniorNet Learning Centers across the United States, and you are eligible for a special AOL subscription rate of $9.95 per month. The rate entitles you to unlimited use of SeniorNet and one hour per month of other AOL services. Additional hours are billed at the regular rate of $2.95 per hour.) For more information see the "SeniorNet Headquarters" selection on the SeniorNet main menu.

P. 75. "One typical SeniorNet regular is 'Yota'...": This and several of the following anecdotes about SeniorNet users are from the *Wall Street Journal*, Dec. 8, 1994, B section.

P. 78. "...among the messages you find there...": All names and screen names in this section (except for "DanAsh," who is an AOL self-helper) and many of the other identifying characteristics have been changed to protect the privacy of the participants. So please don't try to send e-mail to the other self-helpers listed in this section. Instead, check the current messages in this folder on AOL and join in the current discussion. These selections have been edited for readability, and some similar messages have been combined.

P. 87. Todd Daniel Woodward may be best known as the legendary self-help organizer "Dan Ash" on America Online. He is a publisher, host of a depression support group, and a staff member of the Personal Empowerment Network on AOL. He has served on the staff of eWorld's Transformations Forum.

His ongoing projects include the *alt.support.depression* FAQ, the *alt.support.depression* Depression Book List and the Mood Disorders Support Network. Todd would be interested in hearing from individuals and organizations interested in forming a non-profit organization dedicated to helping self-help organizations make the transition to the online medium. Todd can be reached at SHIC@aol.com. His Web site is http://users.aol.com/tdwoodward/index.html.

Chapter 6: CompuServe

P. 92. "This e-mail message from Kentucky-based...": Personal communication from Raymond Green (Phone: [606] 263-2598, extension 207. Mail: 73 Fitch Avenue, Winchester, KY 40391).

P. 93. "a recent article in the magazine *Natural Health*": Meredith Gould Ruch, "Health Online," *Natural Health*, July/August 1994, pp. 78–81.

P. 104. "Another CompuServe self-helper who recently benefited...": Paul Hansen's story is recounted in "Care Takers" by Cathryn Conroy, *CompuServe Magazine*, February 1994, pp. 10–19.

P. 115. "Hammerschmidt brings a personal perspective...": Dr. Dale Hammerschmidt's quote appears in "Care Takers" by Cathryn Conroy, *CompuServe Magazine*, February 1994, pp. 10–19.

Chapter 7: Prodigy

P. 136. "Here are some representative messages...": Unless e-mail addresses are given or it's specified otherwise, all names of self-helpers and other identifying characteristics in this chapter have been changed. These comments have been lightly edited to maintain clarity and to protect the members' privacy.

Chapter 9: Internet Mailing Lists

P. 168. "Here's a representative posting from a recent issue...": E-mail from JFinch@aol.com.

Chapter 10: Internet Newsgroups

P. 201. "USENET Newsgroups...": For an in-depth look at the world of USENET newsgroups, see *The USENET Book: Finding, Using, and Surviving Newsgroups on the Internet,* by Bryan Pfaffenberger, Addison–Wesley Publishing, Reading, MA, 1995.

P. 204. "You find three of these threads...": The postings quoted here and in the rest of the chapter are lightly edited excerpts from actual postings by real online self-helpers in the *alt.support.depression* newsgroup. I've also deleted the long and mostly irrelevant headers and footers from the messages.

P. 206. "researcher, Jayne Butler,...": Special thanks to Jayne, a doctoral student at the University of Toronto, for her help in compiling and verifying the newsgroup listings in this chapter. Jayne asked me to insert this message in the Notes:

> Dear Health Online Reader: I'm a doctoral student in adult education at the Ontario Institute for Studies in Education at the University of Toronto. My research interests center on the health care consumer at home and the use of computer networks to support the health-active, health-responsible empowered patient. I would appreciate hearing from anyone who can help me under-stand--either through recommended reading material or through personal experience--the kinds of support, learning, and empowerment that happen in self-help groups, and in online self-help groups in particular. I look forward to hearing from you.
>   --Jayne Butler (jbutler@oise.on.ca)

P. 219. "Here's a selected list of health- and...": A tip of the hat to John Grohol, author of the outstanding Web page PsychCentral (see p. 242), the definitive online guide to self-help newsgroups (and winner of a Health Online Distinguished Achievement Award) for providing much of the information that was my starting point in researching this chapter.

P. 228. "Here is a list of FAQs...": Special thanks to Bruce C. McKenzie, author of the outstanding online resource *Medicine-Related FAQs,* the definitive online guide to health and support FAQs by e-mail. Bruce's list is more extensive and more up-to-date than the list in this chapter. You can obtain a copy of Bruce's list by sending him a message at bruce-m@cybertas.demon.co.uk. You can find a variety of FAQs at: http://www.cis.ohio-state.edu/hypertext/faq/usenet/FAQ-List.html.

Chapter 11: The World Wide Web

P. 237. "The Web is so compelling...": Walter S. Mossberg, "Untangling the Web," *Smart Money,* April 1995, pp. 127–128.

Epilogue: The Healing Computer

Some of the material in this chapter was adapted, with permission, from "Overview and Summary of the First National Conference on Consumer Health Informatics," by Tom Ferguson and Steve Carrell, in *Consumer Health Informatics: Bringing the Patient into the Loop, The Proceedings of the First National Conference on Consumer Health Informatics* (MailComm Plus, Austin, TX, 1993, (512) 472-1296), pp. 1-6. Additional material was adapted from "From Industrial–Age Medicine to Information–Age Health Care," my introductory essay to the Health and Self-Care section of *The Millennium Whole Earth Catalog*, edited by Howard Rheingold (HarperSanFrancisco, San Francisco, 1994), p. 170. I'd like to thank the editors of the *Catalog* for inviting me to edit the Health/Medical section and for their permission to rework the essay for this chapter. Additional information was adapted from my article "Consumer Health Informatics" in *HealthCare Forum*, January/February 1995, pp. 28–32.

P. 275. "The future of health care in these troubled times...": This quote from Dr. Koop's foreword to *Self-Help: Concepts and Applications,* edited by A. H. Katz, Hannah L. Hedrick, and Daryl Holtz Isenberg, Charles Press, Philadelphia, 1992, p. xviii.

P. 278. "Benefits of a Health-Oriented Online Support Forum": These figures have been excerpted from a summary of the results of Health ResponseAbility Systems' seventy-question member survey conducted at the end of the Better Health & Medical Forum's first year online. Received via e-mail from Sysop Elin Silveous (ESilveous@aol.com) on April 17, 1995.

A Note to Health and Computer Professionals

P. 283. "Online, computer-assisted communication...": Jerome P. Kassirer, "The Next Transformation in the Delivery of Health Care," *New England Journal of Medicine*, January 5, 1995, pp. 32-34.

P. 285. "Notable demonstrations at recent meetings...": For example, the first National Conference on Consumer Health Informatics, held July 17-18, 1993, at the University of Wisconsin, Stevens Point, Wisconsin. The conference was sponsored by the National Wellness Institute of Stevens Point and Healthwise, Inc., of Boise, Idaho. I was the conference coordinator. The proceedings, *Consumer Health Informatics: Bringing the Patient into the Loop—The Proceedings of the First National Conference on Consumer Health Informatics,* edited by Tom Ferguson, are available from MailComm Plus, 2729 Exposition Blvd., Austin, TX 78703; (512) 472-1296; fax: (512) 476-3930.

P. 286. "...calling the customer *boss*": Personal communication, Guy Danielson, M.D., Tyler, Texas, September 13, 1994. You can reach Dr. Danielson at GuyOtis@aol.com.

Acknowledgments

As I LOOK UP FROM MY COMPUTER to see the nearly-complete page proofs stacked neatly on my desk, I realize what a highly-collaborative experience these last two years have been. Many online self-helpers contributed to this work. I received advice and encouragement from and shared personal experiences with hundreds of online friends, colleagues, and acquaintances, many of them much more knowledgeable than I. Thanks to all who helped make my dream of *Health Online* a reality.

Special thanks is due to Ed Madara, director of the American Self-Help Clearinghouse, for his endless supply of help and support through the long process of conceiving, planning, and writing this book. I asked Ed to be my co-author, but in his characteristically humble fashion he all-too-modestly demurred, and no amount of coaxing could change his mind. Even so, he played a key role, flooding me with information, putting me in touch with key online self-helpers, writing the introduction, and providing hundreds of comments on several early manuscript drafts. This is Ed's book as much as it is mine.

In this book as in many previous writings I have benefited from the thinking of two remarkable cultural lead dogs who changed my thinking forever: Marshall McLuhan and Stewart Brand. I owe a special thanks to my Yale

Medical School professors Lowell Levin and Alberta Jacoby for their acceptance and support of my mildly heretical medical notions and for helping me get started on my somewhat unorthodox medical career path.

I owe a great debt of gratitude to all my colleagues at *Medical Self-Care* magazine—Lee Ammidon, Michael Castleman, Carole Pisarczyk, and many others—who helped me think through a vision of medicine based on the idea that intelligent, informed layfolk can serve as the real primary practitioners. I am also grateful to MSC's many faithful subscribers.

Thanks to my colleagues at the Center for Clinical Computing at Harvard Medical School and Beth Israel Hospital—and especially to co-president Warner Slack—for inviting me to help plan and participate in their series of conferences on "The Computer as Patient's Assistant." Warner, Charles Saffran, Steven Locke, Jonathan Wald, and many others at these two august institutions are leading the movement to develop and promote consumer interfaces for in-clinic and in-hospital medical information systems.

Another key supporter was Howard Rheingold, my old Reed College classmate, more recently my editorial colleague at the *Whole Earth Catalog*. He invited me to edit the medical sections of *The Millennium Whole Earth Catalog*, then encouraged me to write a book on self-care in cyberspace. His groundbreaking work, *The Virtual Community*, taught me a great deal about this strange new world and served as a model for reporting on it.

Special thanks to Todd Woodward, online community organizer and creator of the Self-Help Information Coalition on America Online. Todd took me under his wing, answering my questions by the dozen and leading me into the world of self-help forums and chat groups. One of my most memorable early experiences in researching this book was an evening I spent standing behind Todd as he sat at his computer, typing away at blazing speed. In the window in the center of his screen he was moderating an unruly chat group of two dozen opinionated self-helpers, while in six smaller windows he conducted half a dozen private chats with various attendees at the same meeting. And all the while he was carrying on an erudite, side-splittingly funny commentary on the whole process for the benefit of his amazed audience of one.

Thanks to Joe Graedon, my friend, former co-author, and wizened veteran of the authorial path, for his unfailing torrent of moral support—online, on-phone and in-person—and for his unflagging enthusiasm for this project.

Thanks to Elin Silveous and Allan Douma of the Better Health & Medical Forum on America Online, Tom Koch of the Family Health Board on CompuServe, and former board leader Jim Callan of Prodigy's Health & Lifestyles Bulletin Board who reviewed the chapters on their respective services. And thanks to Jim for inviting me to serve as the "Doc of the Day" on his forum, where I had an opportunity to answer online questions from a wide variety of Prodigy self-helpers.

Thanks to Jayne Butler, a doctoral student at the University of Toronto, whose cheery e-mail message offered her research services. She provided invaluable aid in compiling and verifying the newsgroup listings. For a note from Jayne, see the Author's Notes.

Many other colleagues and friends provided ideas for this book and support for its author. Special thanks to Linda Adler, Farrokh Alemi, Linda Allison and Bill Wells, Robert Blank, Eric Boberg, Jan Bozarth and Robert "Beto" Skiles, Patricia Brennan, Linda Chapin, Robert Cooper, Guy Danielson, Deborah Deatrick, Lewis and Brandy Engel, Tony Farrell, Roger Gould, Teresa Graedon, John Grohol, Karen Gurin, David Gustafson, David Hehman, Anne Helmke, Bill Hettler, Don Kemper and Molly Mettler, Tim Kieschnink, Jan Leonard, Michael McDonald, Albert Mulley, Susan Neri, Ben Nolke and Judy Ryser, Dean Ornish, Kenneth Pelletier, Patricia Phelan, Joe Pickard, Bart Rhoades, David Robertson, Sandra "Pinks" Pinkerton, Richard Rockefeller, Samantha Scolamiero, Keith Sehnert, David Sobel, Judith Sokolow and George LaSalle, Allan Stevens, Jim Strohecker, Jack and Ann Swingler, John Travis, John Wennberg, Jean Wooldridge, and Stuart and Beth Yudofsky.

At her day job, Lissa Hattersley kept the Self-Care Productions office running smoothly in spite of my two-year preoccupation with this project. In real life she's a wonderful musician and singer. You can catch her band, Let's Get Big, at selected Austin clubs.

Another important colleague was my online researcher and editorial assistant, Tracy Shuford. Tracy exhibited limitless good cheer, whether typing endless tapes of my stumbling early drafts or fact-checking key resources on the fast-changing byways of the Internet.

Thanks to Regula Noetzli and Charlotte Sheedy at the Charlotte Sheedy Literary Agency for helping me find such a terrific publisher and to impresario Bill Patrick of Addison-Wesley for agreeing to publish *Health Online*.

My Addison-Wesley editor, John Bell (johnb@aw.com), was with me every step of the way. He was an author's dream, supportive, enthusiastic, online-savvy, and easily available by phone. He unfailingly went to bat for this book as needed and took its author out to a memorable literary lunch at the Ritz. The other A-W staffers I worked with were equally professional and personable. Production Supervisor Pat Jalbert shepherded the manuscript through the copyediting and typesetting process with good-natured aplomb. My wonderfully thorough copy editor, Michael Robinson, subjected the manuscript to a level of scrutiny that would have intimidated Shakespeare himself, leaving no turn of phrase unexamined and no gratuitous comma untouched. He went far beyond the call of duty, even going online to check the content of these pages against the electronic originals. Cover designer Suzanne Heiser was gracious enough to listen to my ideas for the book's cover and to make the changes I suggested. Thanks go too to our keen-eyed indexer Alexandra Nickerson. And publicist Alison Pratt (AlisonP@aw.com) worked long and hard to get review copies out to interested journalists and reviewers.

Thanks to Dave Griffith and colleagues at PC/Mac Clean for helping us assemble our computer systems and to Hal Koonstra at MacWorks Consulting who kept them running smoothly and came in to rescue us when we got in over our heads. The technologically inclined may be interested to know that this book was written on Microsoft Word 5.1 running on a Macintosh Duo 280c with 16 megabytes of RAM, a 320-megabyte hard disk, a Global Village PowerPort Mercury 28.8 internal modem, a Duo Dock, a twenty-inch Radius color monitor, an Iomega Zip drive, a one-gigabyte external hard drive, and a desk full of assorted peripherals. It was typeset using QuarkXpress 3.3 on a Macintosh Quadra 650.

Thanks to all those I am unable to thank by name, some to protect their privacy, others because some of the best information in this book was supplied by self-helpers I never met, whose names I never knew. To all those whose online paths crossed mine, thank you for the altruistic dedication, the common vision, and the heartfelt personal experiences that made coordinating this book such a pleasure. It is your knowledge and your wisdom that is reflected in its pages.

Finally, this book would not have been possible without the many years of unwavering support I have received from my wife Meredith and daughter Adrienne; from my family of origin, the devoted and ever-inspiring Ferguson clan, from Oregon to India; and from my gracious and multitudinous in-laws, the Mitchells.

Index